The Skills System Instructor's Guide

*An Emotion-Regulation Skills Curriculum
for all Learning Abilities*

Julie F. Brown

iUniverse, Inc.
Bloomington

The Skills System Instructor's Guide
An Emotion-Regulation Skills Curriculum for all Learning Abilities

The information, ideas, and suggestions in this book are not intended as a substitute for professional advice.
Before following any suggestions contained in this book, you should consult your personal physician or
mental health professional. Neither the author nor the publisher shall be liable or responsible for any loss or
damage allegedly arising as a consequence of your use or application of any information or suggestions in this
book. This book provides general information and diagnosis of individual patient needs is always necessary.

iUniverse books may be ordered through booksellers or by contacting:

iUniverse
1663 Liberty Drive
Bloomington, IN 47403
www.iuniverse.com
1-800-Authors (1-800-288-4677)

Because of the dynamic nature of the Internet, any Web addresses or links contained in
this book may have changed since publication and may no longer be valid. The views
expressed in this work are solely those of the author and do not necessarily reflect the views
of the publisher, and the publisher hereby disclaims any responsibility for them.

Any people depicted in stock imagery provided by Thinkstock are models,
and such images are being used for illustrative purposes only.

Certain stock imagery © Thinkstock.

ISBN: 978-1-4502-9548-2 (pbk)
ISBN: 978-1-4502-8989-4 (ebk)

Library of Congress Control Number: 2011903049

Printed in the United States of America

iUniverse rev. date: 4/23/2011

The images used in the Skills System Instructor's Guide were purchased through Clipart.com.
These images are copyright protected and JUPITERIMAGES requests the copyright notice
"© 2010 Jupiterimages Corporation" appear on this credit page in relation to clip art in Appendix A

Contents

List of Tables

PREFACE

Developing the Skills System

The treasure hunt. The development of the Skills System has been a sixteen-year journey. This adventure began shortly after I graduated from Boston University with my MSW. I was working as a clinician in a behaviorally-based twenty-five-bed residential school for intellectually disabled, emotionally disturbed, adolescent males and females in Massachusetts. One day, a youth who had a significant history of committing sexual offenses, setting fires, treating animals cruelly, and assaulting others was sitting in my office. We were discussing his latest incident of aggression toward a staff member. I posed questions, trying to elicit alternative behaviors to smashing the staff in the head with a padlock. The young man was unable to generate useful options; thus I suggested that he could have played the card game Uno instead.

In the midst of saying the word "Uno," I experienced an epiphany. This boy had suffered numerous traumas and inflicted even more, and my solution was *Uno*! While pulling this suggestion out of my eclectic bag of therapeutic tricks, I became keenly aware that this isolated activity was a woefully inadequate intervention. While the card game may have been a piece of a coping puzzle, the problem was that I did not have an adequate, synthesized framework for coping that I could consistently transfer to this individual in a form that he could understand, generalize, and apply. If I did not have a comprehensive representation of a coping map, there was no way that this intellectually disabled adolescent was going to integrate my random teaching into a technically strong, yet flexible model that could help him manage the challenging internal and external factors that he faced on a daily basis.

I possessed no vision about the path ahead, yet the journey to find the Skills System had begun.

I spent the next three years immersed in treating this diverse and challenging population of youth within the residential setting. I combed the literature for insights; I found more tiny puzzle pieces, but still no map. No comprehensive tools to help youth who have numerous Axis 1 and Axis 2 diagnoses integrate the necessary skills to reduce the need for supervision. No models complex enough and yet simple enough to assist individuals who struggled with effects of neglect, witnessing violence, physical abuse, sexual victimization, and/or social stigmatization. I could not find a program that could help these youths reduce the need for multiple antipsychotic medications, antidepressants, mood stabilizers, and other drugs to control behavior. Although the well-structured token economy within the facility was helpful, it was not sufficient to teach these children, who had complex needs, the necessary skills to regulate their reinforced patterns of dyscontrol in settings beyond residential care. Somewhere there had to be a better solution.

During a monthly consultation in 1997, a well-regarded trauma specialist recommended I find out more about dialectical behavior therapy (DBT) (Linehan, 1993; Linehan, 1993b). DBT was a comprehensive cognitive-behavioral model developed by Marsha M. Linehan, PhD, in 1993 to treat individuals with borderline personality disorder (BPD). Initially I asked myself, "How could a treatment for BPD women who demonstrated suicidal and parasuicidal behaviors apply to my clients?" During my initial phases of DBT training, I discovered that although few of my clients were formally diagnosed with BPD, many experienced the BPD behavioral patterns of emotional, cognitive, and behavioral dysregulation described by Linehan. I was cautiously optimistic that DBT would prove to be a piece of the treasure map.

By 1999 I was fortunate enough to have been intensively trained in DBT and started Justice Resource Institute's Integrated Clinical Services (ICS) in Rhode Island. ICS provided outpatient therapy services for developmentally disabled adults who experienced intense behavioral control problems. Standard DBT individual therapy and coping-skillstraining groups were key ingredients of the ICS program. The comprehensive DBT treatment model was designed to help people change highly reinforced, long-term patterns of behavior associated with impaired emotion regulation. While it was clear that the DBT technology was helpful in improving self-management capacities, accommodations were necessary to allow cognitively impaired individuals to learn and generalize new adaptive coping skills. Adherence to the DBT model was paramount; our challenge was to make DBT technology handicapped accessible without reducing the therapeutic viability of the empirically validated treatment.

Surprisingly, the individual therapy aspects of DBT (Linehan, 1993) required minimal adaptation for this population. While learning DBT individual therapy and treating cognitively impaired people is intellectually demanding for the therapist, participation in the treatment as a client is relatively straightforward. Unfortunately, the skills component (Linehan, 1993b) was a more complex problem. During the first year, we followed the standard DBT skills manual, adjusting teaching strategies to help improve comprehension of the information. The concepts contained in the mindfulness, interpersonal-effectiveness, emotion-regulation, and distress-tolerance modules (Linehan, 1993b) were vital, yet the language and format were barriers for the clients. Many participants struggled to pronounce, remember, and understand the standard DBT skills terms and thus were unable to recall and utilize the concepts within the context of life when emotionally dysregulated.

The DBT skills curriculum did not provide intellectually disabled individuals with a framework that facilitated transitions from one skill to the next within complicated contexts that required multiple skills. I continually felt as though skills-training group for my clients was like playing the game Fifty-Two Pickup when I was a child. I felt, as a group leader, as if I were my mean, elder sister who would invite me to play cards and scream "Fifty-two pickup!" as she squeezed the deck, sending the fifty-two cards into the air and all over the floor for me to pick up. The participants seemed to stare, dazed and confused (as I had as a child staring at all of the cards), looking at the divergent information, without even knowing which skill (or card) to pick up first.

While I was driven to maintain adherence to the DBT model, I had a clear sense that I needed to present coping skills in a vastly different way if my clients were to truly grasp the essential principles. I began creating step-by-step progressions that the intellectually disabled participants could learn and utilize. I knew that I had to find a simple system that offered participants a template for dynamically using skills in a self-generated way that integrated information from both the internal and external experience within each moment. While it was critical that the concepts be uncomplicated, the function had to be highly complex to synthesize these elements. The system had to help the individual be aware of the current moment, mobilize inner wisdom in a consistent way, cultivate effective planning, and embody both the simplicity and the sophistication required to help the person handle life's most abstract and demanding events. I spent months gnawing on these concepts to piece together this intricate puzzle.

One day, as I was driving, merging into a high-speed lane at sixty miles per hour, I noticed the core idea of the Skills System passing through my mind. It was so simple and so complicated at the same time—how dialectical! The treasure had emerged, and I was lucky enough to have noticed it careening through my mind. Fortunately, I didn't know at that moment how exciting this gift was, because I probably would have driven off the road.

The treasure. Since that day on Route 195, the Skills System has become a simple, yet sophisticated emotion-regulation road map for children, adolescents, and adults both with and without significant learning challenges. The nine skills and three System Tools provide a useful structure that helps the person make effective choices in service of personal goals. The ICS single-group, longitudinal pilot study examining reductions in behavioral targets of forty intellectually disabled individuals over a four-year period, showed statistically significant reductions in low-, medium-, and high-risk behaviors (Brown et al., 2010, not yet published). Although this was not a randomized controlled trial, the results support the use of the Skills System and will hopefully encourage other professionals to explore the usage of the Skills System in conjunction with DBT individual therapy and without.

Today I may recommend playing Uno to one of my clients; however, I can be confident that the individual knows several other adaptive coping skills, when to use each skill, how many skills to utilize, and how to implement the skills as a result of his Skills System training. For example, recently in skills group, one client, whose full-scale IQ score is in the moderate range of mental retardation, recounted a stressful situation she had managed successfully during the previous day. She described first getting a Clear Picture of the situation. She stated she was mad at a level 4. Her staff was not listening to what she was saying. This individual reported having strong urges to scream at the staff. Immediately the woman stopped and stepped back. She used On-Track Thinking to reflect upon whether these urges were helpful to her reaching her goal. Knowing that she wanted to increase her independence and improve her relationships, she determined that screaming was not helpful. Realizing that she was too upset to use Expressing Myself or Problem Solving at that time, my client decided to do a Safety Plan and go to her room. She then reported doing an On-Track Action by calmly informing the staff that she was going to go to her bedroom. While in her room she did a few New-Me Activities (listening to music and drawing) that helped her think clearly, feel better, and relax. My client stated that later during the shift, she did her Clear Picture skill again and determined that she was feeling much calmer. She used On-Track Thinking to make a skills plan to talk to the staff about the problem. Because she was calm and focused, she was able to discuss and solve the problem with the staff.

As I listen to my clients recount detailed and effective skills usage as a part of skills-training group, I periodically think of that boy with the padlock so many years ago. I think about how grateful I am to him for showing me my inadequacies. It has been a privilege working with many dedicated people—both group members and co-therapists—to improve the Skills System over the years.

The Skills System Instructor's Guide is an attempt to share this work with other individuals who may benefit from the coping framework. It is our hope that this book supplies professionals with the necessary tools to teach this model to individuals who experience self-regulation as well as learning challenges, to integrate adaptive coping skills into their lives.

The Skills System

The Skills System Instructor's Guide provides people who wish to become skills trainers with the materials and strategies to teach the Skills System in individual and/or group settings. The curriculum, background information, teaching strategies, and visual aids are designed to instruct individuals who experience learning challenges. The simplified materials and systematic teaching approach help people of all abilities surmount intellectual, emotional, and/or behavioral barriers that hinder generalization of new adaptive behaviors. Interestingly, the simplified structure and language used in the Skills System may help people of all intellectual abilities understand, integrate, and generalize adaptive emotion-regulation strategies. The simplicity of the Skills System eases the recollection of strategies even amid strong negative emotions and confusion. Therefore, people diagnosed with moderate mental retardation, as well as individuals of average or higher intelligence, may reap the benefits of the Skills System.

This book presents foundational information for skills trainers who want to teach participants who have learning challenges. In the instruction of individuals with intellectual deficits, not only do materials and teaching strategies need to be adapted, but the skills trainer must also understand common challenges that impact self-management for people who have cognitive impairment. Intellectually disabled participants experience challenges related to emotional, cognitive, behavioral, mental health, developmental, and environmental factors that complicate life and the learning process. These increased vulnerabilities coupled with the realities of reduced resources create legitimate dilemmas that a skills trainer must understand if effective teaching and skills coaching are the goal. Similarly, for trainers working with people who have other special needs (e.g., mental illness or advanced age), additional information about the population and/or specific issues informs effective practice.

Who can be a Skills System skills trainer? A Skills System trainer teaches the Skills System to an individual or group. In most cases, master's- and PhD-level clinicians provide skills training. A skills trainer must fully understand the Skills System, information related to learning impairments, and enhanced teaching strategies to facilitate the transfer information effectively. The skills trainer must also be sufficiently equipped to provide specific supports to the population being instructed. For example, in the treatment of intellectually disabled violent offenders, the skills trainer should be an experienced professional within that specific treatment setting. Clinical knowledge may be helpful not only within the skills-training session, but also in surmounting barriers that impede the integration of skills within the context of the participant's daily life. Issues that are barriers to learning and to the generalization of adaptive coping skills are likely to require therapeutic supports to address.

Who can be a skills coach? Skills System coaches are people who have a strong understanding of the Skills System and are available to provide supports within the context of the individual's life. Skills coaches help the individual use skills, yet do not function as the participant's therapist. Parents, teachers, and friends can be helpful skills coaches. An individual who lives in a residential setting may have a broad array of skills coaches. For example, groupmates, support staff (e.g., administrative, residential, and vocational workers), housemates, roommates, and family members commonly function in the role of skills coaches. Collateral support providers, such as psychologists, nurses, physicians, and social workers, can enhance a treatment team's effectiveness by functioning as skills coaches.

Benefits for support providers. Residential agencies and support staff who work with individuals who require supervision report that the Skills System has been helpful in at least two important ways. First, the materials help professionals provide effective interventions to consumers who exhibit problematic behaviors. Without this knowledge base, support staff may provide inconsistent and even unhelpful coaching advice to participants. As employees increase levels of effectiveness, job satisfaction improves. Second, professionals note that the coping strategies are personally helpful in the management of strong emotions evoked when supporting a person with emotional and behavioral problems. Rather than promoting cycles of staff ineffectiveness that trigger an individual's acting out, thus leading to staff burnout, the Skills System promotes effectiveness and improved relationships. Healthy, reciprocal, balanced relationships between the individual and support staff can cultivate immense personal growth for both parties.

Orientation to The Skills System Instructor's Guide. This resource book provides a comprehensive set of materials to facilitate teaching the Skills System and to begin the process of implementing the model within a residential setting. It is essential that a professional who wishes to become a skills trainer must first learn the Skills System. Chapter 1 offers a brief overview of the Skills System, while Chapter 2 presents detailed descriptions of each of the skills and the System Tools to fulfill this task. It is important to note that the descriptions in both these chapters are intended to teach the skills trainer concepts and may not be in the form that individuals with intellectual deficits can learn. While reading these preliminary chapters, the trainer may question whether the material is too complex for an intellectually disabled person to understand and use, but the reality is that the Skills System needs to be comprehensive to provide the necessary tools to adequately regulate emotions. The information therefore must be designed and taught in ways that gradually build the knowledge base, facilitate recall, and promote generalization of these complex concepts over time. Chapters 5–8 introduce several key components of the teaching model that enable individuals with intellectual impairment to learn and master the Skills System.

One of the great benefits of the Skills System model is that it helps create a common, adaptive emotion-regulation language within support environments. In order to maximize the impact of the Skills System, instructors need to understand how support providers can function as skills coaches. Chapter 3 outlines the information needed to become a skills coach.

It is vital that a trainer has a strong understanding of the diverse issues that may impact the individual's instruction and generalization of skills. Chapter 4 addresses general factors that impact coping and learning, with specific information about individuals with intellectual disabilities. This information is useful for skills trainers and coaches alike.

The Skills System teaching strategies are a vital aspect of this model. Given that emotion regulation is a challenging and abstract set of concepts and tasks, creating fathomable learning experiences is a quintessential element of the process. For example, the training structure, teaching strategies, twelve-week cycle curriculum, and handouts are all carefully crafted to maximize comprehension and retention. Thus, the fifth chapter reviews the structure of skills instruction. Foundational teaching strategies that are used throughout skills training are presented in Chapter 6, while Chapter 7 highlights teaching strategies that are utilized within specific phases of the E-Spiral framework. Chapter 8 includes the Skills System twelve-week cycle curriculum, which offers a detailed week-by-week breakdown and detailed instructions for providing skills training.

The curriculum integrates with numerous handouts, worked examples, and worksheets; these resources are included in Appendix A. Participants will require individual copies of these materials; having a skills notebook is essential for group and home-study activities. The participant can either use *The Skills System Instructor's Guide* as a daily skills notebook, or a three-ring binder can be purchased through the Skills System website (www.theskillssystem.com). The binder format allows for the addition of new Skills System handouts that become available as well as individualized materials that skills trainers and/or individual therapists create with the participant.

This book also provides skills trainers with supplemental materials. Appendix B includes the Skills System Planning Sheet, which integrates the preparation of activities and the documentation of progress through the skills curriculum. It can be challenging to monitor progression through the curriculum because of the participants' differing rates of learning; this form improves the continuity of instruction. Appendix C contains skills scenarios that further develop the integration of skills. These tools may be helpful when teaching clients and/or skills coaches the Skills System. Lastly, Appendix D is a skills test. This competency evaluation may be completed by participants or support providers; it also can function as a skills worksheet.

It is important to note that the format of *The Skills System Instructor's Guide* is designed to teach the reader the Skills System. Therefore, the instructor is exposed to deepening layers of skills information to broaden and expand skills knowledge, as are participants in skills groups. While the reader may notice some repetition of points, the evolving exposure to the material will serve to improve recognition and recall.

ACKNOWLEDGMENTS

Many people have made this book possible. The Justice Resource Institute (JRI) provided an environment that allowed the Skills System to be developed. In particular, I would like to thank Andrew Pond for his unwavering support. My team at JRI-Integrated Clinical Services, David Damon and Deborah Jackson, were central to the development of *The Skills System Instructor's Guide*. Their relentless dedication to helping the individuals we treat, willingness to collaborate, and endless patience with this author elicit gratitude beyond words. My friend and associate, Paige Dibiasio, PhD, also offered vital and ever-evolving support. The consumers who attended therapy at JRI-ICS were key contributors. There are too many to name individually, but please know that each of you were my teachers. The vision and dedication of the state of Rhode Island and of the private residential providers were essential components as well. In the face of many challenges, people like Stephanie Horridge, Lisa and James Rafferty, and Kathleen Ellis assisted the growth of this model.

I would like to extend a special acknowledgment to Cynthia Sanderson, PhD, for her kindness and support. The work of Marsha M. Linehan, PhD, the developer of dialectical behavior therapy (DBT), provided important foundational information for this curriculum. James Gross, PhD, the editor of the Handbook of Emotion Regulation (2007), offered valuable feedback that improved the model. Donald Meichenbaum, PhD, Kelly Koerner, PhD, and many of the DBT trainers were also helpful and encouraging during this lengthy process.

Lastly, I would like to acknowledge the contribution of my family to this project. My husband's perpetual support and encouragement were indispensable. My mother's countless hours of proofreading of the multiple versions of the guide were greatly appreciated. My children were wonderful teachers; they helped me better understand the human growth process and how relationships support and impede this personal evolution.

I am grateful for and indebted to you all.

CHAPTER 1:

Introducing The Skills System

Bernice Johnson Reagon, an African-American scholar and songwriter, wrote "Life's challenges are not supposed to paralyze you—they're supposed to help you discover who you are" (Lewis, 2009). Fully experiencing life's challenges and remaining present within the current moment can be excruciatingly difficult. Painful emotions and overwhelming thoughts may bombard the individual, blurring self-reflection and the course ahead. The person may not choose to be paralyzed; it is what happens when certain events occur and he or she lacks effective coping skills.

While emotions may blind the individual and pose difficulties, they may also be the very vehicle of self-discovery and fulfillment. Emotions are key components of many important and joyful aspects of the human experience. Having the capacity to benefit from emotions, rather than being paralyzed by them, offers the individual the opportunity to mobilize individuality while actively learning valuable life lessons and evolving to reach personal potential. As the individual learns how to regulate emotions, thoughts, and actions, he is not only not paralyzed, but he is able to face life, relationships, and himself with courage, grace, and strength.

Developing effective emotion-regulation skills is an important step toward managing life's complexities, versus becoming paralyzed by them. Knowing how to increase positive effect and reduce negative feelings can help the person improve his or her quality of life. This regulatory capacity allows the person to balance both rational and emotional aspects of situations to reach his or her personal goals. Regulating emotions does not mean erasing them; it means proactively and reactively making adjustments in behavior that help the individual maintain balance. This ability to balance helps the individual remain actively engaged in the process of self-discovery even when experiencing significant life challenges.

The Skills System

The Skills System is a set of nine skills and three system rules that helps the individual cope with life's challenges. The emotion-regulation skills curriculum was developed to help the person organize her internal and external experiences in ways that decrease discomfort and problematic behaviors, while increasing positive affect and goals directed actions. This simple framework guides the person through the process of becoming aware of the current moment, directing

1

attention, and activating behaviors that are in service of personal goals. The person learns to follow steps that mobilize inner wisdom in each unique situation. As the skills and the guidelines are integrated into the context of the person's life, the demonstration of effective coping behaviors within challenging situations increases. Each situation provides the person with an opportunity for self-discovery and for active participation in events. The individual is no longer paralyzed; he or she is a Skills Master.

User-friendly for individuals with learning challenges.

Learning new, more adaptive patterns of behavior is a challenging task for anyone. This is especially difficult when the individual must manage complicating factors such as mental health issues, intellectual impairment, physical problems, or other difficult life circumstances. These life challenges may increase stress and impact the individual's ability to learn new information.

The Skills System and the curriculum contained in this guide are designed to help individuals who experience learning challenges. For example, an individual who is diagnosed with an intellectual disability or mental illness may have difficulty focusing attention, remembering information, and utilizing concepts within complex situations. The Skills System itself and the teaching strategies contained in the *Instructor's Guide* are constructed to maximize learning, integration, and ultimately generalization of the skills into life's contexts. Even an individual who cannot read or write can learn and use the Skills System.

Compatible with dialectical behavior therapy (DBT).

The Skills System was developed as an accessible alternative for individuals with cognitive impairment who were participating in DBT therapy (Linehan, 1993). DBT therapy has two main components: individual therapy and skills-training group. The skills curriculum (Linehan, 1993b) is broken down into four modules. The individual learns skills in the areas of mindfulness, emotion regulation, distress tolerance, and interpersonal effectiveness. The clients learn adaptive coping skills in group and discuss implementation of the strategies within life contexts during individual therapy.

The standard DBT skills (Linehan, 1993b) were not specifically designed for individuals with intellectual disabilities in that the terms are complicated and there is no framework for utilizing the skills. Although the format of the standard skills is challenging, the general concepts are vastly helpful for this population. Merely modifying the teaching of the standard curriculum is not sufficient to capture the essence of DBT in a way that promotes generalization of the principles and skills by this population. The Skills System utilizes DBT principles, while the language and format are adapted to address the needs of individuals who experience significant learning challenges. The Skills System may be conceptualized as pre-DBT skills; the remedial structure of the Skills System model offers the individual basic self-regulation capacities, upon which the standard skills can be added.

Applications of the Skills System

Who can benefit from learning the Skills System? Many people have experiences or physiology that complicates the learning and demonstration of effective emotion-regulation behaviors. Each person has unique clusters of strengths and deficits, abilities and disabilities. Any individual, intellectually disabled or otherwise, may be prone to overwhelming emotions, unclear thinking, or unproductive action. All people have the capacity to make impulsive decisions that hinder the accomplishment of personal goals. Even individuals who practice adaptive coping behaviors experience overwhelming circumstances that can stress such capacities. The Skills System materials are user-friendly concepts that are accessible to learners of all abilities.

The utilization of the Skills System is expanding. Although the Skills System was originally designed for adults with significant cognitive impairment who were participating in DBT, the model is often used within the context of other forms of individual therapy or with individuals not receiving these services. Similarly, although the curriculum was designed for adults, adolescent and children's programs have adopted the model. In addition, the curriculum is being used by a broad spectrum of individuals, from those with severe learning challenges to those with no learning challenges whatsoever. The Skills System concepts and teaching strategies are constructed to facilitate learning and implementation; the ease of learning benefits all.

The Skills System model has been used in many different therapeutic settings. For example, the Skills System has been implemented in residential programs for emotionally disturbed children, as well as within outpatient community mental health settings. Residential programs serving emotionally disturbed adolescents have also utilized the Skills System. In addition, residential programs supporting intellectually disabled adolescents and adults have integrated the model into their programs. Although no empirical data is yet available in these settings, informal reports support the usage of the Skills System with diverse populations.

Overview of the Skills System

There are nine skills in the Skills System; these nine skills form the Skills List. There are also three System Tools that guide utilization of the skills. An individual who tends to become overwhelmed by emotion, has difficulty focusing on thoughts that are in service of personal goals, and/or reacts impulsively to urges benefits from learning step-by-step progressions to manage these factors. A person with these issues may have difficulty transitioning successfully from one strategy to the next in traditional coping-skills education that provides individual elements without offering a system to guide implementation. The unified structure assists the person in remembering strategies and moving fluidly through a multistep coping transaction while experiencing intense emotional-, cognitive-, and behavioral-regulation problems. As the individual learns the skills and the system, he or she integrates the capacity to successfully experience a full range of human emotions, practice self-determination, and acquire the means to navigate toward goals even in challenging circumstances.

The first three skills in the Skills System comprise a core progression that serves as the foundation for skills use. This sequence begins when an individual experiences a change in emotion; he or she begins by getting a Clear Picture (Skill 1). Six steps lead the person to become aware of information within the current moment. This is crucial, because often individuals with self-regulation problems focus attention on the past or future, rather than the present. Not only does focusing on the current moment give the person accurate information to use in making decisions, but it also reduces strong emotional responses.

Once the person gets a Clear Picture, he or she switches to focusing on On-Track Thinking (Skill 2). In On-Track Thinking, the individual moves through a simple four-step sequence that leads him or her through the process of mapping out an effective coping plan. This cognitive framework serves to shape the individual's thinking patterns to promote emotion regulation and goal-directed behaviors. As the person learns the adaptive cognitive structure in group, practices it within his life context, and experiences positive reinforcement, the functional thinking patterns become increasingly sophisticated and automatic over time.

On-Track Thinking requires the individual to make a Skills Plan. This component links the remaining skills together in a chain. Three simple rules (System Tools) determine which skills will be helpful and how many to use within the context of the present moment. Depending on the individual's self-reported level of emotional arousal (using the Feelings Rating Scale), he or she knows whether using more interactive skills (Skills 6-9) are options (using the Categories of Skills). The person learns that at high levels of emotional (and cognitive) arousal, it is necessary to choose more solitary skills (Skills 1–5) that function to reduce the sensations of uncomfortable feelings, to divert attention from problematic urges to effective actions, to minimize risks, and to improve focus. At all levels of escalation, the individual makes a plan to choose a sufficient number of skills (using the Recipe for Skills), targeting specifically the most effective skills according to the demands of the situation.

Next, the individual takes an On-Track Action (Skill 3). On-Track Actions are the behaviors the individual mobilizes to move in the direction of his goal. Therefore, the person gets a Clear Picture, does On-Track Thinking, and executes a series of On-Track Actions. If the individual is over a level 3 emotion, she may engage in a Safety Plan (Skills 4) or New-Me Activities (Skills 5). If under a level 3, the person can also use the Calm-Only skills, which are Problem Solving (Skill 6), Expressing Myself (Skill 7), Getting It Right (Skill 8), and Relationship Care (Skill 9). Once a cluster of skills has been completed, the individual returns to do Clear Picture again to become aware of the new situation that has evolved.

Initially, the individual conceptualizes the Skills System as a series of linear events; when a sequence of skills is finished, he or she returns to doing Clear Picture, On-Track Thinking, On-Track Action, and so on, repeating the process in each subsequent situation. As the individual integrates the Skills System, he or she is more able to utilize Clear Picture and On-Track Thinking throughout the coping process in a dynamic, transacting pattern to adjust On-Track Actions. Even individuals with significant cognitive impairment gradually improve the ability to make subtle adjustments; this flexibility can enhance the person's success in reaching goals and in maintaining on-track relationships. The Skills System is a structured, yet malleable framework that can help an individual reduce reliance on avoidant behaviors, bear increased responsibilities, and fully engage in the human experience.

The Skills List	**System Tools**
All-the-Time Skills	A. Feelings Rating Scale
1. Clear Picture	• 0–5 scale for rating the intensity of
2. On-Track Thinking	emotions
3. On-Track Action	B. Categories of Skills
4. Safety Plan	• Skills 1–5 are All-The-Time Skills
5. New-Me ActivitiesCalm-Only Skills	• Skills 6–9 are Calm-Only skills
6. Problem Solving	C. Recipe for Skills
7. Expressing Myself	• Add one skill for every level of
8. Getting It Right	emotion. (e.g., at a level 2 emotion,
9. Relationship Care	use three skills)

Table 1.1: Skills List and System Tools

The Skills List

The following section includes brief descriptions of each of the skills and System Tools. This is intended as an initial exposure to the information. These concepts are presented in greater detail in Chapter 2. This introduction will serve as a skeleton upon which more information will be layered in the following chapters.

1. Getting started with a Clear Picture.

The first skill in the Skills System is Clear Picture; the metaphor of a television represents having a clear versus a fuzzy vision of a situation. Clear Picture guides the individual through steps that bring focused attention to six aspects of the person's present experience to gain clarity. The first of the Clear Picture Do's prompts the individual to focus on her breath. Next, the person shifts attention to notice what is happening around her. Once the individual has awareness of the environment, attention is then shifted to doing a Body Check; bringing attention to the body begins a series of self-reflections that help orient the person to the realities of her internal experience. The person then labels and rates her emotions and notices thoughts and urges.

There are two important facets of this skill: (1) gaining accurate information about these important internal and external experiences and (2) effectively shifting attention. Some individuals who experience cognitive deficits and/or self-regulation problems have difficulty shifting attention in ways that manage her level of arousal. The Clear Picture skill trains the person to see facts versus fantasies and to focus on making decisions that are in her best interest.

2. Using On-Track Thinking.

Once the individual has a Clear Picture of her internal and external circumstances in the moment, the person strategically transfers attention to Skill 2, which is On-Track Thinking. The name "On-Track" uses the metaphor of a train to represent the concept of the individual moving incrementally toward a destination or goal. Thus, the image of "Off-Track" communicates circumstances that are not in service of the goal.

On-Track Thinking offers the person a series of four tasks to complete to create an effective thinking process. This sequence, (1) Stop, Step back, and Think about what I want; (2) Check the Urge; (3) Turn It to Thumbs-Up; and (4) Make a Skills Plan, provides an adaptive cognitive structuring template for the individual to follow in each situation. These simple steps lead the person to pause before reacting to impulses, reflect on desired outcomes, check the utility of the urge, create useful alternatives, and create a plan to reach the goal.

3. Taking an On-Track Action.

Once the participant gets a Clear Picture and does On-Track Thinking, he uses Skill 3, which is On-Track Action. The reuse of the word "On-Track" is designed to reinforce the concept that the person transitions from On-Track Thinking to On-Track Action. It is challenging for any person to alter problematic patterns of behavior; On-Track Actions mobilize new, adaptive actions that are directly related to personal goals. It is useful to have On-Track Thoughts, but without On-Track Actions, the individual may revert to problematic behaviors.

There are five different elements of the On-Track Action skill. First, this skill includes any action that the individual takes in the direction of her goal. An action is considered on-track if the person has taken time to be self-aware within the present moment (Clear Picture) and has made an effective decision (On-Track Thinking). The remaining functions of On-Track Actions include Switching Tracks, making an On-Track Action Plan, Accepting the Situation, and/or Letting It Pass and Moving On. Each of these concepts give the individual tools to proactively or reactively manage Off-Track Urges.

4. Managing risky situations with Safety Plans.

During the process of getting a Clear Picture and doing On-Track Thinking, the person may identify possible risks that may impede her progress toward goals. In a situation such as this, the individual may take the On-Track Action to create and execute a Safety Plan. Safety Plans, the fourth skill in the Skills System, provide a framework that assists in evaluating the Level of Risk and in choosing the appropriate responses to manage the circumstances. It is important that the person be fully aware of risks, understand various options for managing the problems, and have the ability to implement actions that neither unnecessarily avoid situations nor recklessly engage in problematic ones.

5. Doing New-Me Activities.

New-Me[1] Activities, the fifth skill, are activities that the person engages in throughout each day. The term "New-Me" represents activities that set the person on-track to personal goals. Individuals may engage in Old-Me behaviors that reinforce problematic feelings, thoughts, and actions. Developing a broad array of preferred New-Me Activities can help an individual improve self-regulation and satisfaction.

New-Me Activities serve four basic functions. Focus New-Me Activities assist the client in focusing attention, while other activities promote distraction. Some activities help the person feel good, and others are intended to be fun. The participant learns to evaluate what her needs are in the moment and to choose a New-Me Activity that fits best.

6. Problem Solving.

The individual may determine that she has a problem or has the urge to impulsively take action to change a situation. Problem Solving helps the person strategically evaluate when and how to solve problems so that she reaches personal goals. The individual may have previous experiences that involved rushed, ill-planned, or extreme responses that not only fail to repair difficulties, but also augment problems. Learning when to solve problems is just as important to knowing how to do it.

Problem Solving, the sixth skill, is a multistep process that guides a person to fix problems in her life. During Problem Solving, the participant takes time to gain clarity about the problem, reviews multiple options for solving it, and checks the fit of the choices. The person develops Plans A, B, and C to prepare for inevitable obstacles that occur.

7. Expressing Myself.

In certain situations, the individual experiences the urge to communicate emotions or thoughts. Expressing Myself, Skill 7, assists the individual in making effective decisions about how and when to communicate with others. A person may have a habit of expressing himself while at high levels of emotional arousal. Although this may serve to purge distress, provide distraction, or mobilize the individual in challenging situations, such impulsive expression often damages relationships or causes other problems. The Expressing Myself skill helps the individual to strategically and effectively utilize communication to reach personal goals. The person learns to use other skills, such as New-Me Activities, to reduce emotions at times when he is experiencing discomfort, rather than venting on others.

---

1   The terms "Old-Me" and "New-Me" were used by Petre-Miller, Haaven, and Little in their book *Treating Intellectually Disabled Sex Offenders* (1989). Although the term New-Me is used in many other forums, a special acknowledgment of these authors' contribution to the field of disabilities is warranted. This author wants to thank James Haaven for his support.

It is vital for the participant to understand various types of expression so that he can choose a means of communication that he believes is the best fit in each situation and then plan and execute that communication. Learning about the functions of self-expression, how to craft interactions, and when to use Expressing Myself can improve relationships and assist the individual in reaching personal goals.

8. Getting It Right.

The person may be in a situation where she needs to get something from another person. Getting It Right is used specifically for acquiring what the individual wants or needs. Getting needs met is a vital skill; unfortunately, skill deficits in this area have often contributed to cycles of ineffective behavior and high levels of dissatisfaction. When the person makes requests while at a high a level of emotional arousal, the person fails to elicit help and may reduce the likelihood that her needs will be met. A person may Get It Wrong when she is unable to judge when, how, and with whom to advocate to get needs met. It is essential to have the capacity to self-advocate and negotiate to reach personal goals.

Skill 8, Getting It Right, provides the individual with a simple framework to get what she wants from another person. The participant learns to be in the Right Mind, talk to the Right Person at the Right Time and Place, use the Right Tone, and say the Right Words. The Right Word include (SEALS) using Sugar, Explaining the Situation, Asking for What You Want, Listening, and Sealing a Deal.

9. Relationship Care.

Each of us experiences countless urges each day that potentially harm our relationships. Relationship Care is designed to help the individual effectively assess relationship situations so that she can make personal decisions that improve her quality of life. Many life problems are fueled by ill-timed and impulsive relationship behaviors. While it is challenging to manage all of the changing forces that are continually transacting as part of the human experience, the individual increases mastery within relationships when she gains the ability to use this and the other skills effectively.

The ninth skill, Relationship Care, assists the person in managing her self-relationship and interactions with other people. Building On-Track Relationships, Balancing On-Track Relationships, and Changing Off-Track Relationships are the essential components. As the individual becomes more aware of her personal needs and learns how various actions either enhance personal connections or lead to creating distance between people, the individual is better able to actively manage interactions with others.

System Tools

A person who has coping skills deficits and self-regulation problems may have difficulty accurately evaluating internal and external experiences. Additionally, the person may not have the ability to monitor his levels of self-regulation to strategically choose behaviors that achieve desired outcomes. The Skills System is designed to help an individual develop coping tools and also the ability to use the skills to get needs met. The System Tools are simple concepts that guide the participant's use of the nine skills on the Skills List. There are three System Tools: (A) the Feelings Rating Scale, (B) the Categories of Skills, and (C) the Recipe for Skills.

A. Feelings Rating Scale.

The Feelings Rating Scale is a simple 0–5 scale that the individual uses to rate the intensity of sensations he is feeling. It is an important tool to help the person be aware of and organize his current experiences. The scale concretizes the abstract experience of emotions, which is particularly important for an individual who has intellectual impairments.

Through the skills-training experience, the participant learns to differentiate emotional experiences and categorize the feelings rating. A 0 feeling means that the person is not experiencing sensations related to the emotion. A 1 feeling is when the person is experiencing a tiny amount of the sensation from the emotion. A 2 feeling is when the individual has a small amount of sensation. A 3 emotion is when a medium level of emotion is felt. Generally, the individual's ability to focus and control behavior is intact when emotions are between a 0 and 3 emotion; above a 3, the person's cognitive and behavioral control abilities may be compromised. A 4 feeling is a strong experience of sensations related to an emotion; often some kind of behavioral dyscontrol or urge to execute Off-Track Actions is present. A 5 feeling is when the individual becomes overwhelmed and exhibits behavior that harms self, others, or property.

The scale serves a dual purpose: (1) the Feelings Rating Scale helps the person get a Clear Picture of the current moment, and (2) the individual also uses the rating to determine which and how many skills to use in the situation in On-Track Thinking. The person learns that at lower levels of arousal, he has the capacity to think clearly and interact effectively; therefore, it is possible to use interactive skills at that time. Conversely, a higher rating communicates to the individual that he will have more difficulty thinking clearly and interacting effectively with other people. At high levels of emotion, more skills are indicated to manage the experience, and the goal at that point is to reduce arousal. The Feelings Rating Scale helps the individual build the capacity to manage impulses and productively wait until he is in the proper mind-set to utilize interactive skills.

B. Categories of Skills.

Many behavioral problems result when an individual engages in interactive skills at high levels of emotion. While it is natural to experience strong urges to take action to fix situations, express feelings, demand that needs be met, and exert control over people, acting on these urges often fails to help the individual reach personal goals. The Categories of Skills help the individual know which skills are effective at given levels of arousal.

There are two Categories of Skills. Skills 1–5 (Clear Picture, On-Track Thinking, On-Track Action, Safety Plan, and New-Me Activities) are called All-the-Time skills. All-the-Time skills can be used at any level of emotion, from 0 to 5. The other Category of Skills is called Calm-Only skills. The person can use skills 6–9 (Problem Solving, Expressing Myself, Getting It Right, and Relationship Care) only when he is at or below a level 3 emotion. Therefore, the person can utilize all nine skills if he is at or below a 3 emotion and just skills 1–5 if he is over a 3 emotion.

C. Recipe for Skills.

Another common pitfall happens when a person uses an insufficient number of skills within a situation. When high levels of emotions trigger body sensations, the effects can be uncomfortable and long-lasting. It is essential that the person use multiple strategies to continually manage behaviors throughout experiences.

The Recipe for Skills calls for using one more skill than the level of emotion. For example, if an individual is at a level 2 emotion, at least three skills must be used. If the individual is at a 5 emotion, at least six skills are needed. In this case, since the person is over a 3 emotion, it is necessary for the person to use an extra All-the-Time skill (e.g., using two New-Me Activities), rather than having the sixth skill be from the Calm-Only category.

The goal of the Recipe for Skills is to ensure that the person plans and executes a sufficient number of skills. The number of skills changes related to the severity of the situation; the intensity of the event is calibrated through the emotional impact the circumstance has on the individual. It is not uncommon for individuals with emotion-regulation problems to rush through insufficient strategies that do not adequately address the multiple components of complex internal and external situations. The Recipe for Skills is intended to teach the person to maximize skill use.

Putting It All Together

When a participant begins learning the Skills System, his ability to recall all of the concepts and terms is expectedly inconsistent. Group teaching strategies continually expose the participant to the Skills List and the System Tools within the contexts of the participants' lives. This revolving approach allows the individual to cobble together comprehension over time. Suggestions for structuring skills instruction, teaching strategies, and implementing a twelve-week curriculum are presented in Chapters 5–8.

Relatively early in skills training, the participant learns to be increasingly mindful of the present moment. The individual becomes able to take a quick snapshot of internal and external factors using the Clear Picture Do's. With practice, the person increases his speed and accuracy in these tasks.

The information gathered during the Clear Picture Do's is used to help the person generate On-Track Thinking. For example, the feelings rating score (e.g., level 4 angry) guides the individual to choose which Category of Skills will be helpful at his current level of emotion. The person learns that All-The-Time skills (1–5) may be utilized at any level of emotion, while Calm-Only skills (6–9) are only used when the individual is below a 3 emotion. In the above example, at a 4 emotion, the participant would only engage in All-the-Time skills and not utilize Calm-Only skills. All-the-Time skills allow the individual to reregulate prior to engaging in the more interactive Calm-Only skills. Additionally, the individual learns to use ample skills for the situation. The Recipe for Skills sets guidelines for the minimum number of skills. Quickly the person learns the adage: the more skills, the better.

On-Track Thinking is a relatively complex skill; mastery is a slow and organic process. The participant may initially have primitive self-dialogue. Often as skills capacities develop, more sophistication evolves. For example, the person may initially self-reflect and think, *I feel angry at a 4; I need to go to my room.* As self-awareness continues to evolve, self-statements become more elaborated: *I am at a 4 anger; I have to use my All-the-Time skills. I have the urge to Express Myself, but I must wait until I am below a 3 emotion. If I do it now, I will yell. Instead I will do a Safety Plan and New-Me Activities. I have to use my skills, because I want to reach my goals. I can do this.*

Throughout the skills-training experience, the individual often becomes aware of (and committed to) taking On-Track versus Off-Track Actions. The mindfulness (Clear Picture) training paired with the cognitive structuring (On-Track Thinking) offers the participant a framework that guides the person toward taking effective, self-determined On-Track Actions. The participant becomes increasingly able to strategically intertwine various combinations of skills to manage oscillating internal and external needs. As the Skills System is integrated, mastery in complex and uncomfortable situations is achieved. The nine skills and three System Tools are repeated and reinforced so that the adaptive coping patterns become default settings.

Integration within Living and Learning Environments.

The Skills System may provide a therapeutic language base and adaptive coping skills model for many different environments. The Skills System can be helpful in residential, outpatient, classroom, and/or home settings. Parents can partner with their children to learn and use the material together. The preliminary research is currently limited, yet the opportunities for future study and exploration are broad.

The visual nature of the Skills System can promote integration within environments. The visual aid materials can provide visual cues that prompt skill use for participants and skills coaches. For example, in one children's program, skills posters and personalized decorations were mounted throughout the buildings. When the model becomes immersed in the Skills System, many creative programmatic and individualized interventions are possible.

There are many benefits of integrating the Skills System into group settings. The Skills System provides common language and a framework of information related to managing emotions, thoughts, and actions. This shared framework and language facilitate learning. When participants and support providers both actively engage in positive relating behaviors, opportunities for adaptive learning and relating increase. For example, there are multiple benefits for participants and staff who take part in peer skills tutoring activities. Ideally, participants and support providers learn how to cope effectively and are able to engage in positive social behaviors that are mutually beneficial and reciprocal.

CHAPTER 2:

Learning The Skills System

The first portion of this chapter is designed to provide the skills trainer with specific information about each of the nine skills and the System Tools that guide the utilization of the skills. While the Skills System is a structured model, it is not a prescriptive formula. Rather, it is a revolving process that shifts to respond to the dynamic perceptions and needs of each person within each changing moment. Knowing all of the elements of the Skills System helps trainers, coaches, and, ultimately the individual, make and execute self-determined, finely tuned Skills Plans.

The final section of this chapter introduces the "modal model" introduced by Gross and Thompson in the *Handbook of Emotion Regulation* (2007). This information aids the trainer to better understand how the individual may combine Skills System components to regulate affect. Emotion regulation deficits are key aspects of many psychological disorders, as well as a main treatment focus of DBT.

Skills coaches may also find utility in reading this chapter. It will give the support person a strong understanding of the skills and how the system functions. Specific techniques for providing skills coaching are presented in Chapter 3.

Chapter 2 may also serve as home-study material for the skills group participant. If an individual has difficulty reading or comprehending the language, support providers can read and/or review the material with the participant. The general information can help expand the participant's knowledge about the skills and System Tools. Home study, peer tutoring, and engaging in skills review with support staff can be useful techniques to enhance mastery. Learning concepts in individual or group training sessions, participating in home study, and applying the Skills System within daily living broadens and deepens each person's understanding of emotion-regulation skills.

The Skills List

1. Clear Picture.

Clear Picture is the first skill in the Skills System, and it is an All-the-Time skill. This means that Clear Picture can be used at any level of feeling, 0–5. There are six steps, which collectively are referred to as the Clear Picture Do's. The purpose of Clear Picture is to become aware of what is happening inside and outside of the person in the current moment. The word "clear" helps the individual understand that it is important to see the present moment *as it is* and to have an accurate perception of the facts. The alternative is a Fuzzy Picture. A Fuzzy Picture describes when an individual is experiencing cognitive dysregulation, is disoriented, or is not perceiving actualities within the situation. When the person has a Fuzzy Picture, Off-Track Thinking prevails, and effective coping is impeded by the lack of clarity.

Clear Picture is the first skill for a reason: it must be done first in every situation. Whenever the person notices any feelings or a situation changes, it is important to take a few seconds to get a Clear Picture. The following steps help the individual become aware of internal and external factors that are currently happening.

(1) Breathe: The first step in Clear Picture is to Take a Breath. As the individual takes a few breaths, it is important to bring attention to the physical sensations of breathing. Noticing the air going in and out of the nose, feeling the chest expand, and observing the snugness of her waistband as she brings the air into the belly area are common focal points during breathing.

It is important that the individual notice the breath *as it is* versus needing to do a particular type of breathing. Seeing the breath *as it is* is a first step toward the individual seeing herself and the situation clearly. Gaining awareness that is free of distortions and avoidance is an important skills starting point. This concrete action of breathing can bring the individual into awareness of the intangible aspects of the current moment; being oriented to the reality of the present, the person is more capable of planning and executing effective behaviors. Additionally, when the person brings 100 percent attention to the breath, attention shifts from the escalating emotions and cognitions, and only the breath is in awareness. Managing this one moment becomes more possible.

Teaching awareness of breath as a simple first step that triggers Skills System usage. Not only is the skill construct linked to this one simple step, but the individual has the breath with them at all times, in all contexts. Learning, practicing, and reinforcing the linkages between taking a breath, the Clear Picture Do's, and the other skills helps promote integration and automation of skills use into the person's life.

(2) Notice Surroundings: It is important for the person to Notice Surroundings. He must take a moment to look around to gain a clear understanding of what is happening outside of himself *right now*. This scan includes noticing aspects of the physical environment and of the relationships that are present. Seeing the situations and relationships *as they are* is crucial. When the individual gets emotionally escalated, it is not uncommon for him to blur factors; inconsistencies between the realities of the situation and the perceptions of the individual can impede effective skills utilization. For example, focusing on what happened in the past, what might happen in the future, or what *should* be happening in the present hinders clarity in the present moment. Gathering accurate information about the current situation helps the individual to handle the situation effectively. Noticing Surroundings is a particularly important step if there are environmental factors, relationships, or risks that are necessary to manage.

As the person develops an understanding that it is easier to manage one clear moment in time, he is more likely to evaluate situations accurately. The individual learns that clarity, although potentially uncomfortable for the moment, allows effective coping and the accomplishment of personal goals. The individual may use fewer avoidant strategies as he experiences them as less effective and more problematic in the long term.

(3) Body Check: Doing a quick body scan helps the individual become aware of what is happening inside of him/or her *right now*. For example, the person can use her five senses to do a Body Check. Reviewing what the person sees, hears, smells, touches, and tastes can be one way to do a Body Check. The participant may notice her feet on the floor and her contact with the chair in which she is sitting to be oriented to the present moment. Noticing physical sensations within the body is helpful; heart rate, breathing, aches, and tension are examples of some sensations that emotions produce. Therefore, noticing body sensations can help the person begin the process of understanding reactions, Labeling Emotions, and Rating Emotions. Not only is having clarity within the present moment vital, but as the person continually monitors her physical being, she learns that sensations come and go through the natural course of each day. This awareness helps the person understand the concept of "this too shall pass." Understanding that painful experience comes and goes naturally helps the individual tolerate being present in the moment. The awareness that painful feelings will abate in time helps the individual be present in, tolerate, and manage discomfort.

Label and Rate Emotions.

The fourth step in Clear Picture is to Label and Rate Emotions. The person notices and describes emotions, such as sadness, happiness, hurt, fear, jealousy, love, guilt, frustration, and anger. Once the person labels the emotion, it is important to rate the emotion using the Feelings Rating Scale (0–5). For example, the individual could label and rate an experience as a 3 Sad. Once again, the continual labeling and rating of feelings implicitly teaches the individual that emotions rise and fall, come and go. This awareness helps the person believe that painful states are transient and that emotions are survivable. As skills develop further, the individual begins to become aware that it is possible to decrease painful experiences, while increasing pleasant ones. With practice, the individual can notice, accept, and allow challenging emotions to pass without taking impulsive action or retriggering more painful feelings.

Notice Thoughts.

The fifth step in Clear Picture is Notice Thoughts. The individual learns to pay attention to thoughts as they pass through her mind *right now*. The thoughts "I hate him" or "If I punch him, I will get arrested" are examples of thoughts that may pass through the individual mind. By Noticing Thoughts, the person learns that thoughts continually come and go; being aware of this flow helps the individual see that it is possible not to react automatically to thoughts. Participants learn that thoughts are like city buses. The individual watches as the buses (thoughts) go by and only chooses ones that are going to her preferred destination (helps reach her goal). During the Clear Picture skill, the individual becomes aware of thoughts. This is an essential first step toward exerting attentional control and cultivating the goal-directed thoughts that happen during the On-Track Thinking skill.

Notice Urges.

The sixth step in Clear Picture is to Notice Urges. Becoming aware of action urges that are associated with various emotions and thoughts is a crucial aspect of managing behaviors effectively. Fight and flight are examples of action urges—for example, "I want to punch him in the face" or "I gotta get out of here." Urges, much like sensations, emotions, and thoughts, naturally come and go. Impulsively reacting to urges usually creates diminished levels of effectiveness when compared to taking a few moments to reflect on personal goals, situational options, and likely outcomes. Not only is Noticing Urges a key aspect of getting a Clear Picture, it is also the transition point to utilizing the other skills in the Skills System. Once the individual notices her urge, it is imperative that attention be shifted to On-Track Thinking.

If an individual does not have the capacity to learn all six Clear Picture Do's, it is helpful to focus on a portion of the skill. Taking a breath is a useful cue that enhances focus and begins the skill-utilization process. It is also very important to complete the process of labeling and rating an emotion using the Feelings Rating Scale. Establishing the rating level helps the person decide which Category of Skills to use (Calm Only and/or All-the-Time); this is significant because the person has to understand when she is too upset to interact with others. Lastly, Noticing Urges is a critical step. Becoming aware of the action urge gives the individual an opportunity to Stop and Step Back to think things through in On-Track Thinking. Thus initially, Taking a Breath, Labeling and Rating Emotion, and Noticing Urges are the key aspects of Clear Picture; the individual can learn the other Clear Picture Do's throughout the skills-training process.

2. On-Track Thinking.

On-Track Thinking is the second skill in the Skills System. It is an All-the-Time skill, so it can be used at any level of emotion, 0–5. On-Track Thinking is the second skill because it is always used directly after getting a Clear Picture. The following steps guide the individual to determine which On-Track Action to take, which is the next step below.

Throughout skills training, instructors help participants understand the concepts of short-term and long-term consequences for actions. This helps the person decide if an urge is helpful or not helpful. Discussions and exercises can expose the individual to self-exploration and various perspectives related to outcomes that help increase awareness of these factors. Learning adaptive coping skills is a lengthy process of discovering evolving personal preferences, goals, means to reach goals, and knowledge about how life tends to work.

Stop, Step Back, and Think about what I want.

Once the person has done the Clear Picture Do's and noticed the action urge, he Stops, Steps Back, and thinks about what he wants. The person may not literally take a step back; the intention of this concept is to guide the person to pause for a moment to self-reflect. Thinking about what the individual wants or does not want to happen in a situation can orient the person toward the appropriate adjustments in behavior. Situations may elicit strong emotions and thoughts that fuel action urges. Counteracting this momentum increases the likelihood that actions will be on-track to personal goals.

Check the Urge.

Next, the person Checks the Urge; a thumbs-up is given if acting on the urge will help the person reach his goal. A thumbs-down is given if the action would be off-track to the goal. Using the phrase "check it" with a simple hand signal can prompt a participant to Check the Urge.

Turn It.

If the thoughts and urges are Off-Track or Thumbs-Down Thinking, it is important to Check It and then Turn It. Turning It means to shift attention to On-Track Thoughts. These Thumbs-Up Thoughts help the individual focus on *doing what works* in every situation. The thumbs-up sign is a useful visual aid that gives a tangible representation to thoughts. For example, if the instructor states a thought, such as, *I feel like hitting him*, the participant can evaluate it as a thumbs-up or thumbs-down for himself. The individual can then give an example of how to Turn It to a Thumbs-Up Thought like, *If I hit him, I will be on restriction*. Thumbs-Up Thinking often includes highlighting the desired or unwanted Outcomes. It is important that he individual not only highlight negative consequences, but also generate positive self-statements that promote

On-Track Actions, such as "I will do a Safety Plan now". Continually self-reflecting, Checking, and Turning to On-Track Thinking promotes movement toward goals as the individual executes a skill plan.

Prior to skills training, the individual's self-talk often consists of self-devaluing internal dialogue that undermines motivation and self-efficacy. The individual may need to improve capacities to generate self-encouragement statements that help motivate him to continue skills use and endure challenging states without reverting to problematic patterns. Cheering himself on with self-talk such as, "I can do this," "I have to use my skills," and/or "everything is going to be all right" represents the use of important Thumbs-Up Thoughts.

Make a Skills Plan.

Once the individual has Checked the Urge and Turned It if necessary, he makes a Skills Plan. Choosing which skills and how many to use are key aspects of this process. Initially, the person may need to go through concrete steps to learn how to formulate an effective Skills Plan. As the individual becomes familiar with concepts, the process happens more intuitively.

- *Choosing Category of Skills.* Deciding whether the individual can use Calm-Only skills (Skills 6–9) is crucial. If the individual is over a 3 emotion, All-the-Time skills (Skills 1–5) should be used. Using Calm-Only skills when over a 3 often causes problems for the individual. It may be helpful to validate the individual's urge to solve the problem, express emotions, try to get needs met, or settle relationship conflicts immediately, but using the All-the-Time skills first to reduce arousal is generally more effective.

- *Recipe for Skills.* The Recipe for Skills is used as a general guide for skills use. The main points are (1) use enough skills and (2) generally using more skills is better. Additionally, the Recipe for Skills is a positive teaching concept, as well as a helpful coaching tool. When teaching the process of making a Skills Plan, the instructor can convey using tangible terms about how to calculate how many skills to use. In a skills-coaching situation, the coach can ask the participant to calculate the Recipe for Skills to shift attention from Off-Track to On-Track Thinking and to improve focus.

- *Choosing the best skills for the situation.* Making a Skills Plan is a preliminary step toward charting a course of action to reach personal goals. The individual thinks about outcomes and possible skills that will help him to achieve the desired effect. For example, the individual would often choose to do Clear Picture, On-Track Thinking, On-Track Action, Safety Plan, and New-Me Activities when in a risky situation. As the individual becomes more familiar with the Skills List through skills training and experience, he accumulates more viable options for proactive behaviors. The Skills System Handout 2 (How Our Skills Help Us) is a brief summary of the functions of each skill; learning this information can aid recall related to which skills to use in various situations.

3. On-Track Action.

On-Track Action is the third skill in the Skills System. It is an All-the-Time skill; thus it can be used at any level of emotion, 0–5. The individual completes Clear Picture and On-Track Thinking to determine the On-Track Action in the circumstance. The triad of skills is a core progression of emotion-regulation skills; the phrase "one, two, three" represents the three simple key steps that are the foundation for utilizing all of the skills.

An On-Track Action is when the person takes an action that is a step toward her goal. For example, if the person is trying to lose weight, reaching for the bag of carrots when preparing lunch may be an On-Track Action. Reaching for a bag of chips may be an Off-Track Action. An On-Track Action is when the person does something that helps her reach a personal goal in a situation. Quickly reacting while hoping that an action is on-track may work, yet may not incorporate the totality of available information and may not have maximum positive impact.

It is essential to understand that *only the individual, in that moment,* can decide whether an action is on-track or off-track. For example, perhaps the individual had lost ten pounds and wanted a few chips as a treat; taking chips instead of carrots on that day may be an On-Track Action. The personal decision-making process is a vital opportunity for self-determination and activation of her inner wisdom. The goal is to help the person engage in a skills process prior to taking actions versus leading her to particular choices.

Skills trainers and coaches have to balance the role of being supportive to the individual with encouraging autonomy. For example, the support provider can offer reflections about her own choices in similar situations and the effectiveness of those decisions in terms of reaching personal goals. She can also highlight possible outcomes for certain actions so that the individual is oriented to the results of decisions prior to making a choice. It is generally not helpful for trainers and coaches to dictate whether an action is on-track or off-track for the person unless it is a high-risk situation

There are times when the On-Track Action is to leave the current mind-set, Shifting Tracks to an on-track train of thought and action. To heighten the likelihood of staying on-track, the person can make On-Track Action Plans that proactively engage an abundance of skills. In situations when the individual had done everything possible to improve a situation that she can, it may be necessary to do the On-Track Action of Accepting the Situation. Lastly, there may be times when the individual needs to Let It Pass and Move On to get back or remain on-track.

Shifting Tracks.

On-Track Actions may be actions that shift the person from off-track to on-track. On-Track Actions are particularly important to engage in when the individual is experiencing Off-Track Urges. It is useful to Shift Tracks as soon as possible after going off the right track; the longer the wait, the more challenging the task of getting back on-track. For example, if I am sitting down watching a soap opera during my normal exercise time, it might be helpful to Shift Tracks and go put on workout clothes. Skills Masters realize when they are off their preferred track and shift behavior to do several On-Track Actions to be sure that they are on the right road to their goals. For example, changing into shorts, putting on running shoes, getting my music player, and filling my bottle of water would increase the likelihood that I would exercise. As a general rule, the individual is not advised to take an action unless it is an On-Track Action!

There are times when the individual continues to trigger uncomfortable emotions and/or ruminate about certain thoughts and urges; these behaviors may serve to increase painful emotions and hinder movement toward goals. In this circumstance, it may be helpful for the person to take the On-Track Action to Shift Tracks. An On-Track Action can help the individual Shift Tracks versus remaining stuck in off-track patterns. To Shift Tracks, the individual shifts focus and behaviors from off-track to on-track. Doing opposite of the Off-Track Urges may help reduce the cues that perpetuate problematic patterns. For example, if the individual does not want to get up in the morning and go to work, doing the opposite may help her Switch Tracks. She can bounce out of bed, jump into the shower , and find a great outfit to wear. The Off-Track

Urges will be replaced by on-track behavior. New On-Track Actions are reinforced and start the process of developing on-track patterns of behavior.

On-Track Action Plans.

On-Track Action Plans are activities that become part of the individual's daily routines and schedules. Doing extra positive things each day may help the person maintain balance in her life. For example, the person may take walks, eat healthy food, take proper medications, do Writing Safety Plans prior to medium- and high-risk events, get proper amounts of sleep, and talk to friends as part of an On-Track Action Plan each day. When balancing various aspects of daily living, the person may be better prepared to mitigate and manage stressful situations that arise.

Accepting the Situation.

When the person has done everything possible to manage a situation, it may be helpful to accept the situation *as it is*. There are many times when it is not possible to solve problems right away, and waiting is necessary. There are times when people are unable to get needs fulfilled and do not receive what is desired. Other times, people do things that affect the individual that cannot be stopped. When things happen in life that are beyond the individual's control, doing the On-Track Action of Accepting the Situation may be the most helpful tactic. It is important for the person to use New-Me Activities to help tolerate the discomfort that Accepting the Situation causes. Eventually, the individual will need to engage in Problem Solving to address underlying issues that may have led to the situation.

Let it Pass and Move On.

It may be helpful to do an On-Track Action to Let It Pass and Move On in certain situations. For example, if it is off-track to continue focusing on something because it is increasing the level of emotion, the individual can move on to some kind of On-Track Thinking or New-Me Activity. It can be challenging for individuals to Let It Pass and Move On; in these cases, it is helpful for skills coaches to highlight clear on-track steps to that lead the individual to demonstrate new behavior.

4. Safety Plan.

Safety Plan is the fourth skill in the Skills System, and it is an All-the-Time skill. This means that the Safety Plan can be used at any level of emotion, 0–5. If the individual determines, after doing Clear Picture and On-Track Thinking, that some kind of risk exists in the environment, a Safety Plan is often part of an effective Skills Plan. The person must decide what level the risk is, what kind of Safety Plan to use, and what actions are necessary to manage the current level of risk.

Levels of Risk.

There are three Levels of Risk: low, medium, and high. In a *low*-risk situation, the problem is far away or the contact may cause stress. In a *medium*-risk situation, the danger is in the area or contact may cause problems. In a *high*-risk situations, the danger is close or contact may cause serious damage.

Once the individual has a Clear Picture of the risk, it is necessary to choose the type of Safety Plan to use. It is important not to overrate or underrate risks. Overrating risk can cause the individual to avoid activities that are helpful to engage in. Underrating risk can lead to danger and harm because improper efforts are made to manage the problems. If the individual is not thinking clearly, it is important that he seeks support from someone to discuss options for managing the risk.

The first step in a Safety Plan is to get a Clear Picture of the risk. There are Inside-of-Me Risks, such as Off-Track Thoughts, Urges, Feelings, and Fantasies (TUFFs). There are also Outside-of-Me Risks, like people who upset the individual or situations that are dangerous. The person handles Inside- and Outside-of-Me Risks before larger problems develop.

Types of Safety Plans.

There are three types of Safety Plans: Thinking, Talking, and Writing.

- A Thinking Safety Plan is when the person thinks about how to manage the risk safely. A Thinking Safety Plan is used in low-risk situations.
- A Talking Safety Plan is when the person decides to tell someone about the risk to elicit support. It is generally helpful to use Talking Safety Plans in medium- and high-risk situations. For example, the individual may approach a skills coach and say, "I am having TUFFs right now. Could you help me make a good Safety Plan?" It is important to note that if the person is over a 3 emotion, the focus of the communication during a Talking Safety Plan is strictly on tactics to manage the risk, versus using participating in lengthy and detailed discussions that explore the content of the situation.
- A Writing Safety Plan is when the individual, with or without assistance, writes down the possible risk and dangers, either prior to, during, or after risky events. The person writes or completes an individualized form that highlights possible problems and strategies to manage difficulties that arise. Writing Safety Plans are particularly important in high-risk situations.

Ways to manage risk.

There are three ways to manage risks: refocus on New-Me Activities, Move Away, and Leave the Area

- Refocus on a New-Me Activity. The first, least invasive way of managing risk is to refocus on a New-Me Activity. New-Me Activities are various positive tasks that the individual does throughout the day. For example, if the person notices a low risk while at work, he may choose to focus on the work task he is doing—sweeping the floor, for instance. If the person is not engaged in an activity, participating in one may help the individual remain safe, focused, and on-track. Refocusing on a New-Me Activity prompts the individual to take a positive action versus merely ignoring the risk, which does not guide the individual toward an On-Track Action. It is important to give full attention to the activity, yet be alert to any changes in the environment and risk level of the situation.
  Example: Jim is at work. He hears his co-worker raising his voice in the next room. Through experience, Jim knows that the co-worker is merely venting, and no significant danger exists. Jim also feels that he is at a safe distance from the trouble and thus assesses the situation as low risk. He thinks about what he should do to handle the situation. Jim decides to stay where he is and focus on his work task.
- Move Away. The next way to manage risk is to Move Away from the risk. This means that the individual moves to a safer area and gets distance from the problem. Once the person has Moved Away, she may want to refocus on a New-Me Activity to stay on-track. It is often necessary to Move Away in medium-risk situations when either the problem is nearby or there is the possibility of harm. Continuing to have a Clear Picture and doing On-Track Thinking will help the person use other

skills to effectively manage the situation.

Example: Mary is in the kitchen getting a snack. Before Mary is able to make her sandwich, her housemate, who is also in the kitchen, begins to yell and swear at someone on the phone. Mary feels uncomfortable and wants to Move Away from the disturbance. Mary tells the staff member that she is feeling uncomfortable and that she is going to her bedroom to watch TV. The staff supports the plan and offers to let Mary know when her housemate has left the area, so that Mary can get her snack. Mary is irritated at a 3 about having to wait for her snack, but uses Clear Picture, On-Track Thinking, Safety Plan, and New-Me Activity, taking the On-Track Action of Moving Away to her room. Ten minutes later, after Mary has done a Distraction New-Me Activity (watching TV), the staff lets Mary know that the housemate left the kitchen and that it is safe to make her sandwich.

- Leave the Area. In high-risk situations where there is serious danger it may be necessary to leave the area completely. Under these circumstances, the individual may need to go where she cannot hear, see, talk to, or touch the risk. Similarly, if the individual engages in self-injurious behaviors, it is important to remove all objects that may be used to inflict harm. Doing a Talking Safety Plan and letting another person know about the danger can help ensure the individual remains a safe distance from perpetrators, potential victims, and possible weapons that are creating high Levels of Risk. If there is imminent danger, it is crucial to seek support. After Leaving the Area, it may be helpful to refocus on a New-Me Activity.

Example: Bob wants to plan a family visit, but his stepfather has a history of becoming violent when he drinks. Bob does a Writing Safety Plan that outlines that staff will wait for Bob in the car in case problems occur during the visit. Bob and the staff agree that if the stepfather starts raising his voice, Bob will leave the house. Bob goes on the visit. The stepfather gets angry and begins to yell at Bob. Bob respectfully Leaves the Area, exits the house, and goes to the staff car to return home. It is important to have the necessary resources available when managing high-risk situations.

5. New-Me Activities.

New-Me Activity is the fifth skill in the Skills System, and it is an All-the-Time skill. This means that the individual can use New-Me Activities at any level of emotion, 0–5. New-Me Activities are the on-track activities that the individual does during each day. Different New-Me Activities affect people in various ways. It is important to choose the best activities for each situation. There are four types: Focus, Feel Good, Distraction, and Fun New-Me Activities.

Focus New-Me Activities.

Focus activities improve attention and focus in the moment. When the individual does sorting, organizing, following step-by-step instructions, and/or counting, his mind becomes more focused. Examples of Focus New-Me Activities are sorting cards, playing solitaire, cooking with a recipe, counting money, folding clothes, cleaning, reading, and playing video games.

When a person is highly emotional and not thinking clearly, it can be helpful to do a simple card-sorting activity. First, the individual separates the deck into two piles, with the red cards in one and the black in another. Even this rudimentary task is challenging when a person is in an escalated state. Once that is complete, the person separates the deck by suit, hearts, diamonds, clubs, and spades each in their own pile. Finally, the individual takes each pile containing one suit and puts it in order, either from the highest card down or the lowest card up. The goal is to perform a task that does not increase cognitive load demands and frustration significantly, but rather helps the individual focus attention. If the person is unable to do one of the tasks, it may be useful to return to a simpler version of the sorting activity. Other sorting games can be created, such as separating the deck by number (e.g., placing all four of the aces together and so on).

Feel Good New-Me Activities.

Feel Good New-Me Activities help the individual and his body feel comfortable and soothed. The individual may engage in activities that are pleasant for the five senses. It is important to note that each individual must have an opportunity to define what he finds soothing. Each person's experience of activities and preferences vary. Engaging in activities that trigger memories, problematic thoughts, or painful emotions may not function to help the individual feel good. The following items are self-soothing activities that involve each of the senses.

- *Sight.* The individual may look at pleasant sights to increase positive feelings and experiences. For example, sitting and looking at a beautiful view, taking a walk in nature, and/or looking at pictures may make the individual feel better.
- *Hearing.* The person may listen to things that increase joy. For example, putting on music, listening to birds sing, or hearing water in a stream can be soothing.
- *Smell.* Experiencing pleasant aromas can help a person feel good. Smelling cookies baking, burning scented candles, and using fragrant hand lotion are examples of Feel Good New-Me Activities.
- *Touch.* Various types of touching can sooth an individual. Putting on cozy slippers, taking a warm bath, and petting an animal are common ways to experience comfort through touch.
- *Taste.* Eating and drinking things that have a pleasant taste can provide pleasure and make people feel good. Having a nice meal, sipping hot tea, eating a piece of chocolate, or drinking ice-cold lemonade on a hot day are examples of some Feel Good New-Me Activities.

Distraction New-Me Activities.

Distraction New-Me Activities help the individual focus on something different than the event that is prompting challenging emotions or off-track behaviors. For example, if the person is waiting for a ride at the doctor's office, staring at the clock may increase uncomfortable emotions. Instead, the individual can look at a magazine. Watching television, movies, playing video games, and reading are a few examples of Distraction New-Me Activities.

Engaging in Distraction New-Me Activities that shift attention from one state of emotion and thought to another may also be helpful. For example, eating spicy food or watching a funny movie can help the person experience different sensations; focusing on something different may allow the individual to feel better and to mobilized toward personal goals.

It is important to note that using Distraction New-Me Activities may be most helpful when the person has done everything possible to manage the situation and she just needs to relax or wait. For example, if the person needs to be picked up at the doctor's office, it is important to call to arrange a ride prior to reading a magazine.

Fun New-Me Activities.

Fun New-Me Activities make the individual feel happiness and joy. It is important that the person has the ability to do many different activities that help him increase positive emotions within the context of daily life. Exploring new activities can help the person improve emotion-regulation abilities by providing beneficial alternatives to experiences that tend to elicit problematic emotions and behaviors. Each person finds joy in different ways; drawing, playing sports, video games, working, cooking, cleaning, reading, watching TV, listening to music, talking to friends, going out, and studying skills are just a few Fun New-Me Activities. Creating On-Track Action Plans that include a variety of these types of activities can help a person maintain balance within his life.

Choosing the best New-Me Activity.

Each kind of New-Me Activity has a different function; choosing the proper New-Me Activity in a situation can help the individual reach personal goals. For example, if the person is becoming upset or confused, choosing a Focus New-Me Activity will help promote clear thinking. If the person is feeling tense or stressed, a Feel Good New-Me Activity may increase relaxation and comfort. If the individual has to wait for a few hours and does not want to continually trigger the emotion of boredom, doing a Distraction New-Me Activity may be a beneficial choice. If the individual wants to feel good about life and experience connection with others, doing a Fun New-Me Activity would be helpful.

Some New-Me Activities serve more than one function. For example, video games may help the person focus, distract her from worries, and provide entertainment. Similarly, a phone call to a friend may make the individual feel better, and it may be fun at the same time. The individual uses Clear Picture and On-Track Thinking to determine which New-Me Activities are the best fit within each different situation.

6. Problem Solving.

Problem Solving is the sixth skill in the Skills System, and it is a Calm-Only skill. This means that the individual can use Problem Solving *only* when below a 3 emotion. When a person attempts Problem Solving over a 3 emotion, it generally creates more problems, rather than fewer. Rushing through Problem Solving may lead the individual to miss effective options and choose alternatives that may feel good in the short term, yet are not helpful in the long term. Problem Solving over a 3 tends to be impulsive, thus less likely to aid the individual in reaching personal goals. If the individual is interacting with other people during Problem Solving, it is important that all involved are below a 3 emotion. When anyone is escalated in the situation, it may hinder the Problem Solving effort; waiting may be beneficial. Problem Solving is a complicated, multistep progression. Gaining mastery in the Problem Solving skill is a long-term learning process. The following steps help the individual solve problems:

1. Getting a Clear Picture of the problem. The individual has to determine what he wants in a situation and what the barriers are to reaching the goal.

2. Checking All Options. During this step, the person explores multiple options for solving the dilemma and Checks the Fit (thumbs-up or thumbs-down) of potential remedies.

3. Creating a Plan A, Plan B, and Plan C. The individual creates multiple plans to ensure some level of success.

Getting a Clear Picture of the problem.

The first step in doing successful Problem Solving is for the individual to get a Clear Picture of what he wants and clarifying what is getting in the way of that goal. Clarifying goals and barriers may be simple or complex, depending on the situation. The person may need to take time to self-reflect or contact a skills coach to illuminate the issues. An example of a relatively simple situation would be if Joseph finds out that he has a basketball game in three days. He wants to play in the game. Joseph realizes that he does not have sneakers that fit him. Wanting to play in the game is Joseph's goal, and not having the proper shoes is the problem. Once Joseph understands these factors, he can Check All Options and make Plan A, B, and C to get new sneakers.

Sometimes the individual is unclear about personal goals; a situation can also be confusing or require multiple steps to solve the problem. Additionally, there may be environmental challenges and/or power differentials that make it difficult for a person with significant learning challenges to solve problems within complex social systems. Dissatisfaction in relationships, family conflicts, and vocational problems are examples of multi-faceted problems. It may be necessary for the person to address components of a problem as part of a larger Problem Solving effort. Getting a Clear Picture of goals, addressing components of a complex problem, and executing effective, multifaceted Problem Solving strategies may require the individual to seek consultation from skills coaches, professionals at the work site, and trusted friends. The person has to be realistic about evaluating what can be changed versus what needs to be accepted in each situation.

Checking All Options.

Once the person has clarified what she wants and what is in the way of these goals, it is time to Check All Options. The person generates possible solutions to the problem. It may be useful to review the pro's(positive outcomes) and con's (negative outcomes) for each option. The individual then checks the fit of each option, as to whether the action would be on-track (thumbs-up) or off-track (thumbs-down) to the goal. While Checking All Options, the person thinks about possible outcomes for the action. Throughout this process, the individual weighs both helpful and unhelpful options to develop a Problem Solving plan. Plans may be simple and have a single step or be more challenging, requiring multiple skills. It is often necessary to use Clear Picture, On-Track Thinking, On-Track Actions, Expressing Myself, Getting It Right, and Relationship Care to execute Problem Solving.

Making Plans A, B, and C.

Plan A is the plan that the individual believes will work best to fix the problem. Plan A best fits the needs of the person and has the highest likelihood of solving the problem in an effective way. Consulting with skills coaches or supportive friends prior to taking action, thinking about what to say, and rehearsing tactics can strengthen a plan.

It is sometimes necessary to negotiate with people while doing Problem Solving. It is therefore helpful to have other alternatives in mind when engaging in discussions with people. A secondary plan is called Plan B. Compromising requires give and take on both parts, so a Plan C might even be necessary. Not getting problems solved and/or encountering resistance can elicit heightened emotional responses. The individual will need to get a Clear Picture, use On-Track Thinking, and implement other skills to deal with the new situation.

7. Expressing Myself.

Expressing Myself is the seventh skill in the Skills System, and it is a Calm-Only skill. This means an individual can use Expressing Myself *only* when he is below a 3 emotion. If the individual is using Expressing Myself with other people, it is helpful that all involved are below a 3 to reduce the likelihood of an off-track interaction.

Gross and Thompson (2007), in the *Handbook of Emotion Regulation*, explain that there is empirical support for the notion that "emotion-expressive behavior slightly increases the feeling of that emotion" (p. 15). In light of this trend, it may be helpful to use Expressing Myself at a 0–2 emotion, because the process of expression may naturally bring the individual to a 3 or higher emotion. If the individual begins Expressing Myself at a 3 emotion and the result is increased arousal to a 4, it is important for the person to get a Clear Picture and use On-Track Thinking to determine what On-Track Action and other All-the-Time skills would be best in the situation.

An individual may inhibit expression as a strategy to regulate emotion. Gross and Thompson (2007) explains further that "Interestingly, decreasing emotion-expressive behavior seems to have mixed effects on the emotion experience (decreasing positive but not negative emotion experience)." Overall, Gross and Thompson conclude that individuals appear to regulate emotions more effectively when he or she finds "ways of expressing them in adaptive rather than maladaptive ways" (2007, p. 15). Although venting emotions is a type of Expressing Myself, Gross and Thompson (2007) highlight that there may be increased benefits to communication that promotes "problem solving and interpersonal understanding" (2007, p. 15).

When the individual is over a 3, there is a strong possibility that he will experience urges to engage in emotion expression. Getting a Clear Picture and using On-Track Thinking can help the individual allow these urges to pass, focusing on more helpful thoughts. At higher levels of emotion, it may be more difficult to focus and perform complex, interactive skills. Ultimately, the person must gauge whether the expression is going to be an On-Track or an Off-Track Action. Over a 3, it is more likely that communication can morph from effective Expressing Myself to venting, blaming, ranting, demanding, yelling, and swearing. Unfortunately, in situations where the individual is trying to gain cooperation, these tactics cause the other party to recoil, disengage, and even retaliate. Although these strategies may be effective in specific situations, as a general rule, when a participant is experiencing an emotion that ranks over a 3, it is difficult for him to coordinate all the necessary skills to successfully reach personal goals. Additionally, the individual may feel guilty and experience self-directed frustration. Waiting for the proper time to use Expressing Myself helps the individual maintain positive relationships with himself and other people.

What is Expressing Myself? Expressing Myself is how the individual communicates what she is thinking and/or feeling. It is a way to bring what is happening inside to the outside. For example, the person may want to communicate ideas, concerns, opinions, hopes, dreams, needs, and feelings. The individual can express herself in many different ways. Talking, laughing, crying, and body language can be forms of Expressing Myself. Doing certain New-Me Activities can promote self-expression. Writing, playing music, drawing, painting, and dancing are examples of expressive arts. The individual can also express energy through hobbies and physical activities, such as sports.

Why use Expressing Myself? Improving adaptive self-expression is beneficial for the individual in many ways. The process of Expressing Myself can improve self-awareness and help others understand the individual. Additionally, as the person improves abilities in communication, he is better able to use Safety Plans. Effective Expressing Myself can increase joy and participation during New-Me Activities. For example, coordinating with other people in recreational and/or work settings can help the individual have more fun and be more effective. Self-expression may also enhance the Problem Solving process; the person is able to express emotions and thoughts prior to crisis situations developing. Similarly, effective expression can facilitate the reaching of personal goals. For example, as communication skills improve, the individual may be better able to get needs met using Getting It Right. The demonstration of and receipt of Relationship Care is enhanced through adaptive self-expression. When the person shares what is inside, there is an opportunity to feel a sense of connection with the self, other people, and the world around him.

Expressing Myself helps the individual maintain a sense of control in his life and facilitates the maintenance and adjustment of relationships.

How to use Expressing Myself. Using words is often the clearest way to communicate with people. It is more difficult for people to understand the accurate meaning of body language or attitudes. Relying on mind reading reduces the likelihood of accurate communication. When the individual tries to be a mind reader, or expects others to be one, it may create Fuzzy versus Clear Pictures. Although it can be challenging, it may be best to do an On-Track Action of using clear words to Express Myself. It is important that the individual have to ability to ask for clarification if verbal or nonverbal communication is not understandable. As in all other situations, the individual uses Clear Picture and On-Track Thinking to best determine how to use Expressing Myself effectively.

When to use Expressing Myself. It is important that the individual have a clear versus fuzzy mind when using Expressing Myself. Having the ability to understand how the expression will affect the individual, as well as the other person, is vital. The person will use Clear Picture and On-Track Thinking to determine when to communicate.

8. Getting It Right.

Getting It Right is a series of tactics that the individual considers when attempting to get something that he wants from another person. It is the eighth skill in the Skills System, and it is a Calm-Only skill. This means that the individual can use Getting It Right *only* when below a 3 emotion. It is important to note that the other person also needs to be below a 3 emotion. If either party in the interaction is above a 3, it may be best to wait until a later time when both individuals are less escalated. To successfully acquire things, the person must be in the Right Mind and talk to the Right Person at the Right Time and Place using the Right Tone and the Right Words.

Right Mind. Being in the Right Mind to use Getting It Right means that the person has a Clear Picture and has used On-Track Thinking to make a plan related to the best tactics to get what is desired. The individual must be prepared, focused, below a 3 on the Feelings Rating Scale, and be ready to do what works. As with Expressing Myself, it is common for emotions to rise prior to and during using Getting It Right. It is important for the participant to self-monitor her emotional status. Beginning to be demanding, acting as though she is right and the other person is incorrect, or using intimidation are signs that the person is starting to Get It Wrong.

Approaching another person to make requests can increase emotional responses; it is vital that the individual continue to use all necessary skills to manage the situation. Creating a Getting It Right plan (see page 260) can help the individual be organized; rehearsing and practicing can increase effectiveness as well. These tactics can help the individual remain effective even if she unexpectedly becomes cognitively overloaded in the moment. If the person has a Fuzzy Picture or engages in Off-Track Thinking, Getting It Right will quickly turn into Getting It Wrong. Therefore, if either person begins to escalate to the 4 or 5 range of emotion, it is best to retreat, returning to Clear Picture and On-Track Thinking to make another Skills Plan.

Right Person. When making a Getting It Right plan, it is important to choose the Right Person to talk to. The Right Person is the one who can and will help the individual get needs met. For example, the individual may want to discuss a raise with the employer versus his co-worker. In complex situations, it may be challenging to know who is best. For example, the person may either talk to a supervisor, program manager, or psychologist regarding a change in the person's Individual Service Plan. Seeking consultation from skills coaches to make these choices may be beneficial. Additionally, if the person is not readily available in the person's life, he may need to call to set up a time to talk. There may be delays that are frustrating. It is important to use other skills while waiting to talk to the Right Person. Getting a Clear Picture, using On-Track Thinking, and doing an On-Track Action of a Focus New-Me Activity may help the person wait and remain in the Right Mind.

Right Time and Place. Choosing the Right Time and Place is important. The individual will want to choose an opportunity when the Right Person is able to give full attention to the interaction. The circumstances have to be conducive to the Right Person helping the individual. The individual may want to use Getting It Right at one time, but it isn't the Right Time for the Right Person. Once again, being committed to doing what works, rather than to what emotions are dictating, generally helps the individual Get It Right.

Right Tone. Using the Right Tone is critically important. The individual must get a Clear Picture and do On-Track Thinking to gauge what tone will work best. Usually being too passive or wimpy makes the Right Person not take the individual seriously. Often being demanding makes the Right Person pull away, stop listening, and think that the individual is not able to handle the situation. When the individual utilizes an aggressive tone, it may stress the relationship so much that the Right Person will not want to help again and may make the circumstances more difficult for the individual.

Right Words. SEALS represents the Right Words or tasks in Getting It Right. **S**ugar, **E**xplaining the Situation, **A**sking for What I Want, **L**istening, and **S**ealing a Deal are the Right Words in Getting It Right. When the individual is in the Right Mind, talking to the Right Person at the Right Time and Place, and using the Right Tone and these Right Words, the individual is likely to get what he wants in a given situation.

- *Sugar.* First, the individual uses some Sugar. Using Sugar represents adding sweetness to the situation. This means that the individual is respectful and polite to the Right Person to create a positive relationship environment—for example, "Excuse me, Mr. Smith, may I speak to you for a moment?" Sugar is an ingredient that makes the Right Person want to help the individual get what he needs. Throughout the interaction, the individual responds to the Right Person's needs (showing strong Relationship Care) while advocating for his own agenda: "Mr. Smith, I know you run a business that helps many people. I would really appreciate your help at this time." The individual will want to be positive to the Right Person and create a situation where he may want to return the favor.

- *Explaining the Situation.* Next, the individual Explains the Situation. The individual highlights why it is important that the Right Person help the individual: "Mr. Smith, as you know, there was a huge earthquake in Haiti this year. Hundreds of thousands of people were killed. There are still many hurt and homeless people there." Explaining the Situation helps the Right Person become motivated to do whatever it takes to help the individual. The individual wants the Right Person to feel good about contributing. Rushing to make the request before using ample Sugar and fully Explaining the Situation can fail to mobilize the Right Person's motivation to help.

- *Asking for What I Want.* After using Sugar and Explaining the Situation, the individual Asks for what he wants: "Mr. Smith, my organization is collecting donations of money and supplies to send to Haiti to help build homes for families whose houses were destroyed in the earthquake." It is helpful to be specific, so that the Right Person clearly understands the request. "If you could either donate $100 or send tools to our organization to ship to Haiti, it would benefit many people. A donation of $100 builds one temporary home for a family." Asking in a clear and direct way helps the Right Person reflect on his ability to help and to make a decision about how to proceed.

- *Listening.* Throughout the entire process of Getting It Right, it is important to listen to the Right Person's opinions and feedback. The answer from the Right Person may be no, or perhaps only a portion of the request can be fulfilled. Despite setbacks it is vital that the individual stay on-track. In all cases, the individual uses Clear Picture and On-Track Thinking to remain focused and to do what works. It is possible that the individual may find out the person really is not the Right Person, and changes in tactics may be necessary. Listening carefully is an essential step toward being able to Seal a Deal.

- *Sealing a Deal.* Finally, the individual tries to Seal a Deal with the Right Person— for example, "Ms. Brown, I am going to give $500 and send three tool boxes to your organization." The individual then seals the deal by saying, "Thank you, Mr. Smith, for your generosity. The check is made out to Homes for Haiti. The check and tools can be sent to 22 Main Street in Harrisville. I really appreciate this; do you have a sense of when you will be able to make this donation?" It is very important to pin down the details as part of Sealing a Deal. It is great when the Right Person agrees to help, but it is vital to ensure the execution of the plan.

If the Right Person says no, the individual tries to negotiate. If the Right Person answers, "I'm sorry, Ms. Brown, but our company already made donations to Haiti," the individual might continue, "Mr. Smith, is there any way your company could donate used tools to our efforts?" The reply might or might not be positive. Finding the balance between being assertive enough to maximize the likelihood of success and still being respectful and maintaining the relationship is important. Sprinkling Sugar throughout the interaction can help reach the goal and facilitate future success.

9. Relationship Care.

Relationship Care is the ninth skill in the Skills System, and it is a Calm-Only skill. Managing relationships is a complex task that may require using other Calm-Only skills, such as Problem Solving, Expressing Myself, and Getting It Right. Just as with the other Calm-Only skills, it is helpful to use Relationship Care with other people when all involved are below a 3 emotion. If the individual is in a conversation with someone who shifts to over a 3 emotion, she needs to get a Clear Picture and do On-Track Thinking to plan how to handle the situation.

There are multiple elements of Relationship Care. Building On-Track Relationships, Balancing On-Track Relationships, and Changing Off-Track Relationships are a few aspects of Relationship Care. Healthy, balanced, fulfilling On-Track Relationships with the self and other people can significantly add to the individual's quality of life.

Building an On-Track Relationship with myself.

The concept of the Core Self helps the individual understand what it means to have a strong self-relationship. There are four elements of the Core Self: self-awareness, self-acceptance, self-value, and self-trust.

Self-awareness. Clear Picture teaches the individual steps that foster self-awareness. In addition, On-Track Thinking prompts the individual to reflect on goals. When the individual is clear about goals, it is much more likely that she will implement effective strategies to reach her goal in a situation. As the person understands that it is beneficial to see the moment *as is* in order to manage the circumstance effectively, self-awareness grows.

Self-acceptance. When the individual is able to be present in the moment, he begins the process of self-acceptance. Seeing himself *as is* is more possible when he has the capacities to manage the awareness and realities of the situation. Unfortunately, seeing the self *as is* may generate painful emotions. Factors such as medical issues, physical disabilities, obesity, mental retardation diagnoses, mental health problems, trauma, and chronic behavioral dysregulation are a few examples of challenges that can significantly complicate the person's self-acceptance efforts.

The process of a strengthening the Core Self often continues as the person improves self-awareness and self-acceptance to include increased self-value. Practicing Clear Picture, demonstrating On-Track Thinking, and taking On-Track Actions helps the person accomplish mastery. Experiencing success in more challenging situations leads the person have a positive self-experience versus self-avoidance. The Skills System is built to continually mobilize the person's inner wisdom and guide the person to actively engage in adaptive behaviors. Over time the person discovers self-capacities and in turn develops the ability to self-value.

Self-trust. Each of the previous elements of the Core Self serve to improve the individual's self-trust. The person sees situations clearly, accepts the realities, remains positive in the face of challenges, and makes skillful decisions that help move her toward personal goals. Experiencing these abilities gives the person the knowledge that she can not only survive, but she can also get what she needs. Previous patterns of overdoing and underdoing are replaced by skillful self-management and ultimately improved self-trust.

Building relationships with others.

The elements of the Core Self (awareness, acceptance, value, and trust) may also be helpful aspects of relationships with others. As the individual is able to be aware of other people, it may allow the individual to be more aware of what other people are experiencing. Being more aware of the other person can help the individual be more responsive and empathetic. Similarly, as the individual self-accepts, he may become more accepting of other people. Likewise, valuing and trusting other people may offer the individual opportunities for richer relationships. Having the ability to be aware of, accept, value, and trust other people will improve relationships and enhance the individual's ability to reach personal goals.

Balancing On-Track Relationships with others.

It is the right and responsibility of each individual to make personal decisions related to her level of participation in relationships on an ongoing basis. The person uses Clear Picture and On-Track Thinking to balance the changing needs of the individual and the other person. For example, if a housemate has a brain injury, the person may choose to accept that her housemate repeats statements frequently. Conversely, there may be a situation where the individual seeks to move from the home, because the housemate's behavior is unacceptable. Thus, Relationship Care is not prescriptive, but a process of using skills to make adjustments within each moment that reflects her inner wisdom. Balancing relationships is a dynamic process that requires the individual to use many tools throughout each day.

Types of Relationships. Each individual has many different types of relationships in his life, and these relationship may change through time. For example, the person who has an intellectual disability may need to relate with residential agencies, employers, job coaches, support staff, housemates, friends, organization members, state social workers, family, and significant others. It is important that the individual learn about the socially effective ways to manage each different type of relationship. As the person ages, his individual role and the role of other people may transform. Developing and maintaining effective relationships with all the different people in the individual's life requires utilization of all of the skills in the Skills System on an ongoing basis.

Relationship behaviors. The individual uses Clear Picture and On-Track Thinking to make decisions about relationship behaviors. The person continually assesses and balances what actions reflect her personal preferences, values, and goals within the moment. Therefore, the process of Caring for Relationships is dynamic. This means that it is a sequence of actions that serves to maintain self-respect and respect for other people as the individual changes, other people change, and life changes. Because there are no Relationship Care prescriptions, it is important to use various relationship tools to make adjustments in each moment.

To manage the variability within relationship environments, it is helpful to understand what factors tend to affect relationships so that the person can make adjustments within the current moment. For example, certain Relationship Care behaviors tend to increase positive feelings between people: listening to the person intently, responding with thoughtful comments, appropriate touching, phone calls, giving gifts, paying compliments, sending cards, doing activities together, and so on.

Each person generally has important people and relationships in his or her life. It may be helpful for the person to incorporate Relationship Care behaviors into On-Track Action plans that proactively maintain relationships. Using tools that enhance connection, communication, and support from the individual to those significant friends, family members, or support providers can help the relationships stay on-track.

Conversely, certain behaviors tend to increase negative feelings between people in relationships. Being distracted, changing the subject, only focusing on oneself, being overcontrolling, being judgmental, not calling back, and being disrespectful are forms of poor Relationship Care. There are times when the individual takes these actions with and without intention. Awareness of these tools can help the individual understand the impact of such actions so that relationship behaviors can be strategically utilized to meet personal goals. For example, if the individual has gone out on a date with someone whom she is not interested in seeing again, the situation may be discussed directly, or she may utilize poor Relationship Care behaviors. As the individual becomes more mindful of these diverse tools, increased self-determination and active Relationship Care can improve the quality of the individual's life.

Two-Way-Street Relationships. One goal of the Skills System is to give the individual proper tools to participate in Two-Way-Street Relationships. Although the individual cannot control the behavior of the other person, Relationship Care teaches the individual to act in a way that allows a Two-Way-Street Relationship to happen. A Two-Way-Street Relationship is a reciprocal relationship in which there is mutual respect and communication. The individual must learn to actively participate, both as a giver and receiver, in a Two-Way-Street Relationship. For example, the individual must talk and listen to the other person. He must work to clarify his points of view and be interested in helping the other person clarify his points. Offering these opportunities to the other person allows the individual to enjoy the same opportunities. Within a Two-Way-Street Relationship, the participants are able to be present, discuss, negotiate, and collaborate. Working together creates a synthesis and a heightened development of each person and the relationship.

One-Way-Street Relationships. One-Way-Street Relationships are either (1) when the individual does not want to participate in a relationship or (2) she is experiencing that another person is not reciprocating in a relationship. There are times when the person may evaluate a One-Way-Street Relationship as out of balance, if she is unhappy with the situation or the other person's relationship behavior. At other times, the individual may want a One-Way-Street Relationship, if she is using her relationship behavior to change the relationship.

Changing Off-Track Relationships.

When the individual's self-relationship becomes off-track, it can impede reaching personal goals. For example, Off-Track Thinking that is self-devaluing may undermine the person's abilities to function to his potential. Another common problem is when the person has a Fuzzy Picture about goals and is thus unable to make and execute effective Skills Plans. Additionally, certain behavior patterns may be hindering the individual from reaching goals. Changing off-track habits, such as smoking, alcoholism, drug use, overeating, undereating, and medication inconsistency, may improve the individual's self-relationship and help him be on-track. It is challenging to change any kind of off-track habit. Therefore, it is necessary to use all of the skills in the Skills System to manage Off-Track Urges and create new behavior patterns.

Changing relationships with others: Repairing Relationships.

Repairing Relationships serves a dual function. This strategy is helpful both when the individual does something to cause a relationship problem and when someone else causes relationship imbalance. For example, if a support staff talks to the individual in a demanding tone, the person may need to repair the relationship to get it back on-track. Additionally, if the individual forgets to call a friend back, a relationship repair might be necessary as well. The individual can Find Middle Ground, do the Steps of Responsibility, and/or end a relationship with others.

Finding Middle Ground.

When a relationship problem arises, the individual first Talks It Out with the other person. Having Two-Way-Street communication may help resolve the conflict. One-way-street communication may lead to poor Relationship Care behaviors. It is most productive if both parties are able to See Both Sides of the situation. Understanding the other person's perspective can help facilitate a mutually agreeable solution. Then the pair works it out together by finding a solution that fits for both people. Finding the Middle Ground means that both parties meet halfway and collaborate to make the situation better for both.

Steps of Responsibility.

When the individual feels that she has created a relationship problem, it may be helpful to Repair Relationships by doing the Steps of Responsibility. This process involves (1) clearly admitting the problem, (2) communicating about the impact on the other person, (3) apologizing, (4) committing to change, and (5) doing an On-Track Action. It is not easy to take responsibility, because the individual may feel shame, have the urge to be stubborn, blame the other person, or insist that she is right. Although doing the Steps of Responsibility may cause discomfort, the process can ultimately strengthen the person's self-relationship and the relationship with the other person.

Ending relationships with others.

There may be instances when the individual has made efforts to repair the relationship, but still relationship problems exist. The individual may determine that a relationship is off-track. For example, if the other person is continually demonstrating poor Relationship Care behaviors or encouraging the individual to make off-track choices, perhaps the relationship needs to be ended. The individual can just stop participating in relationship behavior or he can formally end the relationship. The individual uses Clear Picture, On-Track Thinking, and Problem Solving to determine if, when, and how a to stop an Off-Track Relationship. Living with problematic relationships can lead the individual to be off-track, out of balance, and miserable.

The individual must also learn to deal with relationships changing or ending through no actions of his own. For example, staff leaving, romantic partners breaking up, people moving away, and people dying are common reasons for disruptions in relationships. It may be necessary for the person to use many skills to cope effectively with relationships that are ending. Although these are often painful experiences, the individual can remain on-track toward her goals while managing loss and grief.

System Tools

There are three System Tools within the Skills System. The Feelings Rating Scale, Categories of Skills, and the Recipe for Skills help the individual organize his current experience and facilitate him to strategically execute skillful behaviors. The System Tools are designed to help the person know how to effectively combine the nine skills to manage the ever-changing human experience.

Feelings Rating Scale.

The Feelings Rating Scale is a 0–5 self-report scale that is used to rate the intensity of emotions, feelings, and/or sensory experiences during a situation. The focus is initially less on semantics differentiating the type of experience (emotions versus feeling versus thought), but rather, more importantly, what level of impact the situation has on the individual. The Feelings Rating Scale is used to rate both uncomfortable and more pleasurable experiences.

The Feelings Rating Scale serves a dual purpose. First, the individual learns to continually rate her feelings rating as part of getting a Clear Picture. The scale is a tool that provides a simple framework that promotes self-awareness and internal organization. Second, the Feelings Rating Scale is utilized during On-Track Thinking. The person uses the Feelings Rating Scale to determine which skills and how many skills would be helpful in the particular situation. If the person is below a 3 emotion, it is possible to use all nine skills in the Skills System. If the rating is over a 3 emotion, only the All-the-Time skills are used.

The Feelings Rating Scale implicitly and naturally adjusts as a person gains capacities. The individual is able to experience stronger emotions, continue to utilize On-Track Thinking, and remain emotionally, cognitively, and behaviorally regulated in increasingly challenging situations. For example, a situation that would have previously elicited a 4 emotion may only produce a 3 emotion as abilities improve. When this shift happens, the person is more able to handle stressful, demanding, and increasingly intimate interactions.

A **0 feeling** means that no feeling is being experienced. For example, a 0 anger means that the person is not experiencing anger at that moment. Instructors may find that some participants display patterns of underrating feelings at 0. As the person develops the capacity to regulate experiences, the accuracy of rating generally increases as well.

A **1 feeling** is a tiny reaction to something that is just noticeable. For example, if I see a nice car driving by, I may feel a 1 envy. I notice a twinge of the emotion and fleeting thoughts about how nice that car is and how I would like to have one like that. If I allow the emotions and thoughts to pass, the feeling dissipates; if I perseverate about what a piece of junk my car is, the feeling will increase.

A 1 feeling may be as high as the emotion goes; a stronger feeling might be forming; or the individual might have reduced arousal from a stronger emotion. It is crucial that the participant learns to become aware of feelings at the 1 stage, because it can help the person maintain awareness and effective coping throughout the situation.

At a 1 feeling, the person is likely able to think clearly; thus she can use any of the nine skills on the Skills List. Because of the individual's capacity to cognitively regulate, she is able to use Calm-Only skills. The slight sensations and minimal cognitive disruption contribute to the relative ease of managing urges, impulses, and actions at a 1 emotion.

A **2 feeling** is a small feeling. For example, I may have a 2 frustration when I am in line at the grocery store and I look at the candy rack. I experience low levels of irritation as I think about how I should not eat candy. If I let the emotions and thoughts float by, the frustration decreases. If I stare at the yummy goodies, I begin to think about those annoying people who can eat candy anytime they want, and my emotions might increase.

There may be emotions, thoughts, urges, and body sensations associated with the experience of a 2 emotion, yet these are mild, and the person is generally able to manage the feelings without significant cognitive or behavioral disruption. Therefore, the individual is able to use all nine of the skills on the Skills List at a 2 feeling. Optimally, the person is able to experience the situation fully and move strategically toward personal goals.

A **3 Feeling** is a medium feeling. For example, I may experience a 3 fear when I lose my pocketbook. I experience increased nervousness and have racing thoughts about all of the negative consequences I may incur. If I remain focused, I can do Problem Solving to find the purse. If I focus on how stupid I was for leaving it in the shopping cart at Walmart again, the emotion may increase.

This level of emotion will cause noticeable and possibly multiple body sensations. Sweaty hands, stomachache, racing heart rate, and pacing are a few symptoms. At 3, "negative" emotions such as sadness, fear, anger, guilt, or jealousy may be uncomfortable for the person. The person may notice more Off-Track Thoughts and Urges at a 3; it may become challenging to focus attention. Using Calm-Only skills at a 3 is cautiously recommended. If the person begins to use the more interactive Calm-Only skills (Problem Solving, Expressing Myself, Getting It Right, and Relationship Care) and notices that emotions are increasing or the strategies are not working effectively, it is best to return to using the All-the-Time skills (Clear Picture, On-Track Thinking, On-Track Action, Safety Plan, and New-Me Activities) until he is more regulated. If the person is over a 3 emotion, for example rating at a 3.5 feeling, using All-the-Time skills is the best option.

A **4 Feeling** is a strong feeling. For example, I experienced a 4 sadness when my cat was run over by a car and died. I felt heartbroken and cried. The feeling fluctuated in intensity, but when I was reminded of her over a three-day period, the strong feeling and tears would return. I was not able to fully participate in daily life activities when I was at that high level of sadness.

At a 4 feeling, it is likely that the person is experiencing intense emotions and body sensations. For example, the person may cry, tremble, breathe quickly, sweat profusely, or feel nauseated. Thought processes may be disrupted; for example, thoughts may be racing, disorganized, or nonexistent (blank). At this high level, behavioral control may become impaired; the individual may take actions that impulsively function to reduce emotional discomfort versus behaviors that strategically attain goals. Interactive, Calm-Only skills are not recommended at a 4 feeling because of the high level of emotional, cognitive, and behavioral instability. Many people demonstrate behavioral problems when Calm-Only skills are implemented at too high a level of emotion. For example, when an individual is experiencing 4 anger, solutions to problems may include verbally abusing or assaulting people. Enacting All-the-Time skills to lower arousal allows the person to regain the clarity and composure that are necessary for strategic skill use. In situations that are unclear, it is helpful to have a discussion about the rating process. Group dialogue delving into the intricacies of the situation and the person's experience can broaden awareness of the many complex factors; this initial ambiguity may promote interactions that ultimately help the person (and the group) have a clearer understanding.

A **5 Feeling** is an out-of-control feeling. For example, I remember when I was younger, I would get very mad at my sister. We shared a bedroom during my youth, and the close proximity fostered 5 anger and hostility. I remember an occasion when I felt out of control and threw some of her belongings out our bedroom window in retaliation. I was so furious about the injustices I had suffered that I impulsively reacted to even the score.

The body sensations, thoughts, and urges at a 5 are overwhelming. For example, the individual may have uncontrollable urges to fight or escape the situation. At a 5, the person demonstrates some form of harm toward self, others, or property. Certain behaviors, such as slamming doors, storming around, and/or yelling may not directly cause harm, yet may indicate a level of dyscontrol that is problematic for the person and hinder goal-directed actions. Throughout the skills-training process, the individual must learn about his patterns of emotional escalation and define when lines are crossed from being in and out of control.

At a 5, All-the-Time skills are necessary. These skills help the person regain the control and capacity to function safely. The situation may require Problem Solving, Expressing Myself, Getting It Right, and/or Relationship Care at some point, but the individual must utilize other skills to reduce the level of escalation prior to engaging in these interactive skills.

Categories of Skills.

There are two Categories of Skills. The first five skills (Clear Picture, On-Track Thinking, On-Track Action, Safety Plan, and New-Me Activities) are All-the-Time skills. The All-the-Time skills can be used at any level of emotion, 0–5. When a person is over a 3, it is imperative that All-the-Time skills are used. All-the-Time skills are designed to help the person self-regulate internal factors that are foundational to reaching personal goals.

All-The-Time Skills 0–5 Emotions	Calm-Only Skills 0–3 Emotions
1. Clear Picture 2. On-Track Thinking 3. On-Track Action 4. Safety Plan 5. New-Me Activities	6. Problem Solving 7. Expressing Myself 8. Getting It Right 9. Relationship Care

Table 2.1: Categories of Skills.

The second Category of Skills is Calm-Only skills. The last four skills (Problem Solving, Expressing Myself, Getting It Right, and Relationship Care) often require interacting with other people and thus should be used *only* when an individual is calm. If a person is even a tiny bit higher than a 3 feeling, All-the-Time skills should be used first.

The Category of Skills is used during On-Track Thinking when making a Skills Plan. At that point, the person evaluates her current level of emotion and determines which skills can be used. If the level is over a 3, All-the-Time skills are the only option for the moment.

Recipe for Skills.

The Recipe for Skills is a System Tool that helps calculate how many skills are necessary in any situation. It is recommended that the individual use *at least* one skill for every level of feeling, including 0. At a 0, the person should continue to have a Clear Picture; thus there is need for skill use even when there is possibly no prompting event that is evoking responses. The minimum number of skills when a person is experiencing a 2 feeling is three skills. At a 3, at least four skills are recommended, and so on. For example, if my housemate is yelling at staff, and I am afraid at a 3 emotion, I would get a Clear Picture of the present moment by doing the Clear Picture Do's. Next, I would use On-Track Thinking to stop, check my urge, and make a Skills Plan. While making a Skills Plan, I would calculate my level of emotion and determine which Category of Skills I could use, how many skills I needed from the Recipe for Skills, and which skill would help me in this situation. My third and forth skills would be On-Track Action (turn off the TV and put down the clicker) and Safety Plan (moving to my room) to manage the risk. A situation that causes a 3 feeling requires ample skills to be sure the individual is able to regulate the emotion and stay on-track to his goal.

When the person is at a 5 feeling, six skills are helpful. Since there are only five All-the-Time skills, it is necessary to double up and use multiple New-Me Activities. The individual would get a Clear Picture, use On-Track Thinking, take an On-Track Action, do a Safety Plan, and engage in two New-Me Activities (such as playing video games and listening to music in his room).

The Recipe for Skills is helpful when a trainer is doing a skills review in group or in individual skills training. For example, when reviewing homework or skills use in a situation, the instructor may ask the individual to report a stressful event, the level of emotion, number of skills needed, and a list of skills that were used. The Recipe for Skills helps the individual and group understand how to utilize enough skills in a situation. Often a Skills Master uses many more than the recommended minimums; thus the experience validates mastery. (Note: the term Skills Master can be used to describe anyone who is actively engaged in skills instruction; you may use it to encourage individuals even when they have not yet perfected their skills.)

Using the Skills System to Regulate Emotions

An individual can use the Skills System to help regulate emotions. Gross and Thompson in the *Handbook of Emotion Regulation* (2007) describe "five families of emotion regulation strategies" (p. 10): "situation selection," "situation modification," "attentional deployment," "cognitive change," and "response modulation." It is useful for skills trainers to understand these five strategies to better understand how to create skills clusters can be used that regulate emotions effectively. As the person learns the Skills System, she can begin to organize skills effectively to manage challenging emotions, thoughts, urges, and situations.

"Situation selection" (Gross and Thompson, 2007) is when the individual "takes actions that make it more (or less) likely that we will end up in a situation we expect will give rise to desirable (or undesirable) emotions" (p. 11). Clear Picture, On-Track Thinking, and On-Track Actions are a core skills cluster that helps the individual select situation to reach personal goals. Through utilizing this triad of skills, in combination with the other skills in the system and the System Tools, the person is able to strategically move from one situation to the next, crafting experiences while managing both internal and external experiences. A Safety Plan, for example, provides the individual with a framework for evaluating situations and offers alternatives to manage various Levels of Risk.

Gross and Thompson describe "situation modification" as "efforts to directly modify the situation so as to alter its emotional impact" (2007, p. 12). Skills such as Problem Solving, Expressing Myself, Getting It Right, and Relationship Care are commonly used to modify situations. It is important that the individual be aware of arousal levels during these skills due to the interactive nature of these tasks.

"Attentional deployment," which is how the individual "directs attention within a given situation," helps that individual "regulate emotion without actually changing the environment" (Gross and Thompson, 2007, p. 13). During the Clear Picture skill, the individual becomes aware of an experience and then makes a plan to adjust attention during On-Track Thinking; the individual executes attentional deployment while using each of the skills. Managing both distraction and concentration are tactics that help the individual regulate emotions. Focus New-Me Activities can be a vehicle for the person to strategically deploy attention to reduce the attention on whatever is triggering the emotion. Conversely, Distraction New-Me Activities can assist the individual in diverting attention from triggers that may increase emotions. As the individual becomes increasingly able to selectively control attention, she is better able to modulate internal and external experiences. The person improves her ability to manage transitions, such as shifting from one skill to the next within the Skills System. In addition, the individual develops the capacity to divert attention from off-track experiences while shifting attention to more helpful or on-track ones.

Gross and Thompson highlight "cognitive change" as a helpful strategy that modifies "how we appraise a situation to alter its emotional significance" (2007, p. 14). The individual uses On-Track Thinking to make cognitive changes. The individual evaluates whether the thought or urge is helpful or not helpful and then Turns It toward the desired goal. Many people who have learning challenges experience low self-efficacy; learning to consciously self-support though manufacturing On-Track or Thumbs-Up Thinking is a vital component of sustaining skillful behaviors. Additionally, changing cognitions by Shifting Tracks during On-Track Action helps counter Off-Track Urges and mobilize behavior in the direction of the goal.

"Response modulation" describes when the person "influences physiological, experiential, or behavioral responding" of an emotion (Gross and Thompson, 2007, p. 15). Gross and Thompson report that reducing the "physiological and experiential aspects of emotion" can help modulation efforts; behaviors such as "exercise and relaxation" (Gross and Thompson, 2007, p. 15) can enhance emotion regulation. New-Me Activities are generally utilized to help the person participate in self-soothing and fun activities that help the individual manage the sensations created by emotion.

Developing new self-regulation behaviors is a lengthy and challenging process. Altering engrained patterns of behavior and integrating new ones requires commitment—and, in some cases, support. The Skills System can create a framework and language that gives the individual and support providers helpful tools to facilitate this difficult process. The following chapter describes how someone can learn to function as a skills coach.

CHAPTER 3:

Skills Coaching

Skills trainers are practitioners who teach the Skills System curriculum to individuals in either group or individual training sessions. Skills coaches learn the Skills System and provide guidance for other skills users who may benefit from or request support. For example, a nurse who knows the curriculum may offer skills coaching during an appointment with a patient who is attempting to utilize skills to manage anxiety.

To be a Skills System skills coach, the individual must (1) know the Skills System and (2) be willing and able to use Two-Way-Street Relationship skills. It is vital that the coach offers the individual help navigating through the Skills System process in a way that is supportive, yet stimulates autonomous functioning. The skills-coaching process encompasses both offering technical skills advice and the provision of an opportunity to experience an adaptive relationship.

Ineffective coaching can worsen a situation. If a skills coach provides misinformation or inadequate information about the Skills System, this may serve to increase the individual's level of dyscontrol. For example, when a skills coach uses a blanket command such as, "Go use your skills," that coach is not offering the individual the specific guidance that is necessary in most complex situations. Advice that promotes repression or avoidance may ultimately lead to more problems. For example, when a coach says, "You should not feel like that," it derails Clear Picture, hence hindering the completion of on-track skill use. In addition, problematic interaction styles (e.g., demanding, judgmental, disinterested, and/or disrespectful) may also prompt an individual to increase escalation rather than help the person get on-track.

This skills-coaching model utilizes the Skills List and System Tools as a basis for providing skills support. The skills coach walks the person through the steps of getting a Clear Picture, doing On-Track Thinking, and taking an On-Track Action. The coach also follows the Feelings Rating Scale, Category of Skills, and Recipe for Skills guidelines when interacting and developing a Skills Plan. For example, both the coach and the participant follow the rules of the Skills System during a coaching session. If either of the people are over a 3 emotion, it is not advised to do Problem Solving, Expressing Myself, Getting It Right, or Relationship Care. Therefore, it is vital that skills coaches do not engage in Calm-Only skills when either person is over a 3. Asking the individual to use these abilities at a high level of arousal sets the person up for failure. The coach needs a strong working understanding of the Skills System to give the proper technical advice and focus conversation in specific ways to help the individual stay or get back on-track.

The skills coach has to know how to make adjustments in what to focus on in each situation. For example, if the individual is over a 3 emotion and is experiencing urges to go off-track, the coach focuses on reducing arousal and maintaining safety. Although the person may want to discuss the topic that is creating stress, it is the coach's role in this situation to structure the conversation in ways that reduce the emotional and cognitive triggers that are serving to escalate the individual. The content of the problems is not discussed until the individual is below a 3 emotion. Once the person is more regulated, discussing the root issues is advised. Conversely, if the person is under a 3 emotion, the coach may discuss the content of the situation to better assess the application of the All-the-Time and Calm-Only skills.

There are two worksheets that can serve as a guide for the skills-coaching process. Using My Skills Worksheet 1 (pages A125–A126) is appropriate for when the individual is over a 3 emotion. It provides the participant and coach with a framework for completing the All-The-Time skills. Using My Skills Worksheet 2 (page A127) is utilized when the person appears to be below a 3 emotion; this document is more lengthy in form and includes the Calm-Only skills. If the coach assesses that the individual is more escalated than initially thought or has become more aroused, the coach may help the individual complete the front side of Worksheet 2 while avoiding addressing Calm-Only skills on the second page. In this case, perhaps the coach and individual could return to complete the worksheet when the participant is calmer. It is not important who reads and fills out the either of these forms; the pair can made a collaborative decision depending on the situation.

In addition to the Using My Skills worksheets, two documents are included in the appendices of this book that are designed to help skills coaches gain mastery. Appendix C contains scenarios that explain how an individual may use skills within life situations. A skills coach may find these stories helpful in understanding how an individual may effectively integrate skills into daily life. Additionally, Appendix D is a skills test. This competency evaluation may be used by a skill coach or a participant to assess skills knowledge. Agencies may require support staff to have an adequate understanding of skills or may incentivize skills-coaching abilities.

Offering Skills-Coaching Support

The first step in providing skills coaching is to offer support. Asking, "Would you like any skills coaching right now?" allows the participant to decide whether such an option fits his current moment. If the participant declines, the coach may say, "Okay, but if you would like any skills coaching later, I will be happy to help you; just let me know." If the individual does want skills coaching, the coach could reinforce the behavior by saying, "Great On-Track Action!". It is useful to keep interactions simple to engage the person in the process and to reinforce efficacy. For example, "What do you think about us focusing on skills one, two, and three right now to get us started?" Once the individual agrees, the coach commences coaching the individual to get get a Clear Picture. It is important that the coach be self-aware of his current moment, as well as assist the individual to obtain a Clear Picture about his present internal and external experiences. When both individuals have this solid foundation, it is more likely that the coaching and the skills implementation will be effective.

It is important for the skills coach to be aware of the impact the current environment has on the individual's decision and participation in skills-coaching discussions. The skills coach may want to make it clear to the individual that moving to another, perhaps more private, area to talk may be an option. There are times when the vicinity reduces the participant's motivation to engage in a skills discussion.

It is important to note that the individual should be encouraged to be as independent as possible in terms of skills use. The coach balances offering adequate support and facilitating the individual's autonomous performance of the skills process. As the individual becomes more regulated, more open-ended questions (e.g., "What skill do you think you should do next?"), versus informative statements (e.g., "On-Track Thinking is next.") can prompt the individual to recall skills concepts independently in the context. The coach uses shaping to help the participant apply the Skills System in increasingly challenging situations with less support.

Clear Picture

Individual.

The coach begins by helping the person do the Clear Picture Do's. Inviting the participant to Take a Breath by saying, "How about we start with taking a few breaths? How does that sound to you?" is a helpful way to start the process. The coach takes a few breaths to model mindful belly-breathing. The coach then invites the participant to Notice Surroundings, do a Body Check, Label and Rate Emotions, Notice Thoughts, and Notice Urges that she is experiencing *right now*. The coach may have to orient the participant to focus on the present moment if she is reporting information related to the past or future.

Throughout this process, the coach is evaluating whether the individual is experiencing 0–3 emotions or is over a 3. Although it is impossible to anticipate the individual's body sensations, exact emotions, thoughts, and urges, it is possible to observe the person's actions to make this assessment. If the person is raising her voice, making demands, or mentally drifting from the current context, the coach may determine that the participant is over a 3 emotion. If the individual is reporting being below a 3 and all evidence is to the contrary, the coach uses his or her assessment to make decisions about the focus of coaching (e.g. what Category of Skills may be used).

This information is vital, because at a 0–3 emotion, coaching may include all nine skills, while if the individual is over a 3, only the All-the-Time skills will be advised. In addition, if the person is over a 3 emotion, the focus of the coaching session will be on reducing high arousal through using the first five skills, rather than discussing the specific content of the situation. In this kind of circumstance, the coach must only discuss elements of the situation that are necessary to safely manage situation. If the person is below a 3 emotion, delving into the particulars and content of the situation is appropriate.

Coach.

It is helpful if the skills coach gets a Clear Picture of what his or her own internal and external experience is in the present moment before, during, and after the interaction. Taking a Breath, Noticing Surroundings, doing a Body Check, Labeling and Rating Emotions, Noticing Thoughts, and Noticing Urges will help the coach be present. When the coach is focused and aware, the likelihood of providing effective coaching increases. If the coach is unable to provide effective supports, awareness of this is vital so that the coach can seek better alternatives for the individual.

The coach must be aware of many complex aspects of a situation to be able to balance multiple factors. Not only does the coach have to be aware of the individual and himself, but also various tangible and intangible factors within the environment. For example, as the result of an intellectual disability, a person's behavioral plans may prescribe interventions and agency policies may create rules that must be followed, even in coaching. Additionally, certain social settings and relationships can create complex social environments that increase the participant's arousal, yet constrain options for coaches. For example, an individual might need to Leave the Area as part of a Safety Plan, yet it may be impossible if the staff is supervising several other consumers or transportation is not available. If the coach is completely aware of the entire situation, he is better able to manage mitigating factors and create interventions that benefit all involved.

Shifting to On-Track Thinking

Once the coach feels that the individual is oriented to the realities of the moment, he or she can begin to help the individual do On-Track Thinking. The coach guides the individual through the process of performing these four tasks:

1. Stop, Step Back, and Think about what I want. Once the skills coach feels that the participant is oriented to his internal experience in the present moment (Clear Picture), guiding the individual to do On-Track Thinking is helpful—perhaps by asking, "What is the first thing we do in On-Track Thinking?" (Stop, Step Back, and Think about what I want). Next the coach may ask the participant what he wants (e.g., to earn independence) or doesn't want (e.g., to get in trouble). Framing the clarifying question as "How do you want this to work out?" may be more accessible than "What is your goal for the situation?"

2. Check the Urge. Now that the coach has elicited the individual's urge (Clear Picture) and goal (On-Track Thinking), it is important to use the thumbs-up (on-track) and thumbs-down (off-track) signs to prompt the individual to Check the Urge. Ask the person, "Do you think the urge is helpful (thumbs-up) or not helpful (thumbs-down) to reach your goal?" It is important that the individual takes a moment to make this personal decision, rather than strictly or quickly following the advice of others.

3. Turn It to Thumbs-Up Thinking. If the individual reports having Off-Track Thinking, the coach can propose Turning It. (Using the thumb signs as a gauge can help make intangible factors, such as thoughts and goals, be more concrete.) The coach supports the individual's replacement of Off-Track Thinking with On-Track Thinking that (1) guides the person to use skills (e.g., I will go to my room and do a New-Me Activity), (2) motivates him to reach a long-term goal (e.g., I want to stay on-track to earn my independence), (3) highlights negative consequences that he wants to avoid (I will lose my job if I tell my boss off), and (4) cheers the person on and offers self-encouragement (I can do this; everything is going to be okay). A barrage of all four of these types of On-Track Thinking are important to sustain the person through a challenging situation.

4. Making a Skills Plan. Once an individual has generated Thumbs-up Thinking, the skills coach can help her create a Skills Plan. One of the first steps is to help determine which Category of Skills the individual can use. At a 0–3, the person can use the All-the-Time and the Calm-Only skills. Above a 3, the individual is not advised to use the Calm-Only skills. A discussion about the rating of emotions and the Category of Skills can help the individual become more focused.

It is likely that at over a 3, the person may experience strong urges to impulsively do Problem Solving, Express Myself, Getting It Right, and do Relationship Care. Many behavioral problems are the result of using Calm-Only skills at too high a level of emotional arousal. The individual may have to allow urges to use Calm-Only skills to pass. Throughout this process, the coach helps the individual understand that the goal is to do what works, rather than being right or in total control of the outcome of the situation immediately. The coach's role is to help the individual make a balanced, effective decision that serves the person's long-term goals.

Discussing the Recipe for Skills can have two benefits. First, the individual becomes aware of using enough skills for the given situation. Not using sufficient skills is another common problem that leads to behavioral dyscontrol. Additionally, talking about the Recipe for Skills continues the process of the individual becoming more cognitively regulated and focused.

Through a discussion process, the partnership can help the individual determined what skills would be most effective in the particular situation. The coach poses questions that help the individual see and choose options: "Do you think this is a risky situation?" "What skill helps us in risky situations?" If the individual is not thinking clearly, it may be necessary for the coach to be more direct: "Do you think a Safety Plan would be useful now?" Being highly directive is recommended only when there is immediate and significant danger: "We are going to need to use a Safety Plan and Leave the Area." Whenever possible, the coach's job is to cultivate the individual's internalized skills knowledge.

Helpful hints.

- *Linking questions.* The individual may volunteer information that is skillful, but is not framed in Skills System terms. For example, if the person says that he would have to "get out of there," the coach may ask a linking question, such as, "What skill would that be?" The individual may say "Safety Plan," or the coach can supply the answer as a worked example.

- *Rehearsal.* Often, when a Skills Plan includes complex skills such as Problem Solving, Getting It Right, and Repairing Relationships, it is important to plan ahead and rehearse the skills prior to execution. The coach and individual discuss several steps ahead, so that the person is clear about her full course of action. The skills coach can help the individual review tactics and options for the skills. For example, if the individual is going to use Getting It Right, reviewing and practicing Right Mind, Right Person, Right Time, Right Place, Right Tone, and Right Words may increase effective execution of the skill.

- *Highlighting barriers.* It is also the skills coach's job to highlight any possible barriers that the individual may encounter—for example, "You mentioned wanting to talk to the house manager to do Problem Solving, but he is not in until Friday this week. How is that going to affect your plan?" Helping the individual do troubleshooting ahead of time increases the likelihood that the individual will succeed.

- *Summarizing the plan.* Once the individual has formulated a Skills Plan, it may be helpful for the skills coach to review the plan with the person. For example, "Okay, so you have said that you will first do a Safety Plan and Move Away to your room. When you get to your room, you said, you are going to do your hooked rug. You also said that you will listen to your music, the relaxing kind. Then, you said that later, once everything is calmer, you will go to the kitchen and get dinner. Do I have that right?" The coach helps the individual manage transitions by summarizing and highlighting the entire plan with the person. This orienting improves the sustainability of the plan and helps the person cultivate the necessary commitment to perform the various steps of the skills process. The coach may want to confirm that the individual agrees with the summation prior to moving ahead to be sure Two-Way-Street communication is happening.

Executing an On-Track Action

One of the final steps of creating a Skills Plan involves determining and guiding the participant toward executing his On-Track Action. The coach asks, "So, we have a sense of your Skills Plan … what is your On-Track Action going to be now?" In this case, the individual would respond, "I will go to my room." This phase of coaching is not complete until the person actually does the action. If there is hesitation, the coach will need to understand the barriers and help forge an alternative plan.

Offering positive reinforcement is an important element of the skills-coaching process. For example, "I really think you have a strong plan here—great job. Good luck. You can do this!" represents the types of comments that can convey support, confidence, and trust to the individual. Neither the individual nor the coach know if the plan will work, but the process maximizes the likelihood of success and offers the individual relationship support in the situation.

The skills coach may also orient the individual to the opportunity to seek additional supports if necessary: "I will be in the living room if you need to check in again. Just let me know if you need to chat." Conveying changeability of himself, others, and situations to the individual helps him understand the dynamic nature of coping. Oversimplifying or expecting factors to remain static may invalidate the individual's experience and inadequately prepare him to effectively handle life's challenges.

Although the plan may have been a collaborative process, it is important that the Skills Plan is the individual's versus the coaches. Using the metaphor of a car, the individual is in the driver's seat, while the coach is in the passenger seat. The coach must respectfully support the capacities of the individual and thus help the person develop self-awareness, self-acceptance, self-value, and self-trust.

CHAPTER 4:

Understanding Learning Challenges
And Intellectual Disabilities

This chapter highlights three important facets of working with individuals who experience significant learning challenges. First, the concepts of cognitive load theory (CLT)(Sweller, 1988) are introduced. CLT can help the skills trainer understand how diverse factors impact a participant's ability to cope and learn. Second, the chapter presents specific emotional, cognitive, behavioral, mental health, developmental, and environmental factors that affect individuals who have intellectual disabilities. It is essential that skills trainers gain an in-depth understanding of factors that impact a participant's ability to cope and learn. The last section of this chapter will highlight how the Skills System is designed to offer remedial supports to individuals who experience vulnerabilities that impede coping and learning.

Overview of Cognitive Load Theory

A myriad of complex factors influence a person's ability to utilize adaptive coping strategies and to learn new information. Although it is impossible to highlight all of these for the diverse populations that may utilize the Skills System, it is helpful to examine the general impact that these diverse factors may have on cognitive processing capacities. Cognitive load theory (Sweller, 1988) is a construct that helps skills trainers understand how certain factors can reduce an individual's abilities to cope effectively and learn new material. Understanding cognitive load theory helps skills trainers understand how complex personal issues may impede cognitive functioning capacities. When cognitive processing is impaired, the likelihood of maladaptive coping behaviors increases, and the probability of adaptive skill acquisition decreases.

The term "cognitive load" represents the amount of cognitive resources that are necessary for a person to perform a thinking and reasoning activity. When the individual's ability to focus is compromised or the instructional information is not organized properly, cognitive load increases, and the efficiency of processing decreases. Consequently, if stimuli are unmanageable or the individual's ability to process information effectively is compromised, cognitive overload will result. This cognitive overload impairs schema acquisition, later resulting in a lower performance (Sweller, 1988).

Skills trainers must be aware of factors that impact the individual's abilities to manage cognitive load demands when designing teaching activities. Interventions need to be designed to minimize cognitive load, consequently maximizing cognitive functioning and learning. Cognitive load theory heightens the skills trainer's awareness of extraneous processing that impedes efficient integration of information. Skills trainers are mindful of designing proper interventions and continually monitoring the individual's status to assess cognitive load management.

Factors that impede cognitive functioning.

Five factors impede cognitive functioning (Sweller, 1988).

1. Simultaneous processing of information. Simultaneous processing is required when integrating movement, visual stimuli, and auditory information at the same time. For example, when an individual is playing a board game, the activity may require that the person manage visual, auditory, and kinesthetic information to play the game. The activity may tax long-term and short-term memory capacities, as well as involving processing information related to the social relationships and context.

2. High volume and interactivity of information. Cognitive load increases when an individual is asked to (1) recall or manage large amounts of interactive information, (2) assess subtle differences and similarities between elements, and (3) to understand intricate relationships between different parts of a whole (especially when there is a deficit of general knowledge about the topic). For example, when learning, utilizing the skill "DEAR MAN" from DBT. This term refers to seven different strategies that are combined to get what the individual wants from another person. The terms are: Describe, Express, Assert wish, Reinforce, Mindful, Appear confident, and Negotiate (Linehan, 1993b, pp. 79–81). This mnemonic is challenging, because the terms have multiple syllables and are minimally associated. An intellectually disabled person may have difficulty pronouncing these words, never mind understanding the concepts and integrating them into the complex contexts. Additionally, because the skill functions within the context of an interaction, it increases cognitive load demands.

3. Retrieval of divergent information. Information is divergent when it is learned at different times and perhaps within different contexts. For example, if the person learned a piece of information in group and associated that information with specific elements of that experience, it may be challenging to recall the information in a work setting. Multiple cues may be necessary to help the person link the information in divergent contexts.

4. Rapid shifts without transition from one topic to another. Quick movement from topic to topic or context to context increases cognitive load. Individuals with intellectual disabilities often have difficulty transitioning from one event, location, activity, and relationship to another. For example, the person may experience difficulties during shift change or during a transition to and from a vocational site. It requires cognitive resources to manage shifting contexts. Orienting the individual to changes helps reduce the cognitive load of transitions.

5. Strong emotional responses to information or while processing information. If the individual experiences strong emotional responses while processing information, cognitive demands increase. For example, if the comment, question, or teaching point in skills group discussions address "hot" topics (e.g., living with impairments, victimization, losses, and processing past behavioral problems), strong emotions that increase cognitive load may result.

Specific Factors that Impact Individuals with Intellectual Disabilities

The skills trainer needs to understand the numerous challenges individuals with intellectual disabilities commonly encounter. The following sections highlight emotional, cognitive, behavioral, mental health, developmental, and environmental vulnerabilities that often affect an individual with an intellectual disability. These factors frequently transact with each other to contribute to patterns of emotional, cognitive, and behavioral dysregulation. The issues not only impact the skills-training process, but also may influence how skills coaching is performed. People who have alternative disabilities, disorders, or problems may experience similar challenges. Knowing the complex and diverse factors impacting each individual can improve the skills trainer's effectiveness.

Emotional factors.

Although there have been significant strides made to better understand the components of emotion regulation within the nondisabled population, McClure (2009) reported that minimal information regarding emotion regulation, associated factors, or treatment for people with intellectual disabilities and emotional regulation deficits can be found. Therefore, during the development of the Skills System, it was necessary to look beyond the disabilities field to explore a model that addressed emotion-regulation factors for the general population.

For example, dialectical behavior therapy (DBT) is a comprehensive cognitive-behavioral model originally developed by Linehan (1993) to treat individuals with borderline personality disorder (BPD). Linehan postulates that emotional dysregulation is a core dysfunction that is specifically targeted with DBT strategies to build enhanced emotion-regulation capacities. DBT treatment is constructed to treat the complex emotional, cognitive, behavioral, self, and relationship dysregulation commonly experienced by clients with BPD. Several randomized controlled trials have been completed highlighting the efficacy of DBT with BPD clients (Linehan et al., 1994; van den Bosch et al., 2002; Verheul et al., 2003). Interestingly, the application of DBT has expanded to treat other populations of clients who have various types of mental illnesses and who experience intense levels of dysregulation. Randomized controlled studies empirically support the efficacy of DBT in treating substance abuse (Linehan et al., 1999; Linehan et al., 2002), eating disorders (Telch et al., 2001; Safer et al., 2001), female veterans with BPD symptoms (Koons et al., 2001), and depression in older adults (Lynch, 2003). Although there have been few studies examining the application of DBT with individuals who have intellectual impairment (Lew, 2006; Sakdalan & Collier, 2009), the expanding validation for using DBT with diverse populations supports exploring the utilization of DBT with individuals with intellectual disabilities.

Linehan describes the concept of "emotional vulnerability" as "high sensitivity to emotional stimuli, emotional intensity, and slow return to emotional baseline" (Linehan, 1993, p. 43). While emotional vulnerability contributes to patterns of cognitive- and behavioral-modulation problems in people with BPD, similar presentations have been reported within the literature related to individuals with intellectual disabilities who experience behavioral problems, mental health issues, and trauma (Wilson, 1999; Esbensen et al., 2008; Jahromi et al., 2008). The following sections highlight various cognitive, behavioral, mental health, developmental, and environmental factors that may contribute to creating and maintaining emotional vulnerability for this population.

Cognitive factors.

Individuals with intellectual disabilities often have cognitive deficits that reduce processing and, in turn, impact adaptive coping capacities. Impairment of executive functioning, short-term memory, and long-term memory can make emotion regulation and learning more difficult.

Additionally, attention deficits and problematic thinking patterns can impact the abilities to learn and cope. It is helpful for the skills trainer to understand how the individuals' cognitive resources may impact abilities to self-manage and integrate new adaptive strategies. The specific design of the Skills System and the teaching strategies (presented in chapters 5–7) account for these deficits and provide the means for the individual to build self-regulation capacities.

Executive functioning.

Individuals with intellectual disabilities may experience impaired executive functioning (Alloway, 2010). The DSM-IV-TR (APA, 2000) explains that executive functioning involves the ability to think abstractly and to plan, initiate, sequence, monitor, and stop complex behavior. Impairment in abstract thinking may be manifested by the individual having difficulty coping with novel tasks and avoiding situations that require the processing of new and complex information (p. 149).

Vicari (1995) observed that when an individual with an intellectual disability performed a second task, his or her ability to categorize, speed of processing, and accuracy were reduced. The individual's short- and long-term memory capacities may not be impaired, yet the central executive functioning and phonological loop capacity may be affected, impairing performance (Van der Molen et al., 2007). Impaired executive functioning may make generating options and solving multicomponent problems difficult for the person with an intellectual disability. Danielsson et al, (2010) highlighted that shifting attention between tasks during encoding and reduced processing speed impacted accuracy, rather than interruptions at recall, when examining decreases in functioning. The structure of the Skills System helps facilitate self-monitoring, improves awareness of effective options, and aids the individual in executing multistep coping strategies; the skills framework provides accommodations for executive-functioning deficits.

Memory deficits.

It is important for skills trainers to assess the individual's memory abilities. Adaptive strategies, such as visual or verbal cues, may be necessary when a participant has short-term and long-term memory impairment. The Skills System training continually reviews and repeats material to broaden and deepen knowledge to maximize learning and retention.

Impaired short-term memory capacities can be present in many different cases and create varying levels of vulnerability. An individual with attention deficit hyperactivity disorder, communication disorder, delirium, dementia, and/or certain medical conditions may experience memory deficits (APA, 2000). An individual diagnosed with mental retardation does not necessarily have short-term memory deficits. Factors such as impairment in verbal strategies, impaired executive functioning, lack of experience, and low self-efficacy may impact the utilization of memory strategies, hence impacting memory functioning (Belmont & Butterfield, 1977; Jerrold et al, 2000; Henry & McLean, 2002).

The skills trainer needs to be aware of long-term memory deficits experienced by participants. Individuals who are diagnosed with delirium or dementia often suffer from long-term memory loss. In these cases, often memories of the distant past are preserved, while more recent memories are more vulnerable.

Once again, an individual diagnosed with mental retardation does not necessarily experience long-term memory deficits. Jorm (1983) found that there is "fairly consistent evidence that mentally retarded readers had adequate long-term memory for non-verbal material and for semantic aspects of verbal material" (p. 311). Jorm also explains that the intellectually disabled subjects had difficulties with verbal memory due to deficits with the articulation loop, memory span, serial ordering, and phonological confusion. Jorm noted less use of verbal rehearsal with this population. The author states that intellectually disabled individuals tended to use fewer mnemonic strategies such as verbal coding, rehearsal, and organization. Whitman (1990) highlighted the role that language plays in labeling, monitoring, analyzing, and controlling one's own cognitive operations, behavior, and social environment. Verbal-processing capacities can impact the cuing process and integration of adaptive coping skills for this population.

While verbal processing may be a weakness for some people who have intellectual impairment, Nigro and Roak (1987) found that individuals diagnosed with mental retardation demonstrated similar capacity as non-disabled subjects on object and spatial location tests. In a similar study, Ueker and Nadel (1998) determined that intellectually disabled subjects remembered locations of objects, but were unable to recall what the objects were. These studies highlight the significant cognitive processing variability within this heterogeneous population.

Attention control.

Merrill (1992) found that intellectually disabled subjects allocated less attention resources to stimulus encoding and decision-making processes than nondisabled participants. Merrill noted that the individuals tended to have the priority of completing the task, regardless of speed or accuracy, due to the fear of appearing disabled. Fear of stigmatization caused disorganized thoughts, confusion, and difficulty focusing attention. This demonstrates how emotions, cognitions, and behaviors create complex interactions that may elicit maladaptive responses.

Many psychiatric disorders affect an individual's ability to control attention. Intellectually disabled individuals may have co-morbid mental illness issues that affect attention control. Individuals diagnosed with pervasive developmental disorder, delirium, dementia, attention deficit disorder, schizophrenia and/or other psychotic disorders, mood disorders, and/or anxiety disorders often struggle to control their attention.

Various aspects of the Skills System assist individuals with attentional control problems. First, the skills help the individual manage emotions that may stimulate cognitive dysregulation and disorganization. Next, the structure serves as a cognitive framework that helps the individual be oriented to on-track behaviors and assists in reorienting the individual when he or she loses focus and goes off-track. Additionally, the system teaches concrete steps to promote attentional control and awareness during Clear Picture. Learning to be present and then strategically transitioning through skill progressions helps individuals learn to focus attention to execute series of adaptive behaviors.

Problematic thinking patterns.

Spivack and Shure (1982) highlight that an individual with cognitive impairment may develop thinking patterns that contribute to problematic coping behaviors. Spivack and Shure explain that "without seeing the motivational issues and goals, there can be no 'means–end' thought and no consideration of the consequences of different decisions" (p. 325). The authors continue to explain that these deficits contribute to a "no thought" or "repressive style" of managing feelings, thoughts, and actions. This cognitive style contributed to problematic thinking patterns that included static perceptions and reduced ability to seek alternatives. Spivack and Shure highlighted that problem solving is impaired due to decreased problem identification and resolution, because there are no perceived problems. Unfortunately, avoiding problems and emotions serves to increase the strength of cues. This "repressive style" increases vulnerability, because it leads to heightened perceived threats, anxiety, and flooding of emotion.

The authors report that another problem arises from "no thought" (Spivack & Shure, 1982, p. 334) style. Spivack and Shure state that the individual may self-generate thoughts as "counter statements" or "inversions" (p. 336) to manage the inconsistencies between their own perceptions and the realities of the situation. Thinking inversions can happen in which the individual labels negative topics as "not bad." For example, the person may tell himself or herself, "aggression is not a problem." Eventually the behavior is perceived as "not bad." Concrete thinking abilities may link or associate the maladaptive behavior as "not bad" with being "good"; therefore, the individual thinks "aggression is good." As a result, the individual becomes increasingly disoriented and unable to work effectively within societal norms. This is an example of how cognitive vulnerabilities contribute to behavioral dysregulation.

The Skills System helps provide cognitive structuring for participants. Rather than focusing on a multistep cognitive restructuring model, the Skills System provides a clear process for the individual to become oriented to goals, self-reflect on the effectiveness of acting on urges, turn thoughts toward the goal, and practice positive self-talk. Less focus is spent on delving into and evaluating the problematic thought process beyond the individual determining whether the thinking is helpful or not helpful to her. This tactic reinforces that thoughts are transient and that the individual can let go of past problematic patterns to move ahead.

Behavioral factors.

Heightened emotional, cognitive, behavioral, and environmental vulnerabilities often impact the behavioral regulation capacities of people with intellectual disabilities (Wilson, 1999; Esbensen et al., 2008; Jahromi et al., 2008). Although aggression is not included in the diagnostic criteria for mental retardation, prevalence of aggression and severe behavioral problems is reportedly higher within this population than in the general public. Wide variation in the prevalence rates exists in the literature. As few as 14 percent (Tyrer et al., 2006) and as many as 71 percent of individuals with intellectual disabilities in school settings had behavioral problems (Sullivan & Knutson, 2000). Prevalence rates of behavioral problems noted by community mental health centers varied within the range of 30 percent to 60 percent (Benson et. al., 1986; Willner, 2002; Hemmings, 2008). Although there is diversity within these findings, there is a consensus that behavioral problems impact the lives of many people with intellectual disabilities and create significant challenges to support providers.

Factors associated with severe behavioral problems.

The literature offers a multitude of specific factors that are associated with chronic and intense behavioral dysregulation in people with intellectual disabilities. Nezu and Nezu (1991) describe intellectually disabled individuals with aggression as more vulnerable due to psychopathology and lack of opportunity to learn adaptive coping strategies. A lack of assertiveness, difficulty coping with frustration, anxiety, and negative social stress were highlighted as contributing factors to aggression. Reiss and Rojahn (1993) explored the relationship between depression and aggression in adults with intellectual disabilities. The study found that criterion levels of depression were present in four times as many aggressive participants as nonaggressive ones. Similarly, Cromwell (1997) reported that aggression was frequently a reaction to feelings of anxiety, depression, and grief. Cromwell stated that intellectually disabled individuals may express emotions through aggression, rather than processing the feelings verbally. Janssen et al. (2002) reported that intellectually disabled individuals experience heightened anxiety and distractibility, which contributed to behavioral dysregulation. Tyrer et al. (2006) found that symptoms of frustration and mood swings were associated with higher levels of aggression. Crocker et al. (2007)

conducted a cross-sectional study of 296 individuals who had mild and moderate intellectual disabilities to identify typologies of aggression. The author reported that the "violent" group lacked social and vocational involvement, experienced significant mental health factors, demonstrated high levels of impulsivity, and had antisocial tendencies in comparison to the other groups. Although the literature highlights significant variation in prevalence rates and etiology, it appears that difficulties regulating emotions is a core contributor to challenging behaviors.

Common antecedents of behavioral instability.

Understanding antecedents of aggressive and/or abusive behaviors helps the participant, individual therapists, support team members, and skills trainers to proactively address factors that may elicit behavioral problems. The table below presents information from the *American Journal of Mental Retardation* Special Issue (2000) that described various stressors that commonly precipitate behavior problems.

Antecedents	Examples
Transitional phases	Individuals are more prone to behavioral dyscontrol during transitions, such as changes in residence, school, work, and route to work, and the reaching of developmental milestones.
Interpersonal loss or rejection	Loss of a parent, relationships ending, and being fired are high-stress events that may trigger aggressive behaviors.
Environmental factors	Crowded environments, loud noises, disorganized settings, lack of satisfactory stimulation, and lack of privacy can precipitate aggression.
Parenting and social support problems	Triggers such as a lack of support, destabilized visits, restricted phone use, neglect, hostility, and abuse within support relationships can be problematic.
Illness and disability	Experiencing chronic medical or psychiatric illness, having sensory impairment, difficulty walking, and having seizures may increase behavioral vulnerabilities.
Stigmatization	When an individual experiences being taunted, teased, bullied, exploited, overcontrolled, or demeaned, it may elicit aggressive responses.
Frustration	Stress created by an inability to communicate needs, lack of choice, and realization of deficits may contribute to behavioral outbursts.

Table 4.1: Common prompting events for behavioral problems (p. 168)

The Skills System is designed to assist individuals in managing factors such as those listed in Table 4.1. As the person is able to manage emotions and cognition more effectively, behavioral control becomes more likely. Rather than behaving impulsively and reacting to stressful situations, the person learns how to manage difficulties and even reach personal goals during these times.

Mental health factors.

Individuals with intellectual disabilities are four times more likely to experience mental health issues than the general population (Matson, 1984; Nezu et. al., 1992; Reiss and Rojahn, 1993). "Diagnostic overshadowing" (Reiss & Szysko, 1983, p. 396) hinders the accurate assessment and treatment of multiple disorders due to the complex presentation of symptoms. The complexity of these clinical cases confounds the process of prescribing effective medications. Often individuals are prescribed combinations of several medications; it can be challenging to evaluate the negative and positive impacts of the drugs.

Communication deficits can affect the individual's and the physician's ability to effectively diagnose and treat mental illness. The individual may be less able to label internal experiences, explain symptoms, and describe side effects to doctors. The evaluation of the effectiveness of medications and the adjustment of medication levels are impacted by these deficits. Due to a lack of adaptive coping skills, the intellectually disabled person may not be able to be a strong self-advocate and demonstrate assertiveness when discussing mental health issues with physicians and support providers. Unfortunately, intellectually disabled individuals have a higher prevalence of mental illness, while experiencing heightened levels of inaccurate diagnoses, medication trials, and impaired communication to solve these complex mental health management problems.

Skills can help the individual better manage mental health symptoms, as well as his care. Improved self-awareness facilitates improved communication related to the accuracy of self-reports and the person's ability to manage interactions with care providers. The individual needs to use Problem Solving, Expressing Myself, Getting It Right, and Relationship Care to manage health issues and to be an effective self-advocate.

Developmental factors.

People with intellectual disabilities progress through an individualized pattern of psychological development. Greenspan (1981) describes this as a person's "individual developmental time-table" (p. 729). Unique configurations happen as a child ages in years while not progressing developmentally in certain areas. For example, an intellectually disabled teenager may not have achieved developmental tasks from previous phases, yet is faced with the life demands of adolescence. The individual may struggle with inconsistent capacities and increasing demands of the environment while simultaneously managing changing physiology.

Greenspan (1981) states that "catch up" learning occurs and "such learning, however, may have a different developmental sequence and final configuration" (p. 726). Greenspan explains that treatment would entail "strengthening the specific missing components" (p. 731). The author highlights the following capacities as developmentally important (2009):

> the ability to take interest in the world and be calm and regulated, to engage with depth and intimacy, to engage and read emotional gestures, to interact with emotional gestures to solve problems with others, to create ideas, to build logical bridges between ideas, to think in a multi-causal framework, to see shades of gray in one's ideas and relationships and feelings, finally, to think reflectively-to operate in two frames of reference at the same time. (p. 5)

The Skills System model is designed to help individuals continue the developmental process throughout the life span.

It is important that individuals have ample opportunities to build developmentally effective abilities. If people do not have sufficient opportunities to master developmental tasks, a vicious cycle can develop. For example, restricted opportunities for relationship experience may hinder growth. Increased developmental delays may increase relationship dysfunction, further restricting the person from opportunities to learn adaptive skills. The deprivation of social interaction isolates these individuals from experiences necessary to develop competencies (Ross & Ross, 1973).

As individuals address developmental tasks, emotional vulnerability and behavioral instability may result. For example, as a forty-year-old participant improves self-regulatory capacities and learns to organize behaviors, she demonstrates mastery of earlier childhood developmental tasks. As these capacities emerge, it is common to witness behaviors that resemble adolescent patterns of interaction that function to establish the person's identity. It is not unusual for Skills System participants to improve self-regulation skills and then begin to exhibit more self-determined behaviors. Unfortunately, just as with an adolescent, adaptive skill use is variable in these initial stages. The person may demonstrate noncompliant and limit-testing behaviors as part of the developmental learning process.

Skills trainers and skills coaches may become confused and disheartened that the participant seemed to be doing well and then appears to experience setbacks. Conflicted interactions may be an essential aspect of the intellectually disabled individual developing autonomy and self-determination. It is not uncommon for treatment teams to experience the frustrations similar to those of parents who are managing a rebellious (healthy) teenager. Unfortunately, participants and teams may experience polarization during these transitional phases. The individual's behavior may be a positive sign of progress, while the team wonders what has gone wrong. Thus, skills trainers should be cautious not to view all "acting out" behavior as pathological.

It may be helpful for skills trainers to educate support providers about this natural, positive process. Although interactions with the participant may be seemingly ridden with conflict at times, this process can provide relationship opportunities that promote further psychological development. Just as parents alter behaviors to accommodate the emergence of the child as an adult, the support team needs to make adjustments as well. For example, a support team may need to provide more initial structure as the person is gaining self-regulation skills. As the individual internalizes self-control abilities, more autonomy, negotiation, and collaboration may foster enhanced growth. Throughout this developmental process, it is vital that the individuals have an opportunity to learn how to balance demonstrating self-determined behaviors with working effectively with others.

Common psychological milestones.

It may be helpful for individuals, skills trainers, and skills coaches to be aware that common life events may lead to increased emotional vulnerabilities for individuals with significant learning challenges. Table 4.3 introduces the "psychosocial milestones" construct developed by Gilson (1987). These life transitions require the individual to demonstrate new and more advanced skills to effectively cope with the situation. Additional skills supports may help individuals successfully navigate these challenging experiences.

Event	Effects
Diagnosis of mental retardation	Stress and need for resources in the family increases.
Birth of siblings	The family has less time to teach the disabled child.
Starting school	The child experiences the first direct confrontation of cognitive deficits in organized educational settings. The child often experiences being different from chronological age peers, loss of friends, isolation, systems problems, bureaucracy difficulties for family, and stress.
Onset of puberty and adolescence	The adolescent may experience a large gap between psychosocial and sexual maturity. The family or placement must face the issues of autonomy versus vulnerability to exploitation.
Sex and dating	Often the individual has restricted dating or is supervised by staff on these outings. Other complicating factors are exclusion from school activities, limited people to date, communication deficits, stigma, physical handicaps, isolation, "rejection induced fantasy life," and family conflict.
Being surpassed by younger siblings	This experience forces the individual to face his or her limitations.
Inappropriate expectations	The individual may be placed in situations in which they may not have sufficient skills to cope effectively.
Emancipation of younger siblings	When the siblings mature, it may mean the loss of a friend/helper/advocate. It may be a loss of help for parents, which can increase family stress. The individual may experience heightened withdrawal, grief, rejection, anger, envy, and anxiety regarding his own future.
End of education	The end of education may mean the end of opportunities, and the individual may "regress to previous levels of psychosocial attainment and resort to passive entertainment of initiative." It is not uncommon for the individual to demonstrate less autonomy as he experiences the limited capacity of agencies to provide help.
Out-of-home placement	The individual may face many challenges related to moving to a community residence. The individual often is not allowed to choose the location of his or her residence, and the timing generally depends on housing availability. The new setting may mean new rules, housemates, transportation limitations, staffing issues, and the changing role of family.
Aging, illness, and death of parents	The individual may experience a loss of support, as well as experiencing grief, stress, major depression, dependency, fear, and anger at a dead parent or the surviving one.

Death or loss of peers and friends	The individuals may lose valued staff, friends may move away, or friends within the support system may die. The individual may experience emotional numbing and withdrawal from new friendships.
Medical illness	Many complications impact medical care for individuals diagnosed with mental retardation. Consumers may have difficulty describing symptoms, which delays diagnosis.
Mental illness	The onset of psychiatric illness can increase challenges for the individual and the individual's support system; managing symptoms and treatment may be impacted by the person's level of functioning.

Table 4.2: "Psychosocial milestones" (Gilson, 1987).

Environmental factors.

Many individuals with intellectual disabilities face multitudes of environmental challenges. Three specific ones are presented in this section: traumatic experiences, social stigmatization, and environmental triggers. These environmental factors may lead to emotional vulnerability, cognitive overload, and behavioral instability for people who have limited adaptive coping abilities. Environmental forces, such as victimization, social stigmatization, overprotection by support staff, minimal financial resources, lack of opportunity for employment, dependency, and social isolation, are prevalent stressors for this population. These chronic, lifelong forces create challenging situations that may lead individuals with limited coping abilities to exhibit ineffective behaviors to manage overwhelming emotions and circumstances.

Traumatic experiences.

An intellectually disabled person experiences higher rates of neglect, physical abuse, and sexual abuse. Sullivan (2000) collected data indicating that 31 percent of disabled people were maltreated, while 9 percent of nondisabled children were abused. According to these school-based records, a cognitively impaired child is 3.4 times more likely to experience abuse than a nondisabled child. Given the high prevalence rates, problems with diagnostic overshadowing, and lack of treatment tailored for this population, it is likely that unresolved PTSD is an underlying problem for some intellectually disabled people. Additionally, the pervasive social stigmatization that this population experiences may contribute to patterns of behavior associated with the effects of trauma.

Effects of trauma.

It is helpful for skills trainers to be aware of the common effects of trauma. Streech-Fischer and van der Kolk (2000) stated that child trauma victims demonstrated heightened levels of helplessness, distress, and exaggerated fight-or-flight responses to nonemergency stimuli. Individuals also experience increased uncertainty that tended to decrease exploration of novel events and social contacts (Streech-Fischer & van der Kolk, 2000). Additionally, the authors highlighted how trauma impacted individuals' physiology, resulting in impaired memory and learning capacity. These patterns are frequently exhibited by individuals with intellectual disabilities.

Traumatic experiences can impact the participants' ability to learn when in skills-training sessions, as well as when implementing skills in natural contexts. Streech-Fischer and van der Kolk (2000) state that a traumatized child must be calm enough to evaluate stimuli to utilize adaptive coping behaviors. The authors explained, "only when they [traumatized children] are not hyper-aroused, can they activate the frontal cortex, which is needed for subtle stimulus discrimination, learning and problem solving" (p. 908). It is important that any interventions designed to help this population take into account the impact of cognitive dysregulation.

The Skills System design is congruous with these points. The Categories of Skills are constructed to help the individuals differentiate which skills are effective at any given level of emotion and which should only be used when emotionally regulated. A basic tenet of the Skills System postulates that if the participant is aroused, it is not advisable to engage in complex, interactive skills due to cognitive dysregulation. In these cases, the participant learns to be mindful of the current moment and to engage in activities that help reregulate the person before using Problem Solving, Expressing Myself, Getting It Right, and Relationship Care.

Social stigmatization.

Social stigmatization is a significant vulnerability factor for an individual with intellectual impairment. Rowitz (1981, 1988) describes how an individual diagnosed with mental retardation is often stigmatized, teased, rejected, insulted, ignored, and labeled as incompetent. Lindsay (2005) concurs that this population becomes stigmatized through being excluded from participating in work and social activities. Exclusion leads to more idle time, reduced pro-social influences, and an overreliance on "segregated, dysfunctional experiences" (p. 435). Stigmatization contributes to restricted social opportunity and increases the likelihood of victimization.

There are many negative effects of prolonged social stigmatization. Reiss and Rojahn (1993) discuss how prolonged exposure to social stigmatization, negative conditions, and negative public attitudes contribute to the development of mental illness. The authors explain that individuals diagnosed with mental retardation who experience stigmatization may develop problematic patterns of behavior. Reiss states, "hopelessness leads to depression, negative social conditions lead to withdrawal, and rebellion against negative social forces perceived as antisocial behavior" (p. 2). Dagnon (1999) reports that as the intellectually disabled individual internalizes social stigma, the person begins to recognize and accept that evaluation. Reinforcing these messages, society does not offer a wide range of roles for individuals diagnosed with mental retardation. The individuals become highly confused regarding their perceptions about their own abilities, capacities, strengths, and challenges.

Moore (2001) highlighted that when individuals diagnosed with mental retardation were aware of their own emotional vulnerability and impaired capacity, the knowledge affected the individual's functioning abilities. Moore reports that the awareness of disability led to social vulnerability and the perception of negative emotional responses from others toward the individual. The self-devaluing perspective made the individual sensitive to social stigma. Self-invalidation, which is triggered and reinforced by environmental factors, impedes self-efficacy, executive functioning, and cognitive processing. The transactions between individuals' self-perception, their perception of the environment, and the environmental forces contribute to emotional vulnerability.

Environmental triggers.

Community residences and residential treatment settings are complex living environments that often perpetuate ineffective patterns of behavior. An individual often experiences limited opportunity to make choices. For example, few consumers can choose where to live or with whom. Wehmeyer and Metzler (1995) report that when intellectually disabled individuals see that choices are limited or meaningless, negative reactions are more prevalent. An individual also may be overprotected by support providers, rather than guided to demonstrate autonomous skill use. When environments are overly structured and an individual is overprotected, the message is sent that the person is not capable. Many intellectually disabled people report feeling infantilized. The person may exhibit dependency and/or behavioral dyscontrol as a result of experiencing a lack of control in her life.

Individuals living in supported environments often experience boredom and frustration due to limited social options. Community integration is often limited. A lack of employment opportunity is a significant stressor for cognitively impaired individuals, but finding employment can be very difficult. Restricted access to the community, limited funding, a lack of employers, and transportation problems are often barriers for employment. Having limited finances severely impacts the person's quality of life.

Relationships with support staff can be strengths as well as vulnerability factors for individuals who receive these services. There is significant variability of the traits, abilities, ethnic backgrounds, and training of support staff that work with consumers. Low wages, long hours, high-risk consumers, and limited training may contribute to increased variability of staff. The most problematic staff members exert too much control over clients—or the opposite, showing too little attention. Unfortunately, people with an intellectual disability rarely have opportunity to choose the people who are supervising them. It is challenging for a consumer to alter the behavior of the problematic staff due to the power differential. Because of the high variability and lack of control that the individual experiences on a regular basis with staff in some settings, staff may be considered an environmental vulnerability.

The Skills System Design

The Skills List and System Tools create a simple framework that provides support for individuals who wish to develop adaptive coping skills. The structure of the Skills System creates a pathway that guides the individual to navigate through adaptive coping steps that facilitate effective self-regulation. In addition, the Skills System information is continually reviewed and applied in life contexts, a approach that helps compensate for vulnerabilities that impact encoding (Danielsson, 2010). This learning process creates an integrated knowledge base; the repetition helps the individual reduce cognitive load demands. Over time, as adaptive schemas are positively reinforced, the capacity to negotiate more complex situations without becoming cognitively overloaded increases. Decreasing the amount of cognitive resources needed to perform a task helps the individual complete complex tasks more efficiently. The positive cognitive structuring that the Skills System offers allows individuals to navigate through situations, adjust to transitions, and address multiple facets of complicated situations.

Skills System and individuals with intellectual disabilities.
Cognitive overload.
An individual with mental health issues and/or significant learning impairments experiences demanding events on a daily basis that potentially lead to cognitive overload. For example, residing in congregate living situations, managing relationships with staff and housemates, and negotiating transportation needs, vocational workshops, and activities of daily living can create significant cognitive load demands. The individual is often confronted with events that require simultaneous processing of high volumes of information due to the variable nature of community residences and residential settings. The person may have minimal control in many situations; therefore, much of the information is divergent. The individual may not be oriented to the numerous transitions

encountered each day. In addition to these stressful experiences, social stigmatization, impaired freedom, inconsistently structured environments, insufficiently trained staff members, and limited financial resources are likely to create strong emotional responses. The Skills System is specifically built to help an individual with learning challenges to integrate capacities to effectively manage emotions, thoughts, and actions within the complex life contexts.

Skills System provides remedial supports.

The Skills System framework is particularly helpful for participants who have executive functioning impairment. For example, transitions create high cognitive load demands and are particularly challenging for an individual with cognitive impairments. The Skills System pathway leads the individual through transitions that would formerly derail coping efforts. The Skills System rubric helps the individual maintain a consistent internal cognitive process that helps the person make effective transitions during both internal and external changes. This structured, yet flexible design leads the person through a skills process, hence promoting generalization of skills in diverse settings. As the person practices and experiences reinforcement, adaptive coping behaviors become more automatic and are generalized in increasingly challenging situations.

The Skills System is built to utilize the individual's strengths. The individual with intellectual impairment often has capacities for inner wisdom and intuition, yet struggles with cognitive processing activities that require juggling large amounts of complex information. The Skills System's simple steps lead the person through a process that engages the person's intuition or sense of wisdom. Not only does this trigger the individual's strengths, but the activation of the person's self-relationship improves self-awareness, self-acceptance, self-value, and self-trust. This positive cycle is reinforced as the person reaches personal goals, manages challenging situations, and develops mastery. Thus, the individual enhances adaptive coping skills that assist the person in reducing emotional, cognitive, behavioral, mental health, developmental, and environmental vulnerability factors.

CHAPTER 5:

Structuring Skills System Instruction

Each participant, support environment, and therapeutic setting is unique. Exploring various organizational options helps create flexible, effective skills instruction to accommodate the individual's learning needs. This chapter will introduce several concepts that help skills trainers organize skills education for individuals with significant learning challenges.

The first section of Chapter 5 presents information that helps structure individual and group skills training. The next portion of this chapter introduces three important elements of the Skills System teaching model: the E-Spiral framework, Skills System session format, and twelve-week cycle curriculum. The fourth and final component of the Skills System teaching model, enhanced teaching strategies, is described in Chapters 6 and 7. Skills trainers integrate these four elements to construct skills instruction in ways that fit the individuals and the support setting.

While structure is an essential element of Skills System instruction, flexibility is equally vital. All of the concepts described in this chapter are meant to be utilized as a guide to tailor Skills System training, rather than a prescription. Although no session may actually follow these guidelines exactly, awareness of these concepts can help the practitioner design interventions that advance learning.

Individual and Group Skills Training

It may be helpful for skills trainers to meet with group participants prior to joining skills group to discuss the concept of committing to learning skills. Both parties define behaviors that are helpful in group and those that the individual may be prone to exhibit that would hinder positive engagement in group. The parties agree to be respectful and not harm themselves, anyone else, or property during group. Additionally, the participant must agree that if he or she became romantically involved with another person in group, one of the participants would shift to another group. It is important to note that due to the poverty of social relationships that many individuals with significant learning challenges face, it is not uncommon for group members to form friendships. The impact of relationships in group must be monitored to ensure that group process is not adversely affected.

If the skills trainer assesses that a participant is unable to manage the social environment of group and learn information, it may be necessary for the person to have individual skills training first. With the provision of a foundation of information on an individual basis, the person may be better able to develop basic self-regulation skills that help the person learn in the group setting. Although some participants may benefit from beginning in individual skills training, the ultimate goal may be to help the person engage in a Skills System group. Skills groups provide learning experiences that aid in the generalization of skills into the social environment.

The main goal of group is to help the participants build adaptive coping skills. This goal implicitly defines group rules. For example, behaviors that support learning skills are helpful, while actions that work against skills acquisition will need to be addressed. Helpful hints about ways to discuss problematic behaviors can be found on page 67 within the Contingency Management section in Chapter 6. Additionally, participants may have an individualized behavior plan and/or agency guidelines that need to be followed. It is important that the skills trainer is familiar with behavioral plans so as not to intermittently reinforce problematic behaviors. It is essential that the participant and skills trainer agree about how these rules are going to be addressed in group so that the individual is oriented to the procedures.

Group makeup.

The Skills System groups do not need to have a specific number of participants. It may be ideal to have multiple options for group sizes to suit the needs of participants. Small groups of 2–4 participants offer more individualized training and coaching. Groups of between 4 and 7 people allow for individual participation and opportunities for social interaction. Larger groups (7–10 participants) allow the participant to practice skills in a more complex social setting. Unfortunately, logistics and resources can dictate group size; by understanding factors that impact learning, the skills trainer can advocate for program design features that optimize learning. It may be helpful to have instructors co-lead larger groups.

Timeframes of group sessions.

Group sessions generally meet for one hour per week. Group skills training places high cognitive and emotional demands on participants and skills trainers; fatigue is a legitimate concern as timeframes lengthen. In residential settings, it may be useful to run multiple one-hour skills groups per week. Meeting more than once per week may create opportunity for heightened integration of the Skills System concepts; this exposure may foster improved generalization of skills. Shortening groups to less than an hour (and increasing the frequency) may be workable, as long as the E-Spiral framework concepts are integrated into the program design. It is important to design groups so that there is sufficient time for all aspects of the learning process to occur.

Participants revolve multiple times through the twelve-week cycle curriculum.

The pace at which the group and individuals progress through Skills System materials is highly variable. Generally, the basic Skills System material cannot be integrated by individuals with cognitive challenges within a single twelve-week cycle through group. Individuals with cognitive impairment require repetition of the Skills System curriculum to learn and generalize the information. Thus, it is recommended that an individual with significant learning challenges participate in the Skills System for a minimum of one year. During the course of a year, the person cycles through the material four times. This format allows ample time to introduce the basic Skills System concepts and offers opportunity for repetition.

It is optimal for the individual to remain in a skills group on an ongoing basis. As people increase capacities, often they accept more personal responsibilities. For example, the person may move from working in a sheltered workshop to being employed in the community. Skills group continually helps the participant develop improved coping skills as he or she is participating in more demanding tasks. Each accomplishment brings new challenges; group helps the individual to face transitions and continually progress toward personal goals.

Open versus closed groups.

Skills System groups can be either open or closed groups. There is often variability in attendance; due to logistical factors, participants may frequently miss sessions or drop out of skills training. These factors dictate that group be constructed in a way that allows an individual to miss a group and not experience a significant gap in learning. Additionally, it may be important to invite new members into the group. Instruction needs to be adjusted to accommodate this flow, but generally it does not negatively impact the skills-training process.

The design of the Skills System session format and the twelve-week cycle curriculum build in opportunities for review of materials. When a new person joins group, the skills trainer facilitates a discussion during the review phase that serves to orient the person to the basic concepts of the Skills System. The skills trainer must be able to address the learning needs of the new person, as well as the participant who has been studying skills for five years. Often more seasoned participants enjoy teaching and coaching newer members.

Homogeneous versus heterogeneous groups.

The skills trainer must decide whether groups are going to be heterogeneous or homogeneous. Frequently participants have commonalities in one area while being diverse in others. For example, at this author's clinic, groups were homogeneous in that participants were all diagnosed with some form of developmental disability. The groups were heterogeneous in that within each group, participants have a wide range of mental health diagnoses, intellectual capacities, and academic levels. The individual therapist, skills trainer, and individual collaborate to evaluate whether the person is in the proper group. Given the unique presentations of each person, it is important to individualize, rather than generalize, regarding group makeup decisions. Unfortunately, there may not be multiple options for this population due to limited clinical resources.

There may be benefits to grouping participants by academic functioning level. This distribution may allow individuals with more cognitive capacities to move through material at a faster rate and in greater depth. While reading and writing are not prerequisite skills for participating in the curriculum presented in the *Skills System Instructor's Guide*, clustering individuals who can read and write may increase options for instructors to utilize activities that integrate these mediums. For example, skills trainers may create written individual or group homework assignments that reinforce topics addressed in group.

Dividing group by gender may also be helpful. If participants have high levels of emotional, cognitive, and behavioral dysregulation, having a mixed-gender group can create interpersonal dynamics that impede learning. For example, in groups of individuals with intellectual disabilities, it would not be uncommon for victims of sexual abuse to be in group with perpetrators of abuse. The transaction between an participant with unresolved trauma issues and one who has unmanaged deviant sexual arousal can amount to a dangerous exchange. If a setting has the opportunity to divide groups by gender, at least for the initial cycles through group, it may increase the group's ability to focus on skills integration.

Skills System Teaching Model: E-Spiral Framework

The E-Spiral is a teaching framework that guides Skills System teaching practices during skills instruction sessions. This construct was formulated over years of practice and review of literature.

It serves only as a general guide and framework for practitioners to remember the multiple steps within the learning process. There are four phases of the E-Spiral that are completed during individual and/or group training: Exploring Existing Knowledge Base, Encoding, Elaboration, and Efficacy.

- In Phase 1, Exploring Existing Knowledge Base, individuals review past learning related to the topic that is introduced. Active discussion activates recall of past learning that primes individuals for new learning to happen. The goal is to create a relevant context for the learning

- In Phase 2, Encoding, individuals participate in direct instruction and multimodal activities to learn the skill topic. The aim is to teach new information.

- In Phase 3, Elaboration, individuals engage in practice exercises and discussions that expand and link new information to the person's existing knowledge base. The elaboration process is a vital, yet fun step toward deepening understandings about skills. Thus the purpose is to link and expand knowledge to enhance retention.

- In Phase 4, Efficacy, the participants continue to build mastery and confidence through contextual learning activities, such as role play, in-vivo practice, and troubleshooting challenges. It is critical that intellectually impaired individuals experience a sense of self-efficacy as part of the learning process. The E-Spiral is designed to provide contextual learning opportunities that maximize retention and generalization of skills.

As learners move through these phases and activities, knowledge about the topic is broadened and deepened. This learning process guides people through steps that naturally transition skills information from short-term to long-term memory. Thus, the E-Spiral multilayered learning experience helps intellectually impaired individuals gain mastery that promotes generalization of skills.

The E-Spiral functions as a general guide for teaching practices. While issues and time constraints commonly force the skills trainer to make adjustments, the E-Spiral serves as a template for organizing effective teaching strategies. Even when timeframes are limited, skills trainers learn how to quickly review past learning, teach new concepts, and engage in activities that create a bridge from new learning to the individual's existing knowledge base. Organizing teaching in this looping progression helps layer old and new information, which deepens learning, enhances retention, and improves recall. Being mindful of these principles helps skills trainers avoid truncating the teaching process, which would jeopardize the integration of concepts.

Benefits of the Skills System teaching model.

The twelve-week cycle curriculum creates breadth of skills knowledge, while the E-Spiral creates depth of learning. Skills trainers utilize both of these constructs simultaneously. The dialectical interplay of broadening and deepening learning promotes development and generalization of skills. Table 5.1 exemplifies how an individual's knowledge grows in a web shape using these teaching techniques.

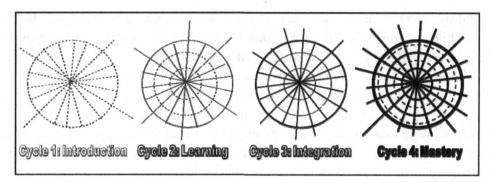

Table 5.1: Learning the Skills System

As the individual learns, practices, and generalizes information, linkages between skills fortify over time. The increased connectivity of the knowledge base enhances recall and recognition of information. As the individual builds a foundation of knowledge, cognitive load demands related to skill-use decrease. The person becomes able to master complex skill behaviors as a result of the integrated skills knowledge base.

Skills System session format.

The Skills System session format (Table 5.2) presents the various tasks within each phase of the E-Spiral. The skills trainer follows these guidelines and designs activities to complete the function of the E-Spiral phase. As the group flows from one discussion point and activity to another, learning happens. Participants do not necessarily need to know this framework, although improving metacognitive understanding about the learning process can increase self-awareness, self-efficacy, and motivation.

Tasks within E-Spiral phases
1. Exploring Existing Knowledge Base: *Recalling past learning*   Mindfulness activity to focus attention   • Review Skills System terms and Skills Practice Review   • Introduce new skills topic   • Discuss existing knowledge on the topic   • Orient to the relevant context of the new learning
2. Encoding: *Teaching the new topic*   • Direct instruction: Reviewing handouts and worked examples   • Multimodal tools: Use diagrams and cue pictures, gestures, and objects
3. Elaboration: *Bridging new and previous learning*   Practice exercises or worksheets   • Discussion: Bridging past and new learning
4. Efficacy: *Bridge to future learning*   Contextual learning activities: Role play, psychodrama, and in-vivo   • Discussion: Highlighting barriers, personal commitment, and troubleshooting for future use of the skill   • Plan for home-study activities   • Group ending: Mindfulness breathing

Table 5.2: Skills System Session Format

It is vital that the instructor understand the necessary steps to enhance comprehension and integration while remaining flexible and responsive to what is happening in the group. Under theoretically ideal conditions, approximately equal amounts of time are spent on each of the four phases. Realistically, a group rarely moves systematically through all of the phases. There are times when certain discussions and activities become more in depth, hence consuming larger percentages of the time. Small groups are more likely to complete E-Spiral tasks. The skills trainer makes decisions about how to manage the tasks and timeframes to maximize opportunities for learning. The twelve-week cycle curriculum continually revisits each skill every twelve weeks; therefore, there are other opportunities to complete a thorough progression through skills material.

Skills System twelve-week cycle curriculum.

The Skills System curriculum revolves in a twelve-week cycle. Each time a participant revisits familiar concepts, understanding and awareness deepens. Through this spiral process, the individual continually integrates new facets of the skills. As the participant learns and practices skills, she gains the ability to utilize skills in increasingly complex situations. The list below presents Skills System topics that are covered during each of the twelve weeks. Chapter 7 presents a detailed explanations of how topics may be reviewed, introduced, practiced, and integrated.

Week 1: Skills List
Week 2: System Tools
Week 3: Clear Picture
Week 4: On-Track Thinking
Week 5: On-Track Action
Week 6: Safety Plan
Week 7: New-Me Activities
Week 8: Problem Solving
Week 9: Expressing Myself
Week 10: Getting It Right
Week 11: Relationship Care
Week 12: Skills Review

Progressing through Skills System content.

The skills trainer adapts the speed of progression through the skills content to the capacities of each group. This is a complex task, given the diverse learning abilities of each participant and the varying levels of knowledge about the Skills System. For example, skills trainers may be able to cover more content during Week 3 related to Clear Picture than a leader of a different group. Notwithstanding, each of the trainers will move on to On-Track Thinking in Week 4. Given the highly diverse population being served, it is necessary to adjust the volume of content taught each week. While the amount of material that is covered varies, the format and progression from week to week remains intact. Skills trainers make adjustments related to the speed of progression through content, knowing that there is only one group during that cycle to address that skill in depth. Although this approach may appear rigid, it allows the participant to be exposed to the entirety of the curriculum in twelve weeks.

It is unrealistic to expect a group to learn a skill completely in a one-hour group session. The twelve-week cycle curriculum forces the group to keep moving through content related to each of the skills. Practitioners may have the urge to spend weeks on one skill to ensure comprehension.

Rather than focusing in-depth on one skill for several weeks, the twelve-week cycle curriculum continually tries to broaden skill knowledge. Although in-depth learning of each skill is helpful, the skills trainer integrates the teaching strategies presented in Chapter 6 and 7 within the twelve-week curriculum (outlined in chapter 8), to expand the breadth and depth of learning for this population over time.

CHAPTER 6:

Foundational Teaching Strategies

Chapter 6 and the following chapter (Chapter 7) will present descriptions of the teaching strategies referenced in the Skills System curriculum. This information serves as a toolkit for practitioners; the strategies were culled from the literature and developed through decades of clinical practice. General strategies used throughout skills-training sessions to manage cognitive load demands and individualize interventions are introduced first. Chapter 7 presents strategies that used within the specific phases of the training sessions. The information contained in these chapters is intended to help skills trainers learn the effective teaching techniques that are an integral part of the Skills System learning experience.

Within the category of foundational teaching interventions there are several strategies that skills trainers utilize throughout all phases of Skills System instruction that function to reduce cognitive load demands: Quick-Step Assessment, simplification, task analysis, mnemonics, worked examples, and orienting. The Quick-Step Assessment is a brief mental exercise that this author developed to explain the process of working with individuals with learning challenges. It is a tool that may help trainers evaluate an individual's cognitive load status and make necessary teaching adjustments. Several other techniques are introduced that can help reduce cognitive load demands and maximize retention for individuals with learning challenges. In addition to enhanced teaching strategies, behavioral techniques are implemented during skills-training sessions: shaping, positive reinforcement, and contingency management. Understanding these foundational strategies helps the skills trainer create an effective initial teaching plan and make necessary accommodations during the session.

Quick-Step Assessment

The Quick-Step Assessment is a strategy skills trainers utilize to evaluate, design, and adjust interventions. The assessment is a three-step process.

Step 1: Assess the cognitive load of the intervention.

Prior to executing any instructional or therapeutic intervention, it is important that the skills trainer consider the cognitive load of the task. Instructors quickly evaluate whether the strategies will present a high or low cognitive load. Interventions that require the individual to do simultaneous processing of information, manage high volume and interactivity of information, retrieve divergent information, shift rapidly without transition from one topic to another, and/or experience strong emotional responses to the information or while processing information increases cognitive load demands.

Step 2: Evaluate cognitive functioning.

In the second step of the Quick-Step Assessment, the skills trainer evaluates whether an individual is cognitively regulated before, during, and after interventions. When an intervention places minimal cognitive demand on the individual, the participant tends to remain cognitively regulated, engaged in the process, and able to learn the material being introduced. If the cognitive load of an intervention is too high, the individual may become lost and unable to follow along in the conversation. As cognitive demands increase and capacities decrease, the participant may experience strong frustration, anger, fear, and shame. This emotional state may further reduce cognitive load capacities and may lead the individual to engage in maladaptive behaviors that function to regulate overwhelming emotions.

The following behaviors may indicate that the individual is experiencing cognitive overload.

- Confused: The individual may be unable to follow the topic of a discussion or perhaps gives incorrect answers.
- Unfocused: The individual may appear distracted, impulsive, fidgety, and/or disorganized.
- Avoidant: The individual may change topics, promote conflict, stare off into space, not answer questions directly, or immediately say "I don't know."
- Dissatisfied or uncomfortable: The person may display hostility, irritability, dissociation, crying, panic, or refusal/nonparticipation; placate the therapist; exhibit flat affect; and/or leave the group.

It is unlikely that the individual will communicate that cognitive capacities have diminished. In fact, the person may try to appear competent, so as not to experience shame related to feeling lost and/or confused. The individual may be interested in participating, yet lacks the skills to inform the skills trainer about the problem. Skills trainers may misattribute behavior of the participant (which may have been the result of skills trainers' mismanagement of the cognitive load demands) as resistance.

Step 3: Choose and shape intervention.

Skills trainers shape interventions throughout a training session. Prior to executing a strategy, she evaluates the design of the tactic, reorganizing the intervention to reduce cognitive load factors. The lower the cognitive load, the more cognitive resources the individual has available to encode and recall the information. When an intervention places low cognitive demand, the individual is able to create associations between bits of information that allow for more information to be stored in long-term memory. The more associations that are encoded, the easier recall is later; this enhances the process of generalization.

When a participant presents as confused, unfocused, avoidant, or uncomfortable during an intervention, the skills trainer weighs the various factors within the situation to make decisions about the best way to proceed. Skills trainers must learn how to find the delicate balance between reinforcing avoidant behaviors by backing off and flooding the individual by continuing with a high cognitive demand activity.

Doing the Quick-Step.

A skills trainers' request for contribution in activities and discussions must fit the individual's current regulation status. For example, skills trainers interact predominantly with group members who are experiencing low cognitive load and who are actively engaged in activities. If an instructor presents a cognitively overloaded participant with a high-cognitive-load-demand intervention, some form of off-track behavioral expression may occur. Skills trainers follow the Skills System rules and do not ask participants to use Calm-Only skills when over a 3 emotion.

The trainer may want to adjust interventions for an individual who is struggling. Avoiding open-ended questions (e.g., "How do you feel about that?") and asking simple, closed-ended questions (e.g., "Did you think that was helpful?") allow for participation, yet do not increase escalation. The instructor may choose to ask obvious questions that he or she is sure participant will get correct. This tactic rebuilds confidence and keeps the individual engaged. When a person is cognitively overloaded, the trainer will want to avoid hot topics or asking for personal disclosure that may further dysregulate the individual. Giving the individual time to regain composure without interaction may also be helpful.

Strategies that Reduce Cognitive Load and Maximize Learning

Several techniques may be utilized to manage cognitive load demands of interventions. These tactics include simplification, task analysis, mnemonics, worked examples, and orienting to new topics and transitions.

Simplification. An individual with cognitive impairment may have difficulty processing abstract, complex, and interconnected information. Simplification of challenging ideas through refinement of language and concepts may reduce cognitive load demands. The simplification process entails finding terms that are easily pronounced, comprehended, applied, and remembered by the individual. For example, the Skills System utilizes the phrase "use sugar" (in Getting It Right) for the concept of reinforcing other people when trying to get needs met. An individual with intellectual deficits can pronounce and readily understand the concept of sugar. A participant has existing knowledge that sugar is a sweetener. By saying, "try using a little more sugar," the participants know that it means to be nicer or more accommodating. The term "reinforce" is long, difficult to pronounce, challenging to comprehend, and less likely to recall. Complex terms increase cognitive load demands and reduce the individual's ability to use the skill. Utilizing simple words that contain high association with the topic are helpful.

Task Analysis. In task analysis skills trainers break complex tasks down into component parts. By reducing multicomponent concepts into a progression of single elements, the person is able to complete the entire task one step at a time. For example, if a person wants to ask someone out on a date, there are several tangible and intangible factors to consider when preparing to successfully complete this task. The skills trainer may want to collaborate with the individual to define specific steps that are required to accomplish the goal. The individual needs to know the various steps and how to make transitions from one step to the next.

Mnemonics. Mnemonics are techniques that organize information in ways that reduce the cognitive load of information. The are several mnemonic techniques that are useful to integrate into intervention design. Chunking, metaphor, cue pictures, peg-word, and acronyms are a few ways to maximize understanding and recall through strategic organization of material.

Chunking information means to organize concepts in ways that improve short-term memory functioning by recoding information. This strategy combines concepts in ways that rely on associations to improve recognition and recall. For example, the random letters S, N, and F are processed as three units, while B, E, and D are processed as one unit due to the association the letters have with the object.

Metaphors are a "bridging strategy" that draws on intuition and existing knowledge of the learner; it provides a "transformation of nonmeaningful information into concrete, meaningful proxies" (Mastropieri, 2000). Metaphors may be words, objects, and/or gestures. These strategies cultivate a semantic knowledge base and teach how things work. For example, a train being on a track to a destination is a metaphor for the individual demonstrating goal-oriented behaviors; the Skills System uses the metaphor of being on-track and off-track to goals. The trainer can integrate using gestures to make additional points. The instructor can pretend to be standing on the tracks and tip his or her body far to one side, almost losing balance; this gesture exemplifies how people can begin to head off-track.

Cue pictures are used to cue memory. The picture explicitly connects new information with prior knowledge by means of visual cues. Thus, cue pictures prompt recall and aid visual encoding. For example, a picture of a TV set represents Clear Picture. Each time the individual sees a TV set in a handout, the participant knows that using Clear Picture is necessary.

The **peg-word method** is when rhyming, songs, numbers or phrases are used to cluster relevant information. For example, "Thirty days has September, April, June, and November ..." These methods use prompt recall by providing acoustic cues.

Acronyms are when the first letter of elements of a larger topic are organized to form another word. For example, SEALS reminds participants about the Right Words in Getting It Right. Although this method may benefit individuals who read more, there are two other associations that enhance recall. The image of a seal and the reference to Sealing the Deal are both designed to prompt recall.

Worked Examples. Worked examples present completed versions of a concept or problem. For example, a skills trainer models how a skill is done successfully. Worked examples help manage cognitive load as well as promote effective integration of adaptive coping skills.

One benefit of using worked examples is that the tactic minimizes cognitive load demands during instruction. Using worked examples reduces cognitive load by eliminating the use of means-end analyzing. Means-end analyzing "directs attention to inappropriate aspects of a problem and imposes heavy cognitive load that interferes with schema acquisition and rule automation" (Sweller, 1989, p. 457).

Sweller (1989) highlights the importance of "schema acquisition and rule automation" to promote learning (p. 457). One way of creating adaptive schema is to use "worked examples" (p. 457) to help the individual integrate accurate information. By demonstrating effective actions or reviewing solved problems, such examples allow the individual to observe how the skill functions. This process facilitates a contextual understanding of the concepts. Studying worked examples promotes increased awareness, knowledge base, and mastery while minimizing anti-learning responses.

Additionally, an individual with intellectual impairment benefits greatly from repeated demonstrations of effective skill use in various contexts. Reviewing information in different ways helps the individual develop perceptions related to the meaning of the material. This semantic encoding may draw on an individual's strengths rather than relying on perceptual skills that may be impaired. Semantic knowledge that builds an awareness of how things work enables the person to generalize information from one setting to another. As the individual makes associations about intrapersonal and interpersonal concepts, adaptive coping in diverse settings is possible.

It may be helpful to use both general and personalized worked examples throughout skills training. Utilizing hypothetical situations about fictitious people depersonalizes the scenario, thus reducing the cognitive load demands. As capacities build, transitioning to reviewing personal examples enhances the relevance, motivation, and contextual learning. Personal examples may stimulate more attention, while also increasing emotionality. Skills trainers use the Quick-Step Assessment to adjust teaching practices to address the needs of each group member.

Orienting to New Topics and Transitions. When changing topics and/or preparing to teach a new concept, orienting is a crucial step. An individual with intellectual challenges may frequently have difficulty managing transitions effectively. Orienting helps the person understand social contexts, which reduces confusion and cognitive load demands: "Great job doing that exercise. Now would it be all right if we take some time to talk about what that activity was like for each of you?" Orienting reduces barriers to learning by decreasing fear of the unknown. As an individual gains skills capacities, transitions will be managed more effectively.

Orienting is an essential element within this teaching model; skills trainers continually orient participants to the next steps. For example, instructors provide logistical information that clearly identifies the next activity and where in the skills book the person needs to go. Trainers provide functional validation by clearly explaining the location of the handouts that will be discussed in group. It is helpful to show participants the handout to be sure the individual is oriented to the current activity.

Additionally, skills trainers ask permission to progress to the next topic as part of the orienting process. For example, asking "Are we all set to move on?" allows the participants to become ready before moving ahead. Rushing and assuming an individual is prepared to progress can create confusion and disengagement. Importantly, eliciting permission creates a reciprocal relationship or an even playing field in the session within which both parties demonstrate on-track control, rather than a hierarchical teacher-student relationship that contains implied power differentials.

When participants have an opportunity to demonstrate self-determination and choice, motivation increases. Carlin (2001) noted that when an individual with intellectual disabilities is allowed to choose what items are going to be remembered, encoding and free-recall rates improve. As skills trainers offer the opportunity for choice, the participants also implicitly learn self-validation and have an opportunity to demonstrate self-determination. Not only does orienting improve encoding and let a participant know what is forthcoming, but it also creates a rich personal-growth experience for the individual.

Behavioral Strategies

It is helpful for skills trainers to have an understanding of basic behavioral strategies; this list does not serve to educate the trainer about behaviorism, but rather highlight particular elements that are useful to be aware of.

Shaping. An individual with learning challenges may need to be taught complex tasks through a gradual process. Shaping is a behavioral technique that reinforces steps of successive approximations. The individual is rewarded for reaching objectives and having behaviors that are in the direction of goals. It is important to use shaping principles during the Encoding Phase so that information is taught in ways that facilitate recall. For example, a learning progression may take steps: A, B, AB, C, BC, and ABC. This type of practice helps the cognitively impaired individual learn to integrate information; schema acquisition is facilitated through this repeated pattern of shaping. Teaching ABCDEFG may introduce more information, yet the person may not have reinforced connections between steps.

There are times in individual or group skills training when it is not possible to teach all the necessary elements of multicomponent concepts. Instructors must individualize and prioritize elements that will help most in the immediate situation. Skills trainers address what is relevant in the moment and trust that other opportunities will arise to teach the remainder of the concept at another time. The individual will learn the relevant material better in that moment; teaching irrelevant information may waste cognitive resources on impertinent information.

Positive reinforcement. Skills trainers provide a significant amount of positive reinforcement for on-track behaviors that are demonstrated in the session. Instructors are continually scanning the participants to notice effort or improvement demonstrated by each person and the group as a whole. Whenever possible trainers highlight the effective behavior, the context, and the positive achievement. Noticing and reinforcing small and large accomplishments are critical.

Contingency management. Participants may have behaviors that are not harmful to group, yet do not enhance the group process. If a behavior is not helpful to the group process, skills trainers utilize extinction. It is important not to respond to the action, so as not to intermittently reinforce the behavior.

Participants may demonstrate behavioral problems or group interfering behaviors that negatively impact the group process. If the behaviors are interfering with the skills trainer's ability to teach or the ability of participants to learn, it is necessary to address the problem by orienting him or her to the issue and offering skills coaching to address the situation.

(1) Orient to the problem. The skills trainer's first assumption is that the individual does not have the awareness or skills to manage the situation effectively. Therefore, the instructor provides coaching prior to enacting contingencies. Premature contingency management can halt the learning process. Orienting the person to the problem is the first step. For example, "Tim, I know you are excited to jump into this discussion, and your ideas are great. When you interrupt us, it is hard to hear everyone's ideas. It is also hard for us to follow what everyone is saying. Do you know what I mean?" Helping the individual see the problem offers the person a chance to self-correct.

(2) Offer skills coaching. If the behavior continues, further orientation, corrective feedback, and coaching about effective alternatives may be necessary. "Tim, I think you are doing a little better with the not interrupting, but it is still a problem for the group. Would you like some skills coaching from me or the group to help you stay on-track?" The skills trainer must pay attention to the goal of teaching skills and not offer positive reinforcement for off-track behaviors.

Coaching during group must be brief and concise. Quickly reviewing Clear Picture and On-Track Thinking with the person can often correct the problem. The following series of questions may be helpful:

- Would you be willing to Take a Breath? (Clear Picture)
- What level of emotion are you feeling? (Clear Picture)
- What urges are you having? (Clear Picture)
- Would it be okay if we Stop, Step Back, and Think about how you want this to go today? (On-Track Thinking)
- Is that urge to _____ helpful (thumbs-up) or not (thumbs-down) helping you get what you want? (On-Track Thinking)
- What skills can you use right now to help you?

- Would you like the group to help you think of some options?
- What will your On-Track Action be?

If possible, the skills trainer and the participant make a plan for how the situation will be improved. When it is clear that the progress of the group is in jeopardy, the individual may need to be asked to take a break for a few moments to gain focus and control. These situations can be excellent skills teaching opportunities for the individual and the group.

CHAPTER 7:
E-Spiral Teaching Strategies

This chapter introduces various teaching strategies and activities that are highlighted within the twelve-week cycle curriculum outlined in Chapter 8. These elements are woven together during various phases of the E-Spiral to enhance the learning process.

Preparing for a Skills-Training Session

Prior to group, skills trainers make a teaching plan to organize the activities, handouts, exercises, and discussions that will happen during the session. The Skills System Planning Sheet (Appendix B) may be a helpful form to use to both plan and track topics. Instructors may plan the basic topics to be addressed, yet exact teaching strategies may be determined during the group. It is important that trainers use relevant information that flows within the group to orchestrate learning.

During a group's first cycle through the Skills System curriculum, it is important to introduce Basic skills information. Instructors may plan on reviewing several handouts in minimal detail to offer a general overview of concepts. Exercises and discussions may be more brief; in-depth exploration of the material will happen in later cycles. As the individual progresses through multiple cycles of the Skills System curriculum, more time is spent on lateral exploration of topics. At that point, the quantity of material introduced is far less important than the quality of the discussions and practice exercises that help an individual integrate concepts.

Teaching plans are adjusted during the group session. As the participants share personal information during the various reviews and discussions in the beginning of group, skills trainers formulate how to link the participants' experiences with the new topics. Just as DBT therapists weave together acceptance and change strategies (Linehan, 1993), the Skills System trainers weave together past and current learning. Practitioners teach through building on existing strengths and motivating the participants by creating relevance. Managing these tasks is a dynamic process; skills trainers are continually making adjustments in the teaching plan to accommodate the changing needs of the group.

E-Spiral Phase 1: Activities that Explore Existing Knowledge

Welcome group. Greeting people is an important initial element of a skills-training session. Instructors engage in lighthearted conversation to initiate a pleasant, egalitarian rapport with participants. During this unstructured time of interaction, skills trainers use the Quick-Step Assessment to evaluate the status of each participant prior to initiating any skills-training activities. For example, as the skills trainer engages in chitchat, he or she is able to evaluate whether the person is calmly maintaining a dialogue or is escalated, unfocused, confused, or disorganized. Instructors monitor for cognitive overload and immediately begin the process of shaping interventions that reflect the current status of the individual. Prior to moving ahead to doing the mindfulness activity, the skills trainer orients the participants to the upcoming event.

Mindfulness activity. Skills-training session formally begins with a mindfulness activity to help participants focus attention in the present moment. Specific activities are described in the sample curriculum provided in Chapter 8. The goal of these exercises is to orient the person to the current context as well as to teach the skill of controlling attention.

Following the mindfulness activity, the participants have a discussion, revealing observations made during the mindfulness exercise. By allowing an opportunity for all participants to describe the experience, individuals practice self-awareness and self-expression behaviors. Mastery of self-awareness behaviors are crucial primary steps that allow for the development of self-acceptance, self-value, and self-trust.

It is crucial that the skills trainer fully explain all activities. Clear step-by-step directions are necessary to be sure the participant fully understands what the activity is and what she needs to do. It is also helpful to highlight any challenges that may be experienced and possible solutions for difficulties. For example, when explaining how to do a breathing activity, the trainer may want to discuss how the individual's attention will drift from the breath; the solution is for the participant to notice the attention wandering and bring it back to her breathing.

Review questions. Review questions are asked to elicit the participants' observations related to group activities or experiences. For example, after the mindfulness breathing exercise, the skills trainer may ask review questions to draw out each group member's experiences of the activity. Instructors query, "What was that activity like for you?" Review questions are generally open-ended to maximize opportunities for self-expression. Expression in group provides a chance for the individual to demonstrate self-validating behavior. The skills trainers will utilize review questions through each of the four phases of group.

The leaders ask review questions and make linking statements that highlight commonalities between participants' observations: "It is interesting that you, James, and Mary were all dealing with challenges with co-workers this week." The instructor consolidates points and moves discussions toward the skills topics that are on the agenda. For example, the leaders may choose to focus on work relationships as a relevant context for learning about the skill for the week. Finding common threads helps create a synthesized body of material that is generated from diverse sources.

Skills System review. Following sharing about the mindfulness activity, the group reviews the Skills List and the System Tools. These activities focus strictly on recalling previously learned information. The skills trainers can review the Skills System Review Questions (Appendix A, page A22) or create fun games that prompt the participants to recall the names and numbers of the skills, as well as the Feelings Rating Scale, Categories of Skills, and Recipe for Skills.

Review skills practice. Following the Skills System review, the individuals share experiences related to using the skill that was assigned for practice the previous week. It may be helpful to use a whiteboard to write down each person's name and the accomplishments; it is important to positively reinforce adaptive skill use and individual progress. Writing down information allows the instructor to link commonalities between individuals' scenarios.

The homework review gives the leader an opportunity to evaluate how well each group member is comprehending the Skills System concepts as well as evaluating his or her level of integration of the skills into life contexts. Additionally, the review process serves to prime the individual's memory to retrieve skills information in preparation for new learning. An individual with cognitive impairment learns most effectively when building on existing knowledge schemes. By placing less emphasis on accommodation and more focus on assimilation, the individual improves learning performance (Scott, 1991). Review helps promote connections and linkage between concepts; continual usage facilitates recognition and recall.

Clarifying questions. Clarifying questions may be helpful during homework reviews to promote a deeper and more detailed understanding of a topic. For example, during Skills Practice Review, the participant may attempt to describe a situation that happened during the week. The details and timeframes may be challenging to follow or vague. Instructors ask clarifying questions like "Can you tell us a little more about that so we can clearly understand?" or "Help me understand … on Tuesday you first had an argument with your co-worker, and on Wednesday you called your boss?" The participant may need assistance recalling the chain of events due to sequencing deficits.

Additionally, clarifying questions can help the person improve self-awareness—for example, "What body sensations did you notice just before you walked in to meet with your boss?" The skills trainer helps the individual and the group gain clarity and improved understanding; experiencing the process of becoming clearer is an important aspect of learning.

Orient to new skill topic. Once the participants have reviewed skills usage from the previous week, it is time to introduce the topic for new learning. The instructor only gives a brief overview of the subject. The goal of this introduction is not to teach the material, but merely to begin the process of exploring existing knowledge related to the topic.

Discussion questions that explore existing knowledge.

Discussions are an essential aspect of Skills System teaching. When participants have an opportunity to self-reflect and express themselves, multiple aspects of growth are served. First, each person is taking skillful action. Additionally, participation in discussions provides an opportunity for the individual to mobilize her Core Self (self-awareness, acceptance, value, and trust) as she joins in the skills exploration. For example, as the person begins to be aware of others and to feel successful, self-awareness is reinforced. Similarly, as the individual listens to others and other people listen to her, self-acceptance is built. Self-value and self-trust develop as the individual interacts and uses skills within training sessions. The person learns a valuable lesson about how each person has a different perspective and that the group members can coexist and collaborate safely.

Assessment questions. Assessment questions are designed to assess the individual's existing knowledge of a given topic. For example, if the topic for the session is Clear Picture, the skills trainer may prompt an initial discussion related to attention control. The instructor may ask, "Who has ever heard the word 'focus'?" and "What does the word 'focus' mean to you?" Skills trainers elicit a baseline of information to evaluate each individual's knowledge and abilities.

Julie F. Brown

Participants may offer inaccurate information during discussions. Instructors acknowledge the inaccurate contribution as a positive effort, yet do not reinforce the content. A neutral response like "Okay," "Very good participation," or "Thank you for sharing" may provide reinforcement for participation when the content is inaccurate. The disclosure of inaccurate information helps skills trainers know who has a basic understanding of the concepts and who does not. To ensure that the group gains an accurate knowledge base, the trainers restate helpful comments and write accurate statements on the whiteboard. Slightly rephrasing and writing comments down in an accurate form can be effective.

The skills trainer must juggle reinforcing accurate information with the need to teach a dialectical perspective. For example, saying "Yes, I have noticed that before, too" sends a different message than, "You are right." The first option conveys a more dialectical perspective that communicates there is value or truth in different perspectives. This tactic teaches that there are many sides in a situation; versus merely right or wrong alternatives. This dialectical attitude helps teach foundational perspectives that enhance the individuals capacities to engage in reciprocal relationships (being connected with others while maintaining identity). Instructors teach participants to see the gray in situations, rather than reinforcing a black or white, polarized perspective. Modeling flexibility allows the participant to engage in a reciprocal relationship; this experience implicitly teaches adaptive coping skills.

Relevant context questions. Relevant context questions are intended to highlight how learning new skills will help participants reach their personal goals. For example: "Have you ever had a time when you felt unfocused?" and "How can being unfocused affect our behaviors?" Additionally, the information shared during this portion of group may be used as examples or exercises in later teaching. Linking these relevant contexts with existing skill deficits can provide motivation for improving skills. Instructors orient the individuals to how the new skills can help manage challenging situations effectively.

E-Spiral Phase 2: Encoding Activities that Teach the New Topic

Once the group has completed all of the above Exploring Existing Knowledge activities, the group is prepared to learn new information. The goal of the Encoding Phase is to have the participants learn accurate new skill information. A wide variety of encoding activities are used within the Skills System teaching model.

While direct instruction and teaching points are necessary, multimodal techniques are essential as well. Multimodal teaching strategies provide "dual coding" (Najjar, 1996, p. 14) of verbal and nonverbal stimuli, which may improve recall. Handouts, diagrams, cue pictures, gestures, and objects are many common strategies used to facilitate encoding of information. Skills trainers must be aware of cognitive load demands when integrating materials; the supplemental information must support familiar points versus presenting divergent information. The Skills System instruction blends encoding visual, spatial, acoustic, and semantic information related to the topic. This multimodal approach helps an impaired learner encode, retain, and retrieve information.

Teaching points. Teaching points are excerpts provided within the twelve-week cycle curriculum in Chapter 8. These points are often presented as quotations. The quotes are not intended to prescribe teaching points, but rather to provide a worked example for skills trainers. The teaching points are also intended to be a sample of how trainers may present information effectively.

72

Teaching within the Skills System is less oriented around lecture format and more focused on question-and-answer periods. It is important that correct information be generated during the encoding process. Therefore instructors ask clear, directed questions to elicit answers that skills trainers knows the individual will answer correctly. For example, "If you are feeling very upset, is your mind usually clear or fuzzy?" Most participants will state that fuzzy is the more accurate answer. Guided discovery questions are not a quiz; they are a way to increase participation and motivation by building on existing knowledge. In between questions and answers, instructors clarify points. Beyond encoding and personal growth benefits, this process allows the trainer to effectively monitor a participant's integration of concepts.

It is useful to assess comprehension following direct instruction. Memory decay may happen for various reasons. Asking a participant to summarize points helps instructors evaluate integration. Summarizing prior to a transition from one topic to another topic helps reinforce the learning.

Handouts. Handouts are a key aspect of Skills System instruction. Not only do handouts provide visual encoding of information, which enhances learning, but they also guide teaching. Participants utilize handouts in skills-training session and home study. Although participants' levels of comprehension of handouts may vary, often individuals improve abilities to utilize materials after multiple twelve-week cycles. Basic handouts are available in this book (Appendix A), but it may be helpful for skills trainers to individualize handouts. Integrating digital pictures, using fun clip art, and scanning photographs may be beneficial. The practitioners must be careful to keep visual aids simple and clear to help minimize cognitive load demands of the materials.

Reviewing handouts. Reviewing handouts is generally an interactive process between the skills trainers and participants. Instructors may invite a participant to read the text on the handout or to offer ideas about what the visual aid is communicating. If time management or the reading level of the participants is low, trainers may choose to read. The participants and the skills trainer make a plan for how the handout is going to be reviewed prior to going over a page. It is important to engage each participant in the learning process, for it fosters investment and self-efficacy.

Skills trainers must be aware of managing the use of handouts in group. Handouts can provide a framework and visual encoding of information. While these are clear benefits, instructors must be aware that cognitive load increases when a participant is required to do two activities at the same time. For example, it may be challenging for an individual to fully attend to a teaching point while looking at a handout. Additionally, transitions may be challenging for participants, so shifting rapidly from one part of a handout to another can increase cognitive load.

Diagrams. Drawing diagrams on a blackboard, large presentation pad, or dry-erase board during discussions can be useful. Diagrams provide visual encoding of information. For example, a diagram of an ascending arc marked with a 0, 1, 2, 3, 4, and 5 can show how a person escalated from a level 1 emotion up to a level 5 emotion. The picture can show the progression from one level to the next; skills trainers can ask the group details about each level and what skills could have been used. A new arc can be drawn to show what the progression may have looked like if the individual had utilized effective skills earlier in the situation. Visually mapping situations can aid comprehension, because the diagram implicitly teaches relationships between various factors.

Utilizing different colors makes activities more fun. Using different colored markers can help the participants understand associations between concepts. For example, using the color orange in every Clear Picture handout creates an association between Clear Picture and orange. Using red to represent On-Track Thinking helps person see the difference between information in orange and in red. Color coding diagrams can improve organization of information and enhance explicit and implicit learning (Gold, 1972).

Gestures. Gestures are a useful technique during teaching. Skills trainers create movements to explain teaching material. For example, when referencing emotions being like a wave, instructors may use their hands to show the movement of the water. The point may be expanded by discussion how a person responds in calm water and then in turbulent water using a whole body movement. These images help people understand some of the realistic challenges of experiencing emotions and the effect emotions have on our thinking and behavior.

Objects. Objects are fun and useful. For example, a Tibetan singing bowl or bell is a basic tool in a Skills System group. Every group begins with various mindfulness activities combined with the ringing of a bell. Other objects, like pom-poms, can be used for cheerleading; red flags can be used to signify risks. Skills trainers can find various objects that represent facets of the Skills System and serve to prompt recall.

Discussion questions that facilitate encoding.

Content Questions. Content questions ask the individual to recall information that has been previously introduced: "What is the first step in the Clear Picture skill?" It is important to expose the group to multiple rehearsals of information, so that material is stored in long term memory. Content questions encourage a participant to repeat concepts; repetition is a vital aspect of improving learning. Practicing recall of information helps the individual integrate skills information; recall is an essential step in generalizing skills into daily living. When the individual gets an answer wrong, the instructor remains positive. Statements like "Almost!" or "You're close—try again!" instead of "No, that's wrong" are helpful.

E-Spiral Phase 3: Activities that Promote Elaboration

Elaboration is an expanded encoding process that creates "additional memory records that improve the ability of the participant to retrieve the original memory" (Najjar, 1996, p. 14). There are two important aspects of elaboration, (1) expanding knowledge and (2) linking knowledge. Elaboration is enhanced when group leaders "help the learner to integrate the stimulus with prior knowledge" (Najjar, 1996, p. 14). Elaboration also happens when the individual is able to assimilate or link new information (learned in the Encoding Phase) with prior knowledge (highlighted during the Exploring Existing Knowledge Base Phase). Worksheets, practice exercises, discussions, and individual skills instruction aid elaboration.

Worksheets. There are many worksheets included in Appendix A of this book. Skills trainers may also design other worksheets for participants. Individualizing worksheets can increase the relevance and impact of the activity. It may be logistically challenging and time-consuming to complete worksheets during group; it may be more advantageous to utilize worksheets as homework assignments.

Individuals in Skills System group often have highly variable levels of academic abilities. Instructors need to personalize the means through which worksheets are completed. One person may be able to complete worksheets independently, while another may require support. The participant may have specific support staff, group members, friends, or family members who help complete paperwork with them. There may be benefits to the person's individual therapist helping fill out the worksheets. Skills trainers ask participants about their plan to complete the homework assignment prior to leaving group.

Practice exercises. Practice exercises are a vital aspect of the learning process. For example, when the group is learning about breathing, it is essential to practice breathing. Talking about breathing teaches about the topic, yet the experience of practicing breathing teaches at a broader and deeper level. As the trainers tries to expand self-awareness during exercises to broaden the individual's knowledge base, contextual learning and practicing heightens facilitates retrieval.

Collaborative feedback. It may be necessary to offer corrective feedback during practice activities. Asking the individual if he or she would like some feedback before offering it gives the person control in the situation and creates a reciprocal interaction—for example, "Mary, would you like to get feedback about the exercise?" Feedback begins as a dialogue about the individual's performance. It is vital to listen to the participant to understand his experience of the point being made. An example of a collaborative approach might be "Matt, I noticed that you were looking down when you asked Jeff for what you wanted. Did you notice that?" "How did he respond to you?" and "Do you think that eye contact would have made him pay attention to you more?" The goal is to help the individual be effective; when effectiveness is determined through a collaborative process, the individual gains in at least three ways. The person learns more effective options, experiences the process of exploring effectiveness, and participates in a healthy reciprocal relationship. When the instructor has a directive style, it may stifle reciprocal communication with an individual who has an intellectual disability.

Similarly, it is best to use consensus to set guidelines for activities. Dictatorial proclamations and interactions may undermine the autonomy of the participant. Group is an opportunity to practice self-validation; group activities and interactions must directly support this process.

Individual instruction. During discussions or practice activities, it may be necessary to provide individual instruction for certain participants. If the teaching point is relatively brief, doing the individualized teaching in group is beneficial for the individual and the group. Another participant may have the same issue and would gain from the clarification. The individual may benefit from observing people growing in awareness after receiving coaching or feedback; it validates how learning is a process. If the participant has significant difficulties or review of the material would disrupt group, meeting with the skills trainer following group to create a plan may be a better option.

Discussion questions that support elaboration.

Discussions are another important tool in cultivating elaboration. Once the group has worked on practicing the skill, it is helpful to engage in a discussion that links previous and present learning. During this phase, the skills trainer asks questions that link information, promote personal disclosure, and expand awareness of topics.

Linking questions. Linking questions are designed to foster elaboration of learning through connecting new with past learning. One example might be, "You mentioned earlier in group that you yelled at a staff member when he did not give you what you wanted. Thinking about what we have learned here today about Getting It Right, what could have you done differently that may have worked better?" It is important to be nonjudgmental during discussions; focusing on highlighting what behaviors tend to elicit desired results is different than saying a person's choice was good or bad. Skills trainers may comment about experiences, but preaching and being overcontrolling are infrequently effective strategies.

Disclosure questions. Disclosure questions prompt a participant to provide personal examples related to a topic: "Has anyone ever had difficulty asking for what they want from people?" "What happened?" "Did it work out like you wanted?" It is important to help the participant be efficient with disclosures; instructors have to guide content and time management with the group to ensure that the discussion is focused and allows everyone to participate. While it is often necessary to address human issues, which are relevant, detailing highly personal or arousing events may lead to dysregulation of group members. Trainers may ask a participant to discuss a certain topic with the individual therapist or skills trainer after group: "Mary, that sounds like a difficult situation. I am wondering if it would be best for you and me to discuss that right after group in a little more detail?" If the individual insists on discussing the issue in group, the instructor may have to reorient to the topic and offer skills coaching to the person relating to waiting until the end of group to discuss the issue. An example: "I can hear that you would like to talk about this issue *and* it is difficult to wait sometimes. What skills might help you focus on group until we are able to check in?" Using the word "and" is helpful. It sends a message of validation and acceptance about situations, yet transitions to mobilizing effective behavior.

Expansion questions. Expansion questions are designed to broaden the scope of the individual's understanding of a concept. For example, the skills trainer may ask, "What other skills would you use in that situation?" Asking the "what if" questions helps the individual learn about various options and the impact on situations. Participants need to know that different actions work well in diverse circumstances. Expansion questions can help a participant understand unusual situations when traditional approaches may be ineffective. For example, the individual needs to know that yelling at people is an important skill in certain situations; the lessons are about using the right skills at the right time. This is an important aspect of learning how to generalize skills into diverse contexts.

E-Spiral Phase 4: Activities that Advance Efficacy

Efficacy-oriented exercises are designed to increase the individual's performance of skills within a contextual learning experience. Retrieval of information is improved if the learning and retrieval contexts are similar. Not only does situational learning promote generalization, but it may also enhance the participant's belief that he is capable of using skills within daily life. Through contextual learning activities, such as role play, psychodrama, and in-vivo practice, the individual enhances mastery and in turn self-efficacy. Although contextual learning may promote improved integration of skills, these activities may elicit higher levels of emotions. It is important to monitor contextual learning activities carefully to manage cognitive load factors.

Role play. Role play activities are an important aspect of Skills System teaching. It is ideal if each participant has an opportunity to participate. Time constraints may impact these activities. Dividing into pairs or small groups may increase opportunities for participation.

The skills trainer and the participants work collaboratively to discuss options and solutions in role play scenarios. The instructors may request a participant to act out various action options to help visualize diverse factors and outcomes. The group can explore how things work and what are natural reactions through role plays. This process provides validation and an experience that advances self-efficacy.

Psychodrama techniques. Psychodrama enactments often expand on traditional role plays by having additional group members play roles that represent various internal and external components within a situation. For example, if an individual is role playing talking to his or her house manager, one group member can role play the participant's On-Track Thinking, and another could give voice to the Off-Track Thinking. This expanded role-play technique is helpful because the participant can listen to both types of thinking and make an on-track decision. This technique makes intangible forces (e.g., thoughts) more tangible for participants. Additionally, this exercise helps the individual experience real-life pressures and sensations related to the context within which skills will need to be demonstrated. If the person is struggling, he can request groupmates to assist as skills-coaching voices. Behavioral rehearsal under these controlled conditions helps shape the individual's capacity toward being able to perform skills outside of group.

It is important to build the complexity of a psychodrama slowly to manage cognitive load demands. Instructors may want to gradually assemble the players so that the activity does not overstimulate the group. It may be useful to pose the rule that one person speaks at a time. Psychodrama techniques "use active/interactive techniques that stimulate more sensory and affective modes of learning than the verbal modality alone" (Tommasulo, 2005, p. 1) While engaging sensory and emotional aspects might have benefits in this process, when working with individuals who experience significant dysregulation, the skills trainer must proceed cautiously.

In-vivo. In-vivo exercises utilize elements of a participant's actual life, rather than creating a contrived environment. Support providers and/or family members may be invited to individual skills-training sessions for in-vivo activities. For example, the skills trainer may ask if the participant wants to practice a skill with her staff, who is in the waiting room. The instructor may function as a skills coach.

Following the exercise, the participant and instructor have a rich opportunity to process the experience. The skills trainer gains a firsthand view of both parties and therefore becomes a more effective skills coach for the participant. In-vivo exercises may be an important vehicle for generalization of skills into daily life and relationships.

Discussion questions that promote efficacy.

Discussions can be designed to improve efficacy. For example, participants can discuss common challenges related to using skills and/or communicating each individual's personal commitment to using skills. Through these discussions, participants communicate personal opinions, make a public commitment, and plan for integrating skills into his life that strengthen the individual's Core Self.

Barrier questions. Generalization of skills may be difficult due to barriers that are encountered in each unique situation. Emotions, thoughts, action urges, and external forces may interplay to create challenges for the individual. The participant must learn to become aware of barriers so that contingency planning is possible. Barrier questions are designed to help a person develop a realistic awareness of challenges that may be encountered. For example, the instructor might ask, "What will be difficult about talking to the house manager?" or "What will make it hard to stay on-track?" It is useful to explore specific factors that may happen before, during, and after events that affect the individual's ability to focus on or perform skills—for example, "What staff is working tomorrow?" and "How will it affect you to be with that staff?" Instructors follow the exploration of barriers with coaching questions that target troubleshooting.

It is important that the individual understand that all people are impacted by seemingly small issues; everyone faces human challenges and skill barriers throughout each day. The self-invalidating person with a disability often assumes that he is highly unique and significantly more dysfunctional than other people. Barrier questions are a great way to expand knowledge base about life, provide validation, and help create realistic expectations.

Inner-wisdom questions. Inner-wisdom questions ask the participant to share personal perspectives about a topic: "Which option do you feel would best fit?" "As you look at all of these choices, which is a fit for you?" "What does your inner wisdom tell you about this situation?" Cultivating an ability to self-reflect, considering personal perspectives, and finding an individual sense of wisdom are important self-validating behaviors. These capacities are not associated with intellectual functioning, although cognitive deficits may impair communication and organizational abilities. These limitations may cause the casual onlooker to incorrectly believe that the individual with significant learning challenges is incapable of utilizing wisdom.

Commitment questions. Commitment questions are a series of queries that guide the individual in deciding whether he or she is going to engage in a certain behavior. The question first poses whether the person values taking the action. For example, an instructor might ask, "James, when are you going to practice Getting It Right?" Once the person commits to using the skill, trainers then try to get the individual to commit to a plan of action: "James, you mentioned that you wanted to learn to use Getting It Right with your house manager. What is your plan to do that?" "You sound as if you are committed to using skills with your house manager. What exactly is your plan?" Third, leaders highlight the barriers and double-checks as to whether the individual is willing, ready, and able to start the plan. An example: "We have already talked about all of the things that are going to be difficult about this; are you sure you are ready to give this a try?" It is vital that the individual knows how to seek skills-coaching support when challenges are encountered.

Coaching questions. Coaching questions prompt the participant to consider what skills would be helpful in a situation. Coaching questions are useful during the Efficacy Phase after the individual makes a public commitment to use skills. Coaching questions help create a plan for when it is challenging to use skills.

Coaching questions may also be helpful when a participant is experiencing stress in skills training. For example, leaders can ask, "What skills could help you handle this situation?" Depending on the individual's level of skills knowledge, instructors may offer suggestions to the participant: "Do you think doing a Safety Plan right now would help?" When the individual is over a 3 emotion, instructors may want to ask the individual to meet with his or her support staff in another area. If the individual rises above a 4 emotion, it may be necessary to move the other participants to another area if there are safety risks.

Highlighting Home-Study Opportunities

The following home-study activities increase efficacy. As the individual increases knowledge about skills, she is encouraged to participate in ongoing, self-directed, skillful behaviors in daily living. The individual actively creates and utilizes On-Track Actions. Skills trainers focus on fostering internal motivation and commitment to maintain skillful behavior. As the individual increases capacities, doing peer and/or staff skills tutoring may reinforce learning through performing teaching tasks.

Homework. The primary homework assignments within the Skills System are to practice skills. The individual is expected to practice the new skill presented during the week. The participant reports in group the following week regarding efforts to use the skill. This process offers positive reinforcement for practicing skills; homework enhances generalization and self-efficacy.

There are worksheets included within the Skills System curriculum that can be assigned as homework. The individual may complete these sheets independently or with support. The focus of these assignments is not the reading and writing, but the content of the worksheet. It is not critical that the individual fill out the paper. When homework assignments are given, each participant makes a plan about how to accomplish the assignment. The Skills System homework assignments are generally simple so that a person can be successful. Instructors may give special homework assignments to a particular participant for individualized study.

Skills notebooks. Each participant needs to have a skills notebook when he or she enters skills training. The notebook contains all of the skills handouts and homework sheets. The individual uses the notebook to carry any individualized paperwork, such as diary cards or Safety Plans. The participant should control as many decisions about the notebook as possible. The individual uses the skills notebook to study skills and to teach skills coaches about skills. Skills notebooks and other study materials are available that the Skills system website at www.theskillssystem.com.

Flash cards. Skills flash cards help an individual learn the Skills List and System Tools. It is helpful when the person knows all of the names, numbers, and pictures associated with the nine skills. Cards with terms or pictures on one side and the answers on the other can be used for a participant and support providers to quiz each other. Making practice fun enhances skill practicing and generalization.

Audio skills CDs and/or MP3s. The Skills System has a Skills CD and/or MP3, which is very helpful for the individuals to listen to. This CD and/or MP3 has multiple tracks, which may be listened to successively or one at a time. Each skill is on a different track. The person may listen to the CD and/or MP3 at home when experiencing distress or just as a homework assignment. It may be helpful to create individual support plans that positively reinforce listening to the Skills CD and/or MP3 outside of sessions.

Phone consultation and skills coaching. It is important that the participant has access to effective skills coaching within the context of daily living. Skills coaches who are well versed in the Skills System can greatly enhance skills integration. It is advantageous when skills coaches are able to lead the individual through getting a Clear Picture and On-Track Thinking to create and execute a Skills Plan. The participant may have an individual therapist, family members, and/or support providers who serve this role.

Skills games. Skills games are a great way to practice skills. Many games can be adapted as a skills game. Who Wants to Be a Skillionaire is a fun skill-trivia activity. Instructors or participants develop skills questions and create a game-show format. A memory game using pairs of skills cards helps provide practice. In this game, several skills cards are placed face down on a table, and each participant tries to find pairs. Many other games can be turned into skills activities by setting a rule that in order to take a move or receive a token, for example, the participant must correctly answer a skills question.

Skills cards. Skills cards are useful home-study tools. The individual can sort the cards to practice organizing skills. The person can also create skills clusters for a particular situation to practice skills planning. The participant can do partnership activities with support providers to enhance skills capacities of both people. This activity may also serve to create a common skills language, as well as promote a reciprocal relationship between the individual and the other person. As the participant teaches the staff, it fosters a sense of mastery and self-efficacy.

Skills journaling. The person may choose to write in a journal by himself or ask staff to do the writing. Focusing on exploring self-awareness, self-expression, and descriptive skills is advantageous. Ruminating on past issues or current problems may be less helpful than highlighting a problem and writing about possible skills that could be used to manage the difficulty effectively.

Peer and staff skills tutoring. Skills tutoring may be an effective form of interactive learning for this population. Skills cards and games may be a helpful vehicle for the work. Both individuals practice recalling information within a relationship setting. When groupmates and/or housemates help each other practice basic skills activities, it provides a contextual learning experience that reinforces generalization and efficacy.

CHAPTER 8:

Skills System Twelve-Week Cycle Curriculum

Chapter 8 contains a sample twelve-week-cycle curriculum. Each week of this framework includes a detailed teaching plan and options for future cycles through the material. Skills trainers will notice that instructions and explanations are presented as quotes. This format is intended to provide a worked example for trainers, rather than to prescribe language. All Skills System visual-aid materials are contained in Appendix: A of this book, beginning on page 157.

It is impossible to predict whether the group will complete a teaching plan. Different settings will have varying timeframes for group sessions. Additionally, skills trainers must remember that the intellectual abilities of group members are unique. Therefore, the collective capacity of each skills group will be variable. This curriculum is a general guide for instructors. It is unlikely that all of the activities will be completed during the timeframes that are available to the group.

In the event that the group does not complete the outlined material, trainers must make determinations whether to return to that week's materials during the next group or whether to move on. If the group continues on, the remainder of the previous week's lessons can be addressed when the group returns to those topics in the following cycle through the curriculum. It is challenging to leave the material unfinished, yet it may be the best long-term alternative. It is vital that a participant develop a broad understanding of the Skills System at first so that the individual can deepen awareness within the full range of Skills System topics. Focusing on a few elements in depth may increase understanding of those topics, yet may hinder the generalization of Skills System concepts. Although it is difficult, it is recommended that the group leave unfinished topics and progress to the following week's teaching. As the skills trainer gains a fuller understanding of the Skills System and the skills group, it will be easier to create realistic and effective teaching plans.

The twelve-week-cycle curriculum presents detailed teaching suggestions. Participants will have a wide variety of responses to the activities and discussion questions. Although the script presented below assumes compliance and participation, the realities may be very different in a training session. For example, the trainer may encounter silence, partial answers, irreverent attitudes, belligerence, and/or dissociation all at the same time! Reviewing the information in Chapter 4, Understanding Learning Challenges and Intellectual Disabilities, may be useful if group interactions are complex; it is likely that issues highlighted in that chapter are interacting and creating barriers. The following are some suggestions to help the skills trainer within moments when the session feels like it is not going well.

- Take a Breath, and get a Clear Picture of the present moment.
- Use On-Track Thinking to check urges to be sure interventions are on-track.
- Utilize the Quick-Step Assessment to evaluate tactics and whether part of the problem is that the intervention is creating high cognitive load. Make necessary adjustments to simplify and/or break down topics further. For example, ask the questions or frame points in ways that use different words to facilitate recognition and recall.
- The trainers may consider offering skills coaching to an individual experiencing stress. The trainer may ask questions to elicit Clear Picture and On-Track Thinking as the first steps; if the person is more dysregulated, the trainer may prompt the individual to use these skills. Reminding the participant about her goal, capacities, and skills can help the person get back on-track. It may be useful to acknowledge skills training as a challenging experience to help normalize the experience.
- Initiating a brief breathing exercise may help the participants and trainers improve focus.
- If the individual or individuals are emotionally, cognitively, and behaviorally regulated (below a 3 emotion) the trainer may focus on Problem Solving to address elements of the situation that need to be changed or Expressing Myself to communicate about the circumstance. Asking the group for feedback related to the activity and/or discussion creates reciprocal communication.
- If a participant is experiencing an emotion of level 3 or higher, Safety Planning is more effective. It may be helpful for the person to focus on a New-Me Activity (skills group), move to a different area in the room, or leave the group. The individual could do a Focus New-Me Activity in the waiting area (e.g., puzzle or card sorting) and return when she is more on-track.
- If the individual refuses to leave the area, the group may have to evacuate the room. It is essential that the skills trainer notice the early warning signs for when an individual is likely to demonstrate violent behaviors. Taking precautions and intervening efficiently is necessary to protect the well-being of the other group members. Having two exits in a group room is optimal. After a problematic event in group, it may be helpful to debrief the other group members to discuss skills that the participants used to manage the event.
- The trainer may need to be cautious about using significant group time to do skills coaching if it is not pertinent for the topic. It may be necessary to ask a participant who does not regain control to step into the waiting area to do Safety Planning with her support staff. Following the group, the trainer may want to review the event and work with the individual to create an On-Track Action Plan for group.

Facilitating any type of therapeutic group can be challenging. It is impossible to know how each individual is going to react. It may be helpful to have co-leaders in groups when the participants are not familiar with each other and the trainers. One leader can manage an individual who is experiencing challenges, and the other can help the rest of the group.

The following sections present options for leading skills-training sessions. Skills trainers can either read this material and design another form of instruction to suit the needs of the specific population or attempt to follow this curriculum. If the trainer chooses to follow this outline, please note that it is merely a guide and should not be followed verbatim if it does not fit for the individual in the session.

Week 1: The Skills List

Preparing for Group
Handouts Needed
- Skills System Review Sheet (page 179)
- Skills System Handout 1 (page 158)
- Skills System Handout 2 (page 159)

E-Spiral Phase 1

Exploring Existing Knowledge Base: Beginning Group

Welcome group. "Hello, everyone! How are you all doing today? (Wait for responses) Okay, it is wonderful to see you all; I am very excited about beginning a skills group with you. Are we ready to get to know each other? We are going to jump in with our first On-Track Action by introducing ourselves. If you are feeling a little shy, notice that feeling and tell us your name anyway! Who is really brave and would like to start?"

Note: Skills trainers may want to consider entering the group and greeting participants in a friendly and positive way. It is helpful to ask participants how they are doing. Allowing an opportunity to hear each person's response to the question conveys validation. Trainers can use the information to begin the process of doing a Quick-Step Assessment in group for each group member.

When the group is beginning or new members join, participants should introduce themselves to each other. Trainers may begin by having each group member share his or her name. The group leader may also have the group share a piece of fun personal information—for example, "What is your favorite kind of pizza?" If the group is already familiar with each other, the leader may request that each person respond to questions like "What are you hoping to learn from this group?" or "What is one of your goals?" The leader is trying to create a comfortable and safe therapeutic environment. Validating the challenges of starting a new group may be helpful.

→*Orient to mindfulness activity: noticing the breath.* "Okay, is everyone ready to learn some skills? Great, let's get started. We are going to begin by noticing our breathing."

Note: After introductions, group leaders will want to orient the group to the first group activity. Inviting the group to begin in a friendly way keeps the tone positive and fun! Skills trainers have to be prepared to deal with a client saying no to invitations; keep invitations open and move on to an individual who is actively participating. It may be helpful to check in with the nonparticipating person after group to do problem solving if necessary. Additionally, it is helpful to have some kind of bell or Tibetan singing bowl that may be rung during group. The auditory cue helps the participants to begin and end tasks.

Instructions for mindfulness exercise. "We begin every group by doing a mindfulness practice. Today we will start with a simple breathing exercise. When we focus our attention on our breathing, we are being mindful. We are using our minds to pay attention to our breathing. Unfortunately, our minds are not always easy to control. That's why we have to practice being mindful. The cool thing is that when we are mindful, we are very focused on what is happening right now. Noticing our breath is actually a really important skill, and it is so simple. When we notice our breathing, it helps us be aware and focused, even in stressful and emotional situations. Are you ready to hear about what we have to do? Are you ready to give 100 percent when we do this exercise? Okay, first, please sit in a comfortable position with your eyes open. Then I will ring the bell six times. When you hear the first ring, begin to notice your breathing. Notice how your body feels as the air goes in and out. Notice whether you breathe through your mouth or your nose. Usually our minds try to wander to other things. Sometimes we think of the past or the future. Notice where your mind goes and gently bring your mind back to noticing your breath. You may notice feelings inside of you; notice your emotions and bring your attention back to your breathing. One of our goals is to learn to control and shift our attention; this activity helps us practice that. Do you have any questions?"

Note: The group reviews the mindfulness activity and shares details about what they noticed. Leaders may want to write down the observations on the board. It is important to reinforce effort and participation. This exercise is intended to teach awareness of attention and the action of reorienting attention to the breath.

- *Review questions.* Choosing one or two of the following questions facilitates sharing: "What did your body feel like when you were breathing?" "What kind of breathing did you notice?" "Did your breathing change at all?" "Did you notice the bell sound?" "Did you notice your attention drifting away?" "What did you do to bring your attention back?"

→**Orient to Skills System review.** "Great sharing. After doing our mindfulness practice each week, we will review the Skills List and other important Skills System information. Today we will look at the Skills System Review Sheet; it is on page 179. It looks like this." (Hold up the page.) "Some of us may already know some of the skills, and if we don't, I will say them."

The group reviews the Skills System Review Questions sheet (P. 179) during this time in group. The skills trainer or participants read the first nine questions on the sheet. A participant answers the questions. It is important to assess a group member's level of skill language acquisition. Leaders try to continually evaluate, shape, and expand each participant's skill knowledge base.

→**Orient to skills practice.** "Great job! Not only do we have to remember the names and numbers of the skills, but we all have to practice using our skills at home. Each week we will share with each other about a time when we used our skills during the week. So, our homework every week is to use our skills and to be willing to talk about it at the next group. Sound okay? Great."

Note: In the first group of Cycle 1, the group discusses generic skills that were used during the week that seemed to help the participants in challenging situations. This helps the individual understand that she already has basic capacities that will be enhanced.

- *Review questions.* "Who would like to tell us about a challenging time this week that they were able to manage? What did you do that was helpful?"

→**Orient to new skills topic.** "I think many of you are already using some of the skills, and you don't know it! We are going to have a chat about focusing our minds to help us get ready for today's learning. I know you might feel shy, but it is great to jump in with both feet and share your ideas and opinions. That's how we really learn a lot. Ready? Perfect."

◉ **Discuss existing knowledge about the new topic.**
- *Assessment questions.* "What are some things that people do that make their situations worse?" "What kinds of things do people to in tough situations to make things better?"
- *Relevant context questions.* Choosing one or more of the following questions helps create a relevant context: "What are some tough situations in life that are hard

to deal with?" "What kinds of situations stress us out?" "Is it sometimes hard for people to do things that are helpful in these situations?" "Why do you think that is?"

→*Orient to relevant context of new topic.* "Great discussion—thank you all. It seems as if all of us have done some helpful and not helpful things when we are in tough situations. Life is very difficult sometimes for all of us (cite specific examples given previously in the group). As we have heard, our thoughts and our feelings can be overwhelming and hard to handle. The Skills System can help us stay on-track even when life gets stressful. We have already learned an important skill today: noticing our breath. See, we are already on our way to being Skill Masters."

E-Spiral Phase 2

Encoding: Teaching the New Topic

→*Orienting to the new learning: Skills System Handout 1.* "The Skills System helps us learn how to control our behaviors so that we can reach our goals. These nine skills help us do things that help us feel better and to reach our goals. Right now we are going to learn the names, numbers, and pictures of the nine skills in the Skills System. How many skills are there in the Skills System?" (Group: "nine!"; Trainer: "All together, how many?"; Group: "NINE!") "Great, see, you are already getting it! I knew you could do this! Are you ready to learn more about how to handle things well? Great."

Instructions for the encoding activity. "Let's all find Skills System Handout 1. It is on page 158 and it looks like this." (Hold up the page and be sure each participant has the page before continuing.) "Would someone like to read, or would you like me to? We are going to read the number and name of each skill. We are also going to discuss each skill picture and what it means. Any questions?"

Note: After reading each skill, the group talks about each skill picture. If a group member reads and the communication is unclear, the skills trainers need to repeat the section so that each group member clearly understands the information. The group needs to move through the teaching material; leaders may have to limit group reading if it hinders progression through the information.

→*Orient to reviewing Skills System Handout 2.* "Okay, fantastic. Now we have to read Skills System Handout 2: How Do Our Skills Help Us. It is on page 159 and it looks like this. Would anyone like to read?"

Note: This handout is used as an overview to give the group members an introduction to the function of each skill. This handout is not intended to be used as an in-depth teaching tool.

→*Orient to end of the Encoding Phase.* "Does anyone have any questions about that handout? Great, now we are going to practice some of what we have learned."

E-Spiral Phase 3

Elaboration: Linking Previous and New Learning

→*Orient to elaboration activity.* "So, we have gone over the Skills List once, and now we are going to practice it more, so that we can learn and remember the information. The more we go over this, the easier it is to remember the skills when we need them."

Instructions for elaboration exercise. Note: Sample exercises A–F are listed below; choose one exercise per cycle. Elaboration exercises ask the participant to practice recognition and recall of skills material in a noncontextual format (e.g., not using the information in a role play). This phase focuses on the participant expanding his capacities to effectively demonstrate the tasks with increasingly less support. Contextual learning formats are described in the next section when efficacy-oriented activities are recommended.

The activities listed below can be completed with or without using visual-aid materials. The group can begin using handouts as a worked example and then shift away from using the cues as confidence builds. The skills trainer may allow each individual to make a personal decision as to whether he wants to look at the sheet, although prompting the participant to stretch and try to close the book may be helpful at some point.

The exercises below become progressively more difficult; thus, during initial cycles through the curriculum, easier exercises will minimize cognitive load demands. Be sure to explain the exercise so that the group clearly understands the activity. Leaders and groups can invent fun ways to practice the numbers and names of skills that fit the learning needs of the participants.

Options for exercises.

A. The skills trainers says a number from 1 to 9 and the group reads the skill name from the handout. The group tries to get quicker and more accurate as the exercise progresses.

B. The group closes their books. A group leader writes 1–9 on the board. The group tries to fill in the blank spaces.

C. With no visual aids, a leader asks the group to say the skills in order.

D. With no visual aids, a group leader says a number, and the group says the skill.

E. A group leader has a client say the first skill, and the next person says the second, and so on.

F. The group does this exercise moving backward from Skills 9 to 1.

- *Review questions.* "How was that exercise for you?"

→*Orient to discussion.* "I think you all did a great job with that exercise. Now, we are going to talk together about skills, so that we can begin to understand them a little better."

Note: The goal of an elaboration-oriented discussion is to begin the process of linking, personalizing, and expanding the participants' semantic knowledge related to the new learning; connecting past and present learning increases integration of the material.

- *Linking question.* "Have any of you used skills like these in the past?"
- *Disclosure question.* "Can you tell us about a time in the past when you had problems handling thoughts or emotions?"
- *Expansion questions.* "Do you think that there are times when knowing skills would help you reach your goals?" "How do you think these skills would have helped you?"

Note: These discussions are not intended to delve into traumatic memory material or detailed accounts of events. The skills trainer listens to the specific point that is being made and then creates a general statement that applies to all participants. For example, "That situation with your housemate sounds difficult. So, are housemate relationships situations when we need to use our skills? Has anyone else had challenges with housemates?"

→*Orient to the end of the Elaboration Phase.* "I can't believe how much you all know about skills already. We are going to do very well with the Skills System."

E-Spiral Phase 4

Efficacy: Bridge to Future Learning

→*Orient to efficacy activities.* "It is important to have fun while we are learning, so that we will like doing it. Right now we are going to play a game."

Note: It is important to have group members participate in activities. During the first cycle through the Skills System curriculum, games, worksheets, and role plays are simple and brief. Over time, leaders can design more complex, lengthy activities that foster generalization of skill information.

Instructions for efficacy activities. "I am going to ask the group some questions. Raise your hand if you think you know the answer. Ready?"

"Question 1: What is the name of the skill that helps us fix our problems?"

"Question 2: What skill helps me know what is going on inside and outside of me?"

"Question 3: What skill is it when I drink a cup of tea and have a snack?"

"Question 4: What skill is it when I do something to get back on-track?"

"Question 5: What skill is when I tell someone how I feel?"

"Question 6: What skill is it when I think things through?"

"Question 7: What skill is it when I try to get what I want?"

"Question 8: What skill helps me handle risky situations?"

"Question 9: What skill is it when I show my friend that I care about them?"

Note: This activity is intended elicit correct answers. When the individual guesses incorrectly, the skills trainer may say "close," "almost," or "try one more time," rather than "no, that's wrong." It may be necessary for a leader to give hints so that the group gets the correct answer. These questions are suggestions; trainers may adapt questions to ensure success for the participants.

- *Review questions.* "How do you think that game went?" "Was it hard to remember the skills?"

→*Orient to discussion.* "I thought you all did really well. We are going to take a few minutes to chat together before we leave for the day."

Note: The goal of these efficacy-oriented questions is to help the individual understand realistic challenges related to the topic. The discussion offers an opportunity for self-reflection about the learning. The participant is invited to make a personal commitment and plan for integrating the skill into her life.

- *Barrier question.* "So far, what is difficult for you about learning the Skills System?"
- *Inner-wisdom question.* "Do you think that it is important for you to learn skills?"
- *Commitment questions.* Asking one or more of these commitment questions can help increase motivation: "Are you willing to face the challenge of trying new things?" "Are you willing to learn and practice skills in group and in your life?" "Are you willing to do some homework for group?"
- *Coaching question.* "How can you coach yourself to learn and practice skills?"

→*Orient to home study.* "We can see that learning skills is challenging. It also sounds as if we all know that practice will help us get better at skills. We may not love doing homework, so it is a good thing that we have our On-Track Action skill to help us jump into our practicing! This week for homework, we are going to notice our breathing as many times as we can. Next week in group, we will talk about when you noticed your breathing and what you noticed about it. Do you have any questions?"

"If anyone would like to study skills at home this week, you can do the Skills System Worksheet 1 or 2. You could also review today's handouts. Going over the Skills System Review Questions on page 179 is very helpful. Perhaps you can go over this sheet with staff. As the staff learns skills, they are able to help be skills coaches for us. Talk to me after group if you would like to go over these."

Note: Be sure the group members are clear about the locations of materials. Skills System Worksheets 1 and 2 and the Skills System Review Questions can be completed as self-study or as homework in later cycles through the material. Following group, meet with any individuals to make a plan for completing the worksheets.

→*Orient to group ending.* "We ring the bell six times at the end of group. It is a chance to notice our breathing. We take a moment to focus our minds as we go back to our activities. Who would like to ring the bell today?"

Week 1: System Component Handouts to Review in Future Cycles or for Home Study

A. Skills System Worksheet 1 (p. 160)

B. Skills System Worksheet 2 (p. 161)

Week 2: System Tools

Preparing for Group
Handouts Needed
- Skills System Review Sheet (page 179)
- Skills System Handout 3 (page 162)
- Feelings Rating Scale Handout 1 (page 163)
- Categories of Skills Handout 1 (page 169)
- Recipe for Skills Handout 1 (page 173)
- Week 2: Group Practice Activity (page)
- Week 2: My Practice Activity (page 178)

E-Spiral Phase 1

Exploring Existing Knowledge Base: Beginning Group

Welcome group. "It is great to see everybody. How are you all doing? Are we ready to learn about skills?"

Orient to mindfulness activity: noticing the air going in and out of my nose. "What do we do first in group? You are right; we ring the bell. Why do we do that? Very good, because we want to focus our minds. Okay, today we are going to learn more about breathing. We are going to notice the air going in and out of our noses as we breathe.

Instructions for mindfulness exercise. "Last week we rang the bell and noticed our breathing. Today we are going to ring the bell six times and notice our breathing again. This time we are going to notice the air going in and out of our nose. Our job is to bring 100 percent of our attention and focus to our noses. Sometimes our minds sometimes act like puppies; they jump all around. We have to be the boss of our minds, so that our attention goes where we tell it to. So, if your attention drifts to other things than your nose, reel it in"—make a gesture of a fishing reel—"and notice the air going in and out of your nose. You may notice other thoughts and feelings too; notice them, allow them to pass, and bring your attention to your nose. This is important to us, because we have to be able to control our attention; we have to direct our minds to what is helpful to us. We have to get our puppies to listen and mind. Any questions? I will ring the bell, and we will start."

- *Review questions.* "What did you notice about the air going in and out of your nose?" "Where else did your attention go?" "Did you bring your focus back to your breathing?" "How did you bring your attention back?"

Note: The group shares details about what they noticed. The leader may want to write observations on the board.

→***Orient to Skills System review.*** "Good job! Now we are going to review the Skills List. How about we turn to page 179, the Skills System Review Questions. Today we will answer questions 1–9. Would anyone like to read, or should I do it?"

Note: Skills trainers or group members read the first nine questions on the sheet. A participant answers the questions. It is important to assess a group member's level of skill language acquisition. Leaders try to continually evaluate, shape, and expand each participant's skill knowledge base.

→*Orient to skills practice.* "Okay, great job. You guys are really starting to be Skills Masters! Let's shift gears and go over our Skills Practice for this week. Our homework was to practice noticing your breath."

- *Review questions.* "Who can tell us about when they noticed their breath this week?" "What did you notice?" "What did you do after you noticed your breathing?" "Did you notice anything helpful while paying attention to your breathing?"

Note: Starting with volunteers is helpful, because it gets the discussion started. Low self-efficacy can hinder volunteering. As a client shares, leaders can include a less participatory group member by asking one or more simple, direct questions, which can reduce the barriers for volunteering: "Bill, did you notice your breathing at all during the week?" "Great, when was that?" "Okay, what did you notice?"

→*Orient to new skills topic.* "Great! I am going to ask a few questions that will help us talk about what we already know about handling strong emotions. Okay?"

◉ **Discuss existing knowledge about the new topic.**

- *Assessment questions.* "How does stress or strong emotion affect people?" "How do strong emotions affect our actions?"
- *Relevant context question.* "Do you think that people ever feel so confused that they just react without thinking?"
- *Clarifying questions.* "Have you ever seen that happen?" "How did it work out for the person?"

→*Orient to relevant context of new topic.* "Today we are going to learn about three important Skills System tools. One is the Feelings Rating Scale. Second is the Categories of Skills. Third is the Recipe for Skills."

E-Spiral Phase 2

Encoding: Teaching the New Topic

→*Orient to new learning:* "We use the Feelings Rating Scale, Categories of Skills, and the Recipe for Skills to know which skills to use in every situation. Having these three tools can help us handle even very stressful and confusing situations! Life can be confusing for all of us. Being able to focus our attention and shift our attention helps us be in control of ourselves and our lives. We are going to learn about a few other tools that can help us organize our actions so that we can feel better and reach our goals. When we know what is going on, we can be on-track. When we are unfocused, often we go off-track. Being focused helps us use our skills well."

Instructions for encoding activity. "Does that sound okay? Great. We are going to look at four different handouts. Please raise your hand if you have a question or feel lost. How about we turn to Skills System Handout 3 on page 162. What is our plan for reading this handout?"

Note: Skills trainers have many options about how to progress through the handouts, worked examples, and worksheets. This teaching plan will review four basic handouts that will serve as a preliminary introduction to the System Tools. There are worked examples and worksheets that are listed below (A-K in the last section) that offer expansion of the concepts in these introductory handouts. The supplemental materials can be used in future cycles of the Skills System curriculum. How the leader decides to utilize these materials depends on the status of the group.

There are four handouts to review in this section. The information in the teaching points below is intended as learning tools for trainers, more so than as scripts to be read in group. As the leaders understand the skill concepts, briefer descriptions can be utilized in group that hit main points without being boring.

Review Skills System Handout 3.

☼ *Section A Teaching Points.* "This means that if you were a tiny bit upset, you would rate the emotion 1. If you were very upset, you would label it as 4. If you were so upset that you were hurting yourself, someone else, or property, it would be a 5 emotion. We will learn more about the Feelings Rating Scale in the next handout. Any questions?"

☼ *Section B Teaching Points.* "Skills 1, 2, 3, 4, and 5 are our All-the-Time skills. We can use them any time, at any level of emotions 0–5. Skills 6, 7, 8, and 9 are Calm-Only skills. We use Calm-Only skills *only* when we are calm. This means we cannot use skills 6, 7, 8, and 9 when we are over a 3 emotion. We have to learn when we can use each skill and when we need to wait to use a skill until we are a little calmer. We will learn more about this on the Categories of Skills handout. Any questions?"

☼ *Section C Teaching Points.* "It is important that we use lots of skills, especially when we have strong emotions. The Recipe for Skills helps us remember to use more skills when we are more emotional. Skills Masters use even more skills than the Recipe for Skills tells us to! The more skills we use, the more on-track to our goals we are. Any questions?"

→**Orient to Feelings Rating Scale Handout 1.** "Good job! Now we are going to take a few minutes to learn more about the Feelings Rating Scale. Please turn to page 163. This is the Feelings Rating Scale Handout 1."

☼ *Feelings Rating Scale Handout 1 Teaching Points.*

☼ "When we are at a 0 emotion, we are not having that emotion. For example, 0 sadness means that the person is not sad at that time."

"A 1 emotion is a tiny emotion. We have a 1 emotion when we have a tiny reaction to something. For example, if I am a 1 sadness, I might feel notice an empty sensation in my chest or feel like looking at the ground."

☼ "A 2 emotion is a small emotion. We may notice different body sensations that a 2 emotion causes. At a 2 sadness, I might notice my face changing, and my smile disappears; my shoulder may drop, because I feel a heaviness. My heart may begin to pound more, and my breathing may be affected. A 2 emotion may be a little uncomfortable if it is a painful emotion."

☼ "A 3 emotion is a medium emotion. A 3 emotion will cause body sensations. For example, I might have a stomachache, feel the urge to pace, and feel muscle tension at a 3 sadness. It is more difficult to be focus at a 3 emotion, and we may have more Off-Track Urges. We can still use All-the-Time and Calm-Only skills at a 3 emotion, but it are important to be careful in case the level increases. If the emotion is even a tiny bit over a 3 emotion, we use only All-the-Time skills and *not* Calm-Only ones.

☼ A 4 emotion is a strong emotion. If it is a painful emotion, we will be very uncomfortable. For example, I would cry at a 4 sadness. I also may want to get angry about what is making me sad. I might have urges to scream, swear, and storm around. At this level, it is difficult to focus, and action urges will be strong. At a 4 emotion, we do not use Calm-Only skills, even though we may have the urge to. We wait until we are below a 3 emotion."

☼ "A 5 emotion is an overwhelming emotion. At a 5, we may harm ourselves, others, or property. At 5 we have to use All-the-Time skills to get back in control. Any questions?"

- *Content questions.* "What might make you have a 1 emotion?" "What would the emotion be?" "How would your body feel?" "What might make you have a 2 emotion?" "What would the emotion be?" "How would your body feel?" "What might make you have a 3 emotion?" "What would the emotion be?" "How would your body feel?" "What might make you have a 4 emotion?" "What would the emotion be?" "How would your body feel?" "What might make you have a 5 emotion?" "What would the emotion be?" "How would your body feel?"

→ *Orient to Categories of Skills Handout 1.* "The Feelings Rating Scale might seem harder than it really is; you will get it! Now we are going to learn more about Categories of Skills on page 169. It looks like this. All set?"

Review Categories of Skills Handout 1.

☼ *Teaching Points.* "There are two Categories of Skills. Skills 1, 2, 3, 4, and 5 are called All-the-Time skills." (Perhaps ask the group what skills 1–5 are.) "These skills can be used at any level of emotion: 0, 1, 2, 3, 4, and even 5. The other Category of Skills is Calm Only. Calm-Only skills can *only* be used when we are having emotions that are between 0 and 3. If we are even a tiny bit over 3, we do not use Calm-Only skills! Any questions?

→ *Orient to Recipe for Skills Handout 1.* "The last handout we will review is on page 173. The Recipe for Skills Handout 1 looks like this. Everyone ready?"

☼ *Teaching points.* "The Recipe for Skills tells us how many skills we need to use in a situation. We add one skill for every level of emotion. So, at a 1 emotion, we have to use two skills. At a 1 emotion, we will use Clear Picture and On-Track Thinking. At a 2 emotion, we have to use three skills. Again, we use Clear Picture, On-Track Thinking, and then we use at least one more skill to handle a 2 emotion. On-Track Thinking helps us figure out which of the other skills we should use. At a 3 emotion, we use four skills. Once again, we use Clear Picture, On-Track Thinking, and two more skills that we think will help us reach our goals. If we are at a 4 emotion, we use five skills. These five skills have to be skills 1–5, because we cannot use any Calm-Only skills at a 4 emotion. At a 5 emotion, we have to use six skills. Once again, at a 5 emotion, we cannot use Calm-Only skills, so all six skills have to be All-the-Time skills. Often we double up on New-Me Activities to help us focus and feel better. Any questions?"

→ *Orient to ending Encoding Phase.* "We have learned a lot today. We learned how to put our skills together. It takes time to understand how to use these tools. Practicing is very important."

E-Spiral Phase 3

Elaboration: Linking Previous and New Learning

→*Orient to elaboration activity.* "If it is okay, we are going to read a story and fill in the blanks. So, let's turn to page 177. It says 'Week 2: Group Practice Activity' on the top and it looks like this. All set? Great."

Instructions for practice exercise. "I am going to read the story, and the group is going to fill in the blanks. We have to work together to find answers for each blank. Ready?"

Story: Mary was running late for work. She was feeling _____ at a level _____. She was thinking _____ _____. That made her feel _____ at a level _____. She had the urge to _____. Mary knew she had to use her skills. At that moment, she was feeling _____ at a level _____. She knew that she could use her _____ skills at any level of emotion. Mary remembered that the All-the-Time skills were _____, _____, _____, _____, and _____ . Because Mary was at a level _____ emotion, she _____ use her Calm-Only skills. Because Mary was at a _____ level emotion, she knew she had to use _____ skills.

- *Review questions.* "How was that exercise for you?"

→*Orient to discussion.* "I thought that was fun. Working together like that is what skill? Right—Relationship Care! Now we are going to have a discussion before we finish for the day."

- *Linking questions.* "How are skills different from how you have handled emotions in the past?" "Have you ever used thinking like Mary did in the story?"
- *Disclosure questions.* "Have there been times in the past when you were confused about what to do in a stressful situation?" "What did you do?" "How did it work?"
- *Expansion question.* "How could the Feelings Rating Scale, Categories of Skills, and Recipe for Skills help you when you are upset or confused?"

→*Orient to the end of Elaboration Phase.*

"Great discussion. I think we are ready to move on to another activity. Okay?"

E-Spiral Phase 4

Efficacy: Bridge to Future Learning

→*Orient to Efficacy Activity: Reviewing questions from Week 2: My Practice Activity.* "If we are ready, let's turn to page 178. At the top it says 'Week 2: My Practice Activity,' and it looks like this."

Instructions for efficacy activity. "I will read the questions on the Week 2: My Practice Activity sheet for each person to answer. You can decide how you would like to fill this sheet out. You can write in, or I can write the answers in for you. Either way is fine; the important part of this is that the answers come from you. Each of us will think back to a stressful situation that happened this week. Then we will label and rate the emotions you had in that situation. After that we will figure which Categories of Skills you could have used. Finally, we will write down how many skills you needed in that situation. Any questions? Who is very brave and would like to go first?"

Note: Each individual speaks briefly about a challenging situation that happened during the week. It is important to keep the discussion focused on the questions rather than on delving into details about the events. The leader may need to help some participants more than others, depending on the individual's level of functioning and knowledge of the material.

- *Review question.* "How was that exercise for you?"

→*Orient to discussion.* "Wonderful job—that isn't easy! We are going to talk now about some of the challenges we face when we use skills like these. Okay?"

- *Barrier question.* "So far, what is hard about using the Feelings Rating Scale, the Categories of Skills, and the Recipe for Skills?"
- *Inner-wisdom question.* "Do you want to be able to use these tools?"
- *Commitment questions.* "Are you willing to learn and practice using these tools?" "When are you going to use these tools in your life?"
- *Coaching question.* "How can you coach yourself to practice using these tools?"

→*Orienting to home study.* "That was a good discussion—thank you. That helps me understand what is challenging for you. Our homework this week will be to practice using the Feelings Rating Scale, the Categories of Skills, and the Recipe for Skills. Whenever you think of it, label and rate what you are feeling. Think about whether you are over or under a 3 emotion. Try to remember which category of skills you can use and how many skills would be helpful. Any questions?

"Also, if anyone is interested in doing home study this week, you can look at the handouts that we have gone over. You could look over the worked examples in that section of your skills book. You could also do the worksheets. Check in with me after group if you need to make a plan for home study."

→*Orient to group ending.* "I thought you all did well. We ring the bell six times at the end of group. It is a chance to notice our breathing. We take a moment to focus our minds as we go back to our activities. Who would like to ring the bell today?"

Week 2: System Tool Handouts to Review in Future Cycles or for Home Study

A. Feelings Rating Scale Handout 2 (p. 164)

☼ *Teaching Points.* This handout is a home-study tool for participants and staff to review the Feelings Rating Scale. Understanding the Feelings Rating Scale helps the individual become more organized and more able to integrate skills at lower levels of emotional arousal. It is critical that the individual learn the difference between a level 4 and level 5 emotion. At a level 4, the person may feel horrible, yet he or she is not acting in an out-of-control way. At a level 5, the person is taking actions that harm himself or herself, others, or property. A participant may say he or she is at a 4.5 to express being nearly out of control. If the person is in group and states he or she is currently at a 5, leaders can ask, "Are you hurting yourself, others, or property right now?" The person can then adjust the rating to a 4 if he or she is extremely uncomfortable, yet is not taking abusive actions.

B. Feelings Rating Scale Worked Example 1 (p. 165)

☼ *Teaching Points.* The group reviews this worked example that shows how the events prompted different levels of emotion. This sheet is presented using a scenario that links all of the answers to help the individual learn how emotions and situations can interact in escalating patterns.

C. Feelings Rating Scale Worksheet 1 (p. 166)

☼ *Teaching Points.* This worksheet is intended to have the individual practice associating events with levels of emotion. The Feelings Rating Scale Worksheet 1 does not have to describe a specific situation as the previous worked example did. The participant can list events that would lead to each level of emotion that are not associated to each other. For example, losing keys might be a 2 frustration, and losing a child would be a 5 sadness.

D. Feelings Rating Scale Worked Example 2 (p. 167)

☼ *Teaching Points.* This worked example focuses on how a singular emotion can escalate. This is useful to help the individual understand the merits of early skill intervention.

E. Feelings Rating Scale Worksheet 2 (p. 168)

☼ *Teaching Points.* This worksheet asks the individual to be aware of how a specific emotion affects them as the emotions escalate.

F. Categories of Skills Worked Example 1 (p. 170)

☼ *Teaching Points.* This worked example shows which Category of Skills the individual would use at various levels of emotion.

G. Categories of Skills Worksheet 1 (p. 171)

☼ *Teaching Points.* This worksheet asks the individual to circle the Categories of Skills that may be used at different levels of emotion.

H. Categories of Skills Worksheet 2 (p. 172)

☼ *Teaching Points.* This worksheet asks the participant to write in an emotion and a rating level. The person then circles which Categories of Skills may be used in that situation.

I. Recipe for Skills Worked Example 1 (p. 174)

☼ *Teaching Points.* This worked example sheet shows how many skills are needed at different levels of emotions.

J. Recipe for Skills Worksheet 1 (p. 175)

☼ *Teaching Points.* This worksheet lists emotions and ratings; the individual circles the number of skills that are necessary.

K. Recipe for Skills Worksheet 2 (p. 176)

☼ *Teaching Points.* This worksheet requests that the participant write down emotions and ratings. The individual then circles how many skills are necessary at that level of emotional escalation.

Week 3: Clear Picture

Preparing for Group
Handouts Needed
- Skills System Review Sheet (page 179)
- Clear Picture Handout 1 (page 181)
- Clear Picture Worked Example 1 (page 182)

E-Spiral Phase 1

Exploring Existing Knowledge Base: Beginning Group

Welcome group. "Hi, everybody; how is it going today? Are we ready to learn about skills? What do we do first in group? You are right; we ring the bell. Why do we do that? Very good—because we want to focus our minds. We are going to learn even more about breathing today!"

→*Orient to mindfulness activity: notice air filling my belly.* "Last week we rang the bell and noticed our breathing. We learned how to turn our attention to the air going in and out of our noses."

Instructions for mindfulness exercise. "Today we are going to pay attention to our breathing again when the bell rings. We will breathe in though our noses again, and this time, we are going to try to feel the air going deep into our bellies. When we do belly breathing, we feel our tummies get bigger. You might notice your pants or your belt getting tighter as your belly fills with air. How about we try it a few times before we ring the bell?" (Observe each participant.) "That looks good. So, I will ring the bell six times. We all will shift our attention to our belly breathing. If your attention drifts away from your belly breathing, try to bring your focus back to the belly breaths. If you notice emotions, gently bring your attention back to your breathing. If you notice other thoughts, gently bring your focus back to … ? Right, your belly breathing! Let's try to keep our puppies in control. We want to practice being the boss of our minds. All set? Any questions?"

Note: Leaders observe the participants and provide individual instruction to those who are not able to perform the task. Additionally, it may be helpful to use the gesture of two hands turning a car steering wheel as the leader is referring to turning attention. The metaphor can be expanded to include acting as though the steering wheel is hard to turn (rusty or no power steering), exemplifying that there are times when our attention is difficult to shift.

- *Review questions.* "What did you notice about the air filling your belly?" "Where else did your attention go?" "Did you bring your focus back to your belly breathing?" "How did you bring your attention back?"

Note: The group shares details about what they noticed. The leader may choose to write observations on the board.

→*Orient to Skills System review.* "Every week we will review the Skills List, the Feelings Rating Scale, the Categories of Skills, and the Recipe for Skills. It is important that we learn these things inside and out, backward and forward. Turn to page 179 which is the Skills System Review Questions sheet. Today we are going to answer all fourteen questions! So exciting; we are getting to be Skill Masters! Would anyone like to read the questions?"

Note: Group leaders can utilize the Skills System Review Sheet or create another way to review this material. The goal is to practice recalling the information so that the terms and concepts become learned and automatic.

→***Orient to skills practice.*** "I think we are doing well; it does take time. The more we practice, the easier it will be to remember these things. This week's homework was to practice using the Feelings Rating Scale, the Categories of Skills, and the Recipe for Skills. Right?"

- *Review questions.* "Who can talk to us about what it was like to use the Feelings Rating Scale?" "Who can tell us about practicing using the Categories of Skills?" "Who can tell us about using the Recipe for Skills?"

→***Orient to new skills topic.*** "Great! Let's see what we already know about getting a Clear Picture."

◉ **Discuss existing knowledge about the new topic.**

- *Assessment question.* "When we are focused, is our mind clear or fuzzy?"
- *Relevant context question.* "How do people handle things when they are in Clear Mind? How do people handle things when they are in Fuzzy Mind?"
- *Clarifying questions.* "How does Clear Mind help people get to their goals?" "How does Fuzzy Mind keep people from reaching their goals?" "How do you think noticing our breathing can help us handle emotions?" "How can noticing our breathing help us manage Off-Track Thoughts?"

→***Orient to relevant context of new topic.*** "From our discussion, it sounds like we agree that emotions and thoughts can become overwhelming. Sometimes we block or avoid emotions. Unfortunately, that makes things worse. Noticing emotions and thoughts helps us know what is really happening inside and outside of us. When we are clear, we can see where we are going; when we are fuzzy, we can't. Clear information about ourselves and our situation helps us make decisions that lead us to our goals. Our Clear Picture skill will help us get a clear mind, so that we can take actions that help us reach our goals. Any questions?"

E-Spiral Phase 2

Encoding: Teaching the New Topic

→***Orient to new learning.*** "Today we are going to learn about the first skill in the Skills System. Skill 1 is Clear Picture. You can tell by the name of the skill that we will be learning how to have a clear mind."

Instructions for encoding activity. "If you are ready, let's turn to page 181. This is the Clear Picture Handout 1." (Hold up the page.) "This is what it looks like. Okay, what is our plan for reviewing this? Would anyone like to read?"

Note: When group members read, it is important that the leader restate terms so that the group is very clear about the information.

Review Clear Picture Handout 1.

☼ *Teaching Points for Clear Picture Handout 1.* "When we get a Clear Picture, we focus 100 percent on what is happening inside and outside of us right now. We pay attention to what is happening so that we understand the facts of the situation. When we are clear about the facts, we can make On-Track Action Plans to reach our goals. When we are fuzzy or try to change the facts, we end up off-track.

"We get a Clear Picture by going through the Clear Picture Do's. These are things we do to become aware of what is happening inside and outside of us in the moment. We take a Breath, Notice our Surroundings, do a Body Check, Label and Rate Emotions using the 0–5 scale, Notice Thoughts, and Notice Urges. When we go through the Do's, it is like taking a picture of what is happening right now. It is like taking a snapshot." (Snap fingers to show how quickly and easily this can be done.)

"It is important to have a clear picture of situations, so we can figure out how to do what works. We want to make strong Skills Plans. If we have a fuzzy picture, we usually do what doesn't work. We need a Clear Picture of ourselves, others, and the situation to make on-track choices that help us reach our goals."

→*Orient to Clear Picture Worked Example 1.* "Does anyone have any questions about that handout? Okay, now we are going to learn more about getting a Clear Picture. Let's turn to page 182. This is the Clear Picture Worked Example 1 sheet. It looks like this." (Hold the page up.) "Would anyone like to read?"

Review Clear Picture Worked Example 1. The group reviews the worked example. If this worked example is not relevant to the population being treated, skills trainers can create a worked example on a copy of the Clear Picture Worksheet 2. The group leader tries to explain each concept, so the participants understand each of the steps of the Clear Picture. It is not necessary that the participant be able to recall each concept initially; that knowledge base will build as the person is exposed to Clear Picture repeatedly.

→*Orient to ending Encoding Phase.* "Does anyone have questions about Clear Picture so far? Okay, are we ready to practice some of the things we have learned?"

E-Spiral Phase 3

Elaboration: Linking Previous and New Learning

→*Orient to elaboration activity.* "Great, let's practice getting a Clear Picture!"

Instructions for practice exercise. "I am going to say one of the Clear Picture Do's and then I will ring the bell. When I ring the bell, I would like you to do the Do. For example, when I say "Breathe," we will all listen to the bell and take a few breaths as the sound gets quiet. Then I will ring the bell and say, "Notice Surroundings." As the bell ring fades, we will all notice what is happening around us. We will do this for Body Check, Label and Rate Emotions, Notice Thoughts, and Notice Urges. Together we will listen to six rings, and we will do all six Clear Picture Do's. If you get lost, notice what getting lost is like and try to follow along at the next bell ring. Any questions? Great, here we go."

- *Review questions.* "What did you notice about your breath?" "What did you notice when you noticed surroundings?" "What did you notice during the Body Check?" "What emotion did you notice, and how strong was it?" "What thoughts did you notice?" "What urges did you notice?"

→*Orient to discussion.* "Good job. Now we are going to take a few minutes to talk a little more about what it is like to get a Clear Picture."

- *Linking questions.* "Have you ever had a Clear Picture in the past?" "What actions did you take?" "Have you ever had a Fuzzy Picture in the past?" "What actions did you take?"

- *Disclosure questions.* "What is it like to be more aware of things inside and outside of you?" "Can it be difficult to see how things really are?" "What do you do when it is hard to face what is really happening?"
- *Expansion questions.* "What other skills do we use with Clear Picture?" "How can having a Clear Picture help you reach your goals?" "Does a fuzzy or clear picture help you reach your goals?" "Why?"

→**Orient to the end of Elaboration Phase.**

"That was a good discussion. I was thinking that it would be helpful to read a story that teaches us more about how we use Clear Picture in our lives."

E-Spiral Phase 4

Efficacy: Bridge to Future Learning

→**Orient to efficacy activities: reading a story.**

I will read this story, and we will answer some questions when we are done. Is everyone all set?"

Instructions for efficacy activity. Story: "There is a man named Robert, and he is twenty-two years old. Robert works in a grocery store, stocking shelves. One day at work, Robert was kneeling and putting cans on a bottom shelf. Suddenly an older lady pushed her cart into him when he was working. He did not see the woman coming toward him; he only felt the cart hitting him. Robert did a Body Check and noticed a sharp pain in his back. Right away, he knew he had to get a Clear Picture, because he was feeling confused at a level 4. He noticed an urge to scream, "Look out! What are you doing? Didn't you see me working here?" As he stood up to see what had happened, he took a few breaths. He checked around him and saw the old woman looking the other way at some spaghetti sauce. He noticed the thought, *I don't think she knows that she ran into me.* Robert did another Body Check, and the pain in his back was nearly gone."

- *Review questions.*
1. Do you think Robert had a Clear Picture of the situation?
2. How long did it take for Robert to do the Clear Picture Do's?
3. Do you think Robert ended up screaming at the woman?
4. What do you think he did next?
5. What would happen if he had yelled at that old woman?
6. Do you think Clear Picture helped Robert reach his goals?

→**Orient to discussion.** "It sounds like Robert is learning to be a Skill Master. Before we finish for the day, we are going to have a brief discussion. Okay?"

- *Barrier questions.* "What is hard about taking a few seconds to get a Clear Picture?" "We have to use Clear Picture all day. What is difficult about that for you?"
- *Inner-wisdom questions.* "Would the Clear Picture Do's help you?" "Do you think you want to use Clear Picture?"
- *Commitment question.* "When will you use Clear Picture?"
- *Coaching question.* "How can you coach yourself to use Clear Picture every day, all day?"

→**Orienting to home study.** "This week our homework will be to jump in with both feet to practicing Clear Picture. As many times as you can, please notice your breathing, surroundings, body, feelings, thoughts, and urges. You might find that the more you practice, the more quickly you can do the Do's. We can learn to do it in a snap!" (Snap fingers.) "At first it might be hard to remember all six Clear Picture Do's. Try to take a few seconds to be aware of what is happening inside and outside of you before you take action. Good luck; we will talk about it next week. Also, if you want to study skills at home, review all the handouts we have gone over so far. You can also do Clear Picture Worksheets 1 and 2."

→**Orient to group ending.** "As you know, we ring the bell six times at the end of group. We do one ring for each of the Clear Picture Do's. It is a chance to notice what is happening inside and outside of us right now. We take a moment to get a Clear Picture as we go back to our activities. Who would like to ring to bell today?"

Week 3: Clear Picture Handouts to Review in Future Cycles or for Home Study

Note: Skills trainers use these handouts, worked examples, and worksheets to develop teaching plans in future cycles through the Skills System curriculum. Orienting, questions, exercise, and skills practice are created to teach expanded material through subsequent cycles.

A. Clear Picture Worksheet 1 (p. 183)

☼ *Teaching Points.* This worksheet helps participants practice recalling the six Clear Picture Do's.

B. Clear Picture Worksheet 2 (p. 184)

☼ *Teaching Points.* This worksheet is helpful for participants to use in the moment at home. The pictures prompt the individual to Take a Breath, Notice Surroundings, do a Body Check, Label and Rate Emotions, Notice Thoughts, and Notice Urges. This is a useful activity for the person to do when he or she needs to get a Clear Picture.

C. Review Clear Picture: Breathing Handout 1 (p. 185)

☼ *Teaching Points.* The Clear Picture Breathing Handout 1 guides the participant to focus attention on breathing to tolerate distress. The handout shifts the person's focus from the stressful situation to awareness of breathing. The awareness of breathing shifts from being aware of current breathing to doing diaphragmatic or belly breaths. Belly breathing can help the individual remain regulated so that the person can think things through.

D. Review Clear Picture: Checking Around Handout 1 (p. 186)

☼ *Teaching Points.* This worksheet helps the participant understand how we observe our surroundings. Practice exercises can include sensory awareness activities.

E. Review Clear Picture: Checking Around Worked Example 1 (p. 187)

☼ *Teaching Points.* The Clear Picture: Checking Around Worked Example 1 helps the participant understand how to get a Clear Picture of their surroundings.

F. Review Clear Picture: Checking Around Worksheet 1 (p. 188)

☼ *Teaching Points.* This worksheet helps the participant understand how to get a Clear Picture of their surroundings.

G. Review Clear Picture: Body Check Handout 1 (p. 189)

☼ *Teaching Points.* This handout is used by the individual to describe what is observed in various situations.

H. Review Clear Picture: Body Check Worksheet 1 (p. 268)

☼ *Teaching Points.* This worksheet helps the participant individualize awareness of body sensations. It is important for the person to observe and describe his or her personal sensory experience.

I. Review Clear Picture: Body Check Worksheet 2 (p. 269)

☼ *Teaching Points.* The Clear Picture: Body Check Worksheet 2 helps the participant associate body sensations and emotions. Increasing awareness can help assist the individual in Labeling and Rating Emotions.

J. Review Clear Picture: Body Check Worked Example 1 (p. 190)

☼ *Teaching Points.* This worked example provides the participant with an example of how a person may experience an emotion at each level of escalation.

K. Review Clear Picture: Body Check Worksheet 3 (p. 191)

☼ *Teaching Points.* This worksheet asks the participant to observe and describe the impact of an emotion at each level of escalation. This practice helps the individual be more aware of how emotions progress. The goal is to teach the participant that utilizing skills while the emotion is at lower levels may be more effective than waiting.

L. Review Clear Picture: Body Check Handout 2 (p. 193)

☼ *Teaching Points.* This handout leads the individual through a progressive relaxation exercise. The visual aid helps the participant integrate the information learned about body awareness and practice that can assist the individual in their daily life.

M. Review Clear Picture: Label and Rate Emotions Handout 1 (p. 194)

☼ *Teaching Points.* The Clear Picture: Label and Rate Emotions Handout 1 introduces eleven different emotions. These labels serve as a starting point to describe many other emotions that people experience; it is fun to have the group create a brainstorm list of all different emotions.

N. Review Clear Picture: Label and Rate Emotions Handout 2 (p. 195)

☼ *Teaching Points.* This handout teaches the participant how emotions function. The participant comes to understand that events prompt emotions. The person learns that chemical changes happen in the body when emotions happen. People communicate what is happening inside of them through their facial expressions and body language. Awareness of these factors can help individuals understand themselves and other people better. It is important for the participant to understand that emotions create action urges. By being aware of these forces, the participant is better able to observe them, describe them, and make decisions versus reacting quickly without thought.

O. Review Clear Picture: Label and Rate Emotions Worked Example 1 (p. 196)

☼ *Teaching Points.* This worked example lists events that may elicit various emotional responses.

P. Review Clear Picture: Label and Rate Emotions Worksheet 1 (p. 197)

☼ *Teaching Points.* This worksheet asks participants to list situations that elicit specific emotions. This activity helps the individual understand linkages between prompting events and his or her emotional responses.

Q. Review Clear Picture: Notice Thoughts Handout 1 (p. 198)

☼ *Teaching Points.* The Clear Picture: Notice Thoughts Handout 1 teaches participants about how thoughts are continually produced by the brain. It is important that the individual understand that some thoughts are helpful and others are not. The goal is for the person to observe thoughts and allow unhelpful thoughts, or Off-Track Thoughts, to pass without taking action. The metaphor of thoughts being like city buses can be helpful, because the individual only gets on a bus that is heading to the desired destination. Getting on the wrong bus or responding to Off-Track Thoughts, will hinder the individual from reaching goals.

R. Review Clear Picture: Notice Thoughts Worked Example 1 (p. 199)

☼ *Teaching Points.* This worked example sheet highlights thoughts that can elicit certain emotions. It is important that the individual understands how thinking patterns can affect emotional status.

S. Review Clear Picture: Notice Thoughts Worksheet 1 (p. 200)

☼ *Teaching Points.* This worksheet gives the individual an opportunity to list thoughts that may elicit specific emotions.

T. Review Clear Picture: Notice Urges Handout 1 (p. 201)

☼ *Teaching Points.* The Clear Picture: Notice Urges Handout 1 highlights how emotions function to help people. An individual may have avoidant responses to emotions; this handout facilitates a discussion to expose the participant to the positive aspects of emotions. The handout and discussion can be utilized to introduce the concept of urges. When the participant understands that emotions and urges give him or her vital information, the individual is able to accept the experience and manage the information effectively.

U. Review Clear Picture: Notice Urges Worked Example 1 (p. 202)

☼ *Teaching Points.* This worked example outlines examples of urges that a person may experience when having specific emotions.

V. Review Clear Picture: Notice Urges Worksheet 1 (p. 203)

☼ *Teaching Points.* The Clear Picture: Notice Urges Worksheet 1 asks the individual to list urges that the participant notices when experiencing certain emotions. Increasing awareness of emotions and action urges facilitates management of action urges.

W. Review Clear Picture: Notice Urges Worked Example 2 (p. 204)

☼ *Teaching Points.* This worked example sheet demonstrates how action urges intensify as an emotion strengthens.

X. Review Clear Picture: Notice Urges Worksheet 2 (p. 205)

☼ *Teaching Points.* This worksheet asks the individual to observe action urges that happen at increasing levels of emotion. This activity helps the participant improve awareness of affective experiences; enhanced awareness during preliminary escalation can result in proactive skill use.

Y. Clear Picture Summary sheet (p. 180)

Week 4: On-Track Thinking

Preparing for Group

Handouts Needed

- Skills System Review Sheet (page 179)
- On-Track Thinking Handout 1 (page 207)
- On-Track Thinking Worked Example 1 (page 208)
- On-Track Thinking Worksheet 2 (page 211)
- On-Track Thinking Handout 2 (page 210)

E-Spiral Phase 1

Exploring Existing Knowledge Base: Beginning Group

Welcome group. "Hello, everybody! It is wonderful to see you all! How are you doing today?"

→*Orient to mindfulness activity: breathing at the same time as the bell rings.* "Are we ready to get started with our mindful breathing?"

Instructions for mindfulness exercise. "Today we are going to practice being the bosses of our minds again. We are going to practice being aware of and controlling our breathing. During this exercise, we are going to breathe at the same time as we ring the bell. So, I will ring the bell, and we will all take a belly breath. I am going to wait until the sound of the bell has disappeared completely before I ring the bell again. Once the sound is gone, I will ring the bell again, and all of us will take another belly breath. We will do this six times. I think you will notice that your breathing is a little slower than normal. If you notice your mind drifting to other things, try to gently bring your mind back to the ringing of the bell and your belly breathing. If you feel emotions, notice them and bring your attention back to the bell and the breath. Our goal is to work together 100 percent with the bell; other things can wait until the exercise is over. Any questions?"

- *Review questions.* "What was that like?" "Were you able to breathe with the bell?" "What was challenging about that?" "Why might it be important to be able to control your attention and actions like this?"

→*Orient to Skills System review.* "You guys are really doing well. Learning about breathing is an important skill. The cool thing is that we always have our breath with us. If we need to focus, all we have to do is bring our attention to our breathing. Okay, now we are going to do our review of the Skills System. Let's turn to page 179; the Skills System Review Questions look like this. Would anyone like to read these?"

→*Orient to skills practice.* "Very good—I think we are doing well. Okay, let's talk about how we did practicing Clear Picture this week."

- *Review questions.* Choosing one or more of these questions can help participants review the use of Clear Picture: "What are the six Clear Picture Do's?" "Who used Clear Picture?" "Could you tell us how it went?" "Which of the Clear Picture Do's did you do?" "Which of the Clear Picture Do's didn't you do?" "Did you find that Clear Picture was helpful?"

→*Orient to new skills topic.* "It sounds as if using our skills helps us focus more and feel better. It also sounds as if we can feel pretty out of control and uncomfortable when we don't use our skills. Unfortunately it is really hard to reach goals when we are off-track. I am going to ask a few questions that will help share what we already know about thinking things through."

◉ **Discuss existing knowledge about the new topic.**

- *Assessment questions.* "What is it like to be confused?" "What kinds of situations make people confused?" (Brainstorm this list on the board.)
- *Relevant context questions.* "What kinds of plans do we make when we are confused?" "What kinds of actions do we take when we are in Fuzzy Mind?" "What kinds of plans do we make when we are in Clear Mind?" "What kinds of actions do we take when we are focused?"
- *Clarifying questions.* "When we take actions when we are fuzzy or unfocused, how does it usually turn out?" "When we take actions when we are focused and clear, how does it usually turn out?"

→*Orient to relevant context of new topic.* "It is important to use On-Track Thinking because, as we know, life can be confusing. Stress and strong emotions happen every day. It is difficult to reach goals when we are upside-down or out of our minds. So, to reach our goals, we have to be in our minds and make good plans. Getting organized helps us handle stressful situations. On-Track Thinking helps us think clearly so that we can handle what is happening inside and outside of us to reach our goals. Any questions?"

E-Spiral Phase 2 - Encoding: Teaching the New Topic

→*Orient to new learning.* "Okay, today we are going to learn about Skill 2 which is On-Track Thinking. We use On-Track Thinking after we get a Clear Picture. On-Track Thinking helps us think things through to make an On-Track Skills Plan to handle every situation.

Instructions for encoding activity. "Now we are going to learn about the different parts of On-Track Thinking. Please turn to page 207. This is the On-Track Thinking Handout 1."

Note: Skills trainer reads through the handout.

Review On-Track Thinking Handout 1.

☼ *Teaching Points for On-Track Thinking Handout 1.* "When we do Clear Picture, we are finding out what is happening inside and outside of us. We do On-Track Thinking before we take any actions; we have to be sure to have an On-Track Skills Plan before we move ahead. When we notice an urge to take action, we Stop, Step back, and Think about what we want. Next, we Check the Urge. We take a few seconds to Check It to see whether the urge is helpful or not helpful to us. We ask ourselves, 'If I do this, will it help me reach my goals?' When we notice an urge is not helpful, we allow it to pass. We give helpful thoughts a thumbs-up and unhelpful thoughts a thumbs-down. We do not want to get on that city bus, because it is not going where we want to go! We turn our attention to Thumbs-Up Thoughts. So, we Check It and Turn It to On-Track, Thumbs-Up Thinking.

"Once we have Checked It and Turned It to On-Track Thinking, we make a Skills Plan. This is when we think about what skills will help us in this situation. First, we check to see whether we can use Calm-Only skills at this time using the Category of Skills. If we are over a 3, we only use All-the-Time skills." (The trainer can ask the group to verbally list the All-the-Time skills and Calm-Only skills.) "Then, we figure out how many skills to use by using the Recipe for Skills.

We have to be sure to use enough skills. Then, we decide what other skills will help us reach our goals. We think about whether we need to use a Safety Plan. Safety Plans help us handle risky situations. Maybe doing a New-Me Activity would be helpful. It may help us keep busy and focused. If we are under a 3, we might want to use Problem Solving to fix problems, Expressing Myself to help us communicate, Getting It right to get what we want, and Relationship Care to balance relationships.

"After we make a Skills Plan, we decide what our On-Track Action will be. An On-Track Action is when we take a Positive Step toward our goal. So, we think things through before we take any action. Making and then doing a Skills Plan can be difficult, so we have to cheer ourselves on with Thumbs-Up Thinking. We cheer ourselves on to help us stay on-track and reach goals! We say things like 'I can do this' and 'I am going to be okay' to cheer ourselves on. Any questions?"

Note: Leaders use gestures of a thumbs-up and -down to represent helpful and unhelpful. Placing the thumbs-up or thumbs-down in front of the leader's chest signifies that the person looks within one's heart to find the answer. Checking the fit of an urge or a plan utilizes the individual's wisdom or personal sense of right and wrong in the moment.

- *Content questions.* "How often do we use On-Track Thinking?" "How do we know when something is helpful or unhelpful?" "What is Off-Track Thinking?" "How does Off-Track Thinking affect us?" "What kinds of things do we say to ourselves to cheer ourselves on?"

→*Orient to On-Track Thinking Worked Example 1.* "There is a lot to learn about On-Track Thinking. Let's go through On-Track Thinking Worked Example 1 on page 208 together. It looks like this."

Note: The On-Track Thinking Worked Example 1 is self-explanatory. Skills trainers read through the worksheet with the group.

- *Content questions.* "How does On-Track Thinking go together with the other skills we have learned?"

→*Orient to ending Encoding Phase.* "Excellent job! Any questions about On-Track Thinking so far?"

E-Spiral Phase 3

Elaboration: Linking Previous and New Learning

→*Orient to elaboration activity.* "Great, are we ready to practice On-Track Thinking? Now, we are going to fill out On-Track Thinking Worksheet 2 together. Turn to page 211. This is what it looks like."

Instructions for practice exercise. "This worksheet helps practice checking urges. I will read a list of eight urges. You will think about each one and decide if the urge would be helpful or unhelpful for you in this moment. If it is helpful, circle the thumb that goes up. If the urge is not helpful, circle the thumb that goes down. If you have a hard time reading, you can get the person next to you to help, or you can just show the group a thumbs-up or thumbs-down for your answer. Any questions?"

☼ *Teaching points for On-Track Thinking Worksheet 2.* "Each of us has to decide what is on-track and off-track for ourselves. No one can tell you what is right for you; we have to search within ourselves to find those answers. This worksheet is a chance to practice looking inside you to see if an urge is helpful or unhelpful. Our goals change, so we have to be sure to check within our hearts to find out if something is helpful or unhelpful in this moment. Every situation is different. So, it is best to check urges each time you use On-Track Thinking. Any questions?"

- *Review questions.* "What was that exercise like for you?" "How did you decide whether the urge was helpful or unhelpful?" and "How long did it take for you to Check the Urge?"

→**Orient to discussion.** "You guys did really well with that. We are going to talk together for a few moments about using On-Track Thinking."

- *Linking question.* "How is On-Track Thinking different from how you have dealt with situations in the past?"
- *Disclosure questions.* "Have you ever just reacted quickly without thinking things through?" "How did that work?" "What was a decision that you felt really good about?" "How did that feel to you?"
- *Expansion questions.* "What other skills do we use with On-Track Thinking?" "When can On-Track Thinking help you in your life?"

→**Orient to the end of Elaboration Phase.**

"Now that we know a little more about On-Track Thinking, are we ready to do a role play together?"

E-Spiral Phase 4

Efficacy: Bridge to Future Learning

→**Orient to efficacy activities: role play.**

"Doing a role play helps us practice using a skill. Some of us get nervous acting in front of other people. It may be helpful for you to do an On-Track Action to jump in to participate if you feel like avoiding this exercise. All set?"

Instructions for efficacy activity. "I am going to walk up to a person in the middle of group and say something to you. It will be meant to cause a small level of emotion. After I say the statement, I would like us all to stop and get a Clear Picture and do On-Track Thinking. We are going to use the On-Track Thinking Handout 2 sheet on page 210 to help us remember all of the steps of these skills in a real-life situation. The group and I will help you remember the step, and you have to do each one as we go through them. Which brave person would like to try it first?"

Note: Examples of what the skills trainer might say to a participant: (1) "There is a problem. Can I see you in my office?" (2) "A letter has arrived with your name on it." (3) "You have a phone call. You can take it in my office." (4) "You have won a prize for being a Skill Master."

Once the leader makes the statement, immediately he or she coaches the participant through the Clear Picture Do's and On-Track Thinking. Focusing on the current moment is important. It is best if all group members understand that this is a role play and that they each participate if possible. If there is only time to do one role play, other participants can contribute answers and help coach the person.

- *Review questions.* "What did you notice during that role play?" "How do you think the skills worked?"

Note: It may be useful to list observations on the board.

→**Orient to discussion.** "I thought you guys did an awesome job. It isn't easy to use skills, but you will find it gets easier and easier with practice. Let's talk for a few minutes about some of the challenges of using skills before we finish for today."

- *Barrier question.* "What is difficult about using On-Track Thinking for you?"
- *Inner-wisdom question.* "Do you think it is important for you to use On-Track Thinking?"
- *Commitment question.* "Are you going to use On-Track Thinking?"
- *Coaching question.* "How can you get yourself to use On-Track Thinking?"

→**Orienting to home study.** "It sounds as if we know it is hard, and we still have to use skills. When we understand that, we really are on our way to being Skill Masters. Skill Masters practice skills outside of group. So, this week we will work on using On-Track Thinking. Practice whenever you have a chance do Clear Picture and On-Track Thinking. Good luck!

"Also, if you want to study skills at home, review all the handouts we have gone over so far. You can also do On-Track Thinking- Worksheet 1. Choose a situation, and fill out the sheet. You can do it by yourself or ask staff to help. Any questions?"

→**Orient to group ending.** "As you know, we ring the bell six times at the end of group. We do one ring for each of the Clear Picture Do's. It is a chance to notice what is happening inside and outside of us right now. We take a moment to get a Clear Picture as we go back to our activities. Who would like to ring the bell today?"

Week 4: On-Track Thinking Handouts to Review in Future Cycles or for Home Study

A. On-Track Thinking Worksheet 1 (p. 209)

Instructions: The individual chooses a situation to review and completes each of the questions.

B. On-Track Thinking Handout 2 (p. 210)

☼ *Teaching points.* "This handout helps us handle Off-Track Thoughts and Urges. When we notice any thought or urge, we Stop, Step back, and Think about want we want. We check whether the thought or urge is helpful or not helpful (Use thumbs-up and -down gesture.) Helpful thoughts and urges keep us on-track to goals. Off-Track thoughts and urges lead us away from our goals. We allow Off-Track Thoughts and Urges to pass without taking actions on them. Any questions?"

C. On-Track Thinking Summary Sheet (p. 206)

Week 5: On-Track Actions

Preparing for Group
Handouts Needed
- Skills System Review Sheet (page 179)

E-Spiral Phase 1
Exploring Existing Knowledge Base: Beginning Group

Welcome group. "How is everyone doing today? Okay, ready to learn some skills? Great! How do we get started? Exactly—we ring the bell. All set?"

→*Orient to mindfulness activity: breathing and Body Check.* "Today we are going to breathe and do a Body Check. Practicing doing a Body Check can help us be more self-aware. The more we notice what is happening inside of us, the clearer we are. It helps us label and rate our emotions when we notice how our body is reacting to a situation."

Instructions for mindfulness exercise. "Okay, I will ring the bell, and we will bring our attention to our bodies. You may notice your breathing and how it feels. You may notice other sensations, like the texture of chair that you are sitting on or the hardness of the floor under your feet. You may notice aches, pains, or muscle tightness. You may notice muscle relaxation and calmness in your body. Notice whatever is happening in your body. If your mind drifts away from doing the Body Check, gently bring your mind back to your body. I will ring the bell six times, and then we will share what we noticed. Any questions?"

- *Review question.* "What did you notice during your Body Check?"

Note: It may be helpful to write the different observations on the board.

→*Orient to Skills System review.* "Fantastic! How about we go through our Skills System review? Let's turn to page 179. The Skills System Review Questions sheet looks like this. Would anyone like to read?"

→*Orient to skills practice.* "Great! It is getting a little easier, isn't it? Okay, let's go over our homework. This week we were going to practice using Clear Picture and On-Track Thinking."

- *Review questions.* "Who would like to share about how they use Clear Picture and On-Track Thinking this week?" "How did it work?" "Do you wish you had done anything differently?"

→*Orient to new skills topic.* "That is a good start. Shall we talk about taking On-Track Actions?"

◉ **Discuss existing knowledge about the new topic.**
- *Assessment questions.* "Are there times when people have urges to go off-track?" "What kinds of things make us want to go off-track?" "Do people feel out of control sometimes?" "Why do you think that happens?"
- *Relevant context questions.* "What is it like to be off-track?" "Do you ever feel as if you are stuck off-track, and you can't get back on-track?" "Do we ever think about getting back on-track but then not do anything to make it happen?"
- *Clarifying questions.* "Do Off-Track Actions help us reach our goals?" "Where do Off-Track Actions take us?" "Do On-Track Actions help us reach our goals? How?"

Note: It is helpful to orient the participants to the possible short-term benefits of Off-Track Actions to validate the urge. Then highlighting the long-term results can help the participant make an informed decision.

→*Orient to relevant context of new topic.* "From our discussion, it is clear that we all have Off-Track Urges. It sounds like it is hard to stay on-track. We have to use Clear Picture and On-Track Thinking to stay on-track. Thinking about being on-track must be followed by action. Taking action means that we do something on-track."

E-Spiral Phase 2

Encoding: Teaching the New Topic

→*Orient to new learning.* "Great discussion. Today we are going to learn about On-Track Actions. We will learn about how we get a Clear Picture, use On-Track Thinking, and take an On-Track Action reaching toward our goal. Let's turn to page 213. We are going to work on the On-Track Action Handout 1. It looks like this. All set?"

Instructions for encoding activity. "Great, we are going to go through the handout together. I will talk a little about each main point, and then we will have a discussion, okay?"

☼ *Teaching Points for On-Track Action Handout 1.* "Clear Picture and On-Track Thinking help us do On-Track Actions. First, we use Skill 1, Clear Picture, to know what is happening inside and outside of us. We check our emotions, thoughts, and urges and Turn It to Skill 2, On-Track Thinking. Then we make a skill plan and figure out what our On-Track Actions, Skill 3, will be to reach our goal. When we start with Skills 1, 2, and 3, we can usually stay on-track to our goals. (Point to the line that leads to the star.) Sometimes we get a Fuzzy Picture and have Off-Track Thinking that lead to Off-Track Actions. (Point to the line that leads to the crash site). The good news is that once we are off-track, we can get back on-track by doing 1, 2, 3! What are skills 1, 2, 3? Right: Clear Picture, On-Track Thinking, and On-Track Action! Staying on-track is as easy as … (Say "1, 2, 3" with everyone at once.) Right: 1, 2, 3! Any questions?"

→*Orienting to On-Track Action Handout 2.* "Okay, let's learn more about On-Track Actions. Turn to page 214. On-Track Action Handout 2 looks like this. Ready?"

☼ *Teaching Points for On-Track Action Handout 2.* (1–5)

1. "There are lots of different kinds of On-Track Actions. An On-Track Action is the first step toward our goals. For example, if we want to learn skills, practicing at home is an On-Track Action. Practicing will help us be a Skills Master. Throwing our skills book in the garbage would probably be an Off-Track Action in that situation."

2. "Sometimes we need to do the On-Track Action of Shifting Tracks when we are heading off-track. It might be helpful to do an On-Track Action that is opposite of our Off-Track Urges to Shift Tracks. For example, if we want new friends, and we are standing in the corner at a party, we may need to take actions to be very friendly and introduce ourselves to people, rather than hiding in the corner. Our urge may be to hide, yet doing the opposite may be a great idea to help us reach our goal."

3. "It is often helpful to make an On-Track Action Plan. Doing on-track things every day that make us healthy and happy can help us feel good and make on-track choices. For example, if we eat well, exercise, and sleep in balanced ways, we are less grumpy and moody. When we feel good, we are more able to be on-track."

4. "There are times when we need to Accept the Situation. Sometimes we have done everything we can in a situation, and we just have to accept what is happening. We may not like it, but we have to realize that it must be accepted. The great thing is that we have skills to deal with waiting for things to get better! Skills Masters learn to make the best of a bad situation or make lemonade when life gives us lemons."

5. "There are times when we need to Let It Pass and Move On. For example, if we broke a favorite mug, we can be sad for a while, but at some point, we are dwelling on problems. When we dwell on problems for too long, it can make us more emotional. We have to learn when enough is enough for ourselves. We may have the urge to get stuck on certain things, but getting stuck can keep us from our goals. Any questions?"

→*Orient to ending Encoding Phase.* "On-Track Actions are our friends! They keep us on-track! Are we ready to practice On-Track Actions?"

E-Spiral Phase 3

Elaboration: Linking Previous and New Learning

→*Orient to elaboration activity: practice exercise.* "Okay, we are going to read a short story and think about On-Track Actions. Please turn to page 215. The On-Track Action Practice Exercise looks like this.

Instructions for practice exercise. Note: Read the instructions and scenario on the On-Track Action Practice Exercise. The group then discusses the Skills Plan and options that the person has for On-Track Actions.

- *Review questions.* "How did that exercise go for you?"

→*Orient to discussion.* "Okay, let's talk a little more about On-Track Actions."

- *Linking questions.* "Who can describe an On-Track Action you have done in the past?" "How did it work?" "Describe an Off-Track Action you have taken." "How did it work?"
- *Disclosure questions.* "When was a time when it was difficult to do an On-Track Action?" "What was going on that made it difficult?"
- *Expansion questions.* "What are other skills we use with On-Track Action?" "Could On-Track Action help you in your life?" "At home?" "At work?" "Your relationships?" "Your family?"

→*Orient to the end of Elaboration Phase.* "Great discussion. It is important for us to understand how to use our skills in difficult situations. In tough situations, it can be easy to go off-track and hard to reach goals."

E-Spiral Phase 4

Efficacy: Bridge to Future Learning

Orient to efficacy activities: role play a scenario. "So, now we are going to do a role play. We are going to have a little, tiny argument! I am actually going to irritate you on purpose, so that you can practice Clear Picture, On-Track Thinking, and On-Track Action. Who would like to start?"

Instructions for efficacy activity. "I am going to walk up to you and accuse you of stealing my CD. As I am talking, I would like you to quickly get a Clear Picture and do On-Track Thinking.

I am not going to keep talking too much, because I want you to have time to figure out what to do. Once you make a Skills Plan, take an On-Track Action. You can ask the group for help whenever you need to. Now, group, if you have a suggestion, raise your hand. Our volunteer may point to you, and you can give the advice. The person can ask for volunteers or try to handle it on his or her own. We are going to do this in slowly to practice putting these skills together. Any questions?"

Note: It is helpful for the skills trainer to stop and prompt the group to help the participant through the Clear Picture Do's, On-Track Thinking, and figuring out an On-Track Action that fits for the participant. Depending on the level of skills knowledge the group has, the trainer gauges how much depth to go into, as well as how much support to offer.

- *Review questions.* "What did you notice during this role play?" "How do you think the skills worked together?" "Would you have done anything differently?"

→**Orient to discussion.** "Great job on the role play. Before we finish, would it be okay if we have a brief discussion about some of the challenges involved in taking On-Track Actions?"

- *Barrier question.* "What is difficult about using On-Track Action?"
- *Inner-wisdom question.* "Do you feel it is important for you to use On-Track Action in your life?"
- *Commitment question.* "When are times you will use On-Track Action?"
- *Coaching question.* "How can you coach yourself to use On-Track Action when you feel stuck?"

→**Orient to home study.** "Good discussion about On-Track Actions. Homework time! This week we are going to practice using On-Track Actions. Let's try to take actions that are the Positive Steps toward a goal. Also, please practice Switching Tracks when you have Off-Track Urges. And finally, Accept the Situation and Let It Go and Move On if it helps you reach your goals.

"Also, if you want to study skills at home, you can review all the handouts we have gone over so far. You can also do On-Track Action Worksheet 1. Any questions?"

→**Orient to group ending.** "As you know, we ring the bell six times at the end of group. We do one ring for each of the Clear Picture Do's. It is a chance to notice what is happening inside and outside of us right now. We take a moment to get a Clear Picture as we go back to our activities. Who would like to ring the bell today?"

Week 5: On-Track Action Handouts to Review in Future Cycles or for Home Study

A. On-Track Action Handout 3 (p. 216)

☼ *Teaching Points.* The participants review the top section of this handout and discuss other situations, Off-Track Urges, and possible positive actions that would be helpful. The group then discusses the bottom section. The group thinks of situations when doing the opposite of Off-Track Urges may be helpful. Skills trainers discuss the benefits of jumping in with both feet versus only giving partial effort. Using the gesture of jumping in with both feet is fun. Countering the point using the gesture of merely touching a toe in the water gives a visual message about the differences. It is important to validate the challenges of jumping into something when we are unsure or afraid and the possible need to do it anyway. (This discussion teaches a dialectical perspective.)

B. On-Track Action Handout 4 (p. 217)

☼ *Teaching Points.* This handout outlines different components of an individual's On-Track Action Plan. It is important to focus on the concept of balance versus absolute rules. The individual needs to be able to make adjustments as his or her life changes.

C. On-Track Action Worked Example 1 (p. 218)

☼ *Teaching Points.* This is a worked example of an On-Track Action Plan. This sheet is intended to highlight realistic options, rather than providing a prescription. The individual must explore personal options and make individual choices that fit his or her life at that time.

D. On-Track Action Worksheet 1 (p. 219)

☼ *Teaching Points.* The individual creates a personal On-Track Action Plan. It may be helpful for the person to fill this On-Track Action Plan with his or her individual therapist.

E. On-Track Action Handout 5 (p. 220)

☼ *Teaching Points.* This handout discusses the process of practicing acceptance in challenging situations. The woman in the picture is waiting for an important phone call. She is getting frustrated as she waits and stares at the phone. She gets a Clear Picture that the phone is frustrating her. She does On-Track Thinking and decides that she cannot make the phone ring. So, instead of staring at the phone and getting more frustrated, she chooses to take an On-Track Action of accepting the situation as it is. She then does a New-Me Activity of drawing while she waits for her call. If the woman kept staring at the phone, she may have gotten more upset.

Content questions. "How do you think her phone call would go if she kept staring at the phone and was very upset?" "How do you think the call would go if she went to do artwork while she was waiting?"

F. On-Track Action Handout 6 (p. 221)

☼ *Teaching Points.* This handout addresses the benefits of the On-Track Actions of letting go and moving on. The top picture shows the effects of a person perseverating on anxious thoughts. The bottom picture shows the same person moving ahead using skills to deal with stress and problems. The image of a rainbow is to exemplify how when it is raining, sometimes it is possible to find positive element in one's life.

G. On-Track Action Handout 7 (p. 222)

☼ *Teaching Points.* This handout highlights how we use Clear Picture, On-Track Thinking, and On-Track Action with the other skills. This handout is a helpful visual aid when reviewing making and implementing skill plans in various situations.

H. On-Track Action Summary Sheet (p. 212)

Week 6: Safety Plans

Preparing for Group

Handouts Needed
- Skills System Review Sheet (page 179)
- Safety Plan Handout 1 (page 224)
- Safety Plan Worked Example 1 (page 225)
- Safety Plan Handout 2 (page 227)
- Safety Plan Worked Example 2 (Page 228)
- Safety Plan Handout 3 (page 230)
- Safety Plan Handout 4 (page 231)
- Safety Plan Worked Example 3 (page 232)
- Safety Plan Worksheet 3 (page 233)

E-Spiral Phase 1

Exploring Existing Knowledge Base: Beginning Group

Welcome group. "Welcome back! How is everyone doing today? Well, how about we get started?"

→*Orient to mindfulness activity: breathing and noticing surroundings.* "Would you like to hear about the mindfulness that we are doing today? Great!"

Instructions for mindfulness exercise. "Okay, as we listen to the bell, we are going to notice our surroundings. Noticing Surroundings is one of the Clear Picture Do's. So, I will ring the bell, and your job is to notice what is happening around you. We use our five senses to notice what we see, hear, smell, taste, and touch. If your mind drifts to something other than your surroundings, gently bring your mind back to the bell and your senses. Having a Clear Picture about what is happening around us helps us make on-track choices. Having a Fuzzy Picture about what is happening around us can help us go off-track.

- *Review questions.* "What did you notice during this exercise?" "Did your mind drift?" "Were you able to bring your mind back?"

→*Orient to Skills System review.* "Good observations. Now how about we do our Skills System review? Okay, please turn to page 179. The Skills System Review Questions look like this. Who would like to read?"

→*Orient to skills practice.* "Great job—we are getting there! Now, we are going to review our skills practice. We were practicing doing On-Track Actions this week. Let's not forget how we also use Clear Picture and On-Track Thinking to do what works."

- *Review questions.* "Who would like to share about how they used On-Track Actions this week?" "What were some of the positive things people did as an On-Track Action?" "What did we do that was opposite of Off-Track Urges?" "Did anyone use 1, 2, 3?" "What things did we accept this week?" "When did people Let It Go and Move On this week?"

→*Orient to new skills topic.*

"Excellent! Before we get started on our now skill for this week, can we talk about what we already know about keeping ourselves safe?"

◉ **Discuss existing knowledge about the new topic.**

- *Assessment questions.* "What does the word 'risk' mean?" "What is a risky situation?"
- *Relevant context questions.* "What are some examples of risky situations that you have noticed?" "How do we know when a situation is not safe?" "What are some situations that may be helpful to avoid?"
- *Clarifying questions.* "What can happen if we move toward risky situations?" "What happens if we move away from risky situations?"

→*Orient to relevant context of new topic.* "Sometimes there are difficult situations in life. Much of the time, it is best that we face challenging situations so that we learn how to deal with them. Avoiding can make things worse sometimes. Other times, situations should be avoided, because there is risk that can cause us problems. In these situations, we use our Safety Plan. We use our Clear Picture and On-Track Thinking to make these important decisions."

E-Spiral Phase 2

Encoding: Teaching the New Topic

→*Orient to new learning.* "The Safety Plan is the fourth skill in the Skills System. Safety Plans help us handle risky situations. We are going to go over several handouts today; it seems like a lot! I do not expect us to learn all about Safety Plans today, but we will review the three types of Safety Plans, the three Levels of Risk, and the three things we can do when we notice risk."

Instructions for encoding activity. "Let's get started by turning to page 224. The Safety Plan Handout 1 looks like this. All set?"

Note: The skills trainer reads the handout.

☼ *Teaching Points for Safety Plan Handout 1.* "Safety Plans help us handle risks that come from inside of us and outside of us. Inside-of-Me risks are ones that happen inside our bodies. When we have TUFFs—Off-Track Thoughts, Urges, Feelings, and Fantasies—we need to use Safety Plans. TUFFs make it more difficult for us to stay on-track.

"Things outside of us, such as people, places, or things, can be risky. Certain people, places, or things can cause us problems. These Outside-of-Me risks can make us have Off-Track Thoughts, Urges, Feelings, and Fantasies that make the situation dangerous for us or other people. Any questions?"

→*Orienting to Safety Plan Worked Example 1.* "Let's turn to the Safety Plan Worked Example 1 on page 225. It looks like this."

☼ *Teaching Point for Safety Plan Worked Example 1.* "Let's read through this worksheet together to learn more about inside and outside risks."

- *Content questions.* "Let's list the risks in this situation." "What should this person be careful of having contact with?"

Note: Write the list on the board.

→*Orienting to Safety Plan Handout 2.* "Okay, good start. Now let's learn about the three levels of risk. Please turn to page 227. The Safety Plan Handout 2 looks like this."

Note: The leader reads through the handout with the group.

☼ *Teaching Point for Safety Plan Handout 2.*

"There are three Levels of Risk: low, medium, and high. To identify risk, ask yourself 1) How much damage can the thing cause? and 2) How close is the thing to us?

"In a high-risk situation, there is a chance for there to be serious damage or the thing is very close to us. In a medium-risk situation, the risk can cause us problems or it is in our area. In low-risk situations, the risk may cause us some stress or the risk is far away from us.

"So, the more damage something can cause, the higher the risk. The closer the risk is to us, the higher the risk is. For example if a rattlesnake is next to us, it is high risk. If the snake is a hundred feet away, the risk is lower. Any questions?"

→***Orienting to Safety Plan Handout 3.*** "Great! I know there is a lot to learn about Safety Plans. It will take time to know it all. Okay, let's turn to page 230. The Safety Plan Handout 3 looks like this."

☼ *Teaching Point for Safety Plan Handout 3.* "Let's read this together to learn about the three types of Safety Plans. We have to do more Safety Planning as the situation becomes more risky. For example, in a low-risk situation, it might be all right to just do a Thinking Safety Plan. In a medium-risk situation, it is usually best to do a Thinking and Talking Safety Plan. In a high-risk situation, it is helpful to do a Thinking, Talking, and Writing Safety Plan to be sure the danger is managed well."

Note: The leader or group reads through the handout with the group.

→***Orienting to Safety Plan Handout 4.*** "So far we have learned about low, medium, and high risks. We have also learned about writing, talking, and thinking Safety Plans. Next we are going to learn about what we do in these situations to handle risk. Please turn to page 231. The Safety Plan Handout 4 looks like this."

Note: The leader or group reads through the handout with the group.

☼ *Teaching Point for Safety Plan Handout 4.* " When there is a low risk, it may be possible to focus on the New-Me Activity that we are doing at the time. For example, if I notice a small issue far away, I can just focus on my activity. I am not ignoring the problem; I am choosing to focus on something helpful. Next, if there is a risk that is closer or will cause me problems, I move away to get distance between me and the risk. For example, I may move my seat in a room if someone is bothering me and then continue focusing on my New-Me Activity. If there is a high-risk situation, I will want to leave the area completely. I want to be sure I cannot hear, see, talk to, or touch the risk. For example, I would go to my room and close the door.

- *Content questions.* "Why is it dangerous to be able to see, hear, talk to, or touch the risk?" "How do we know where to go when we have to move or leave an area?" "Why is it good to do a New-Me Activity?" "What New-Me Activities are helpful to focus on?" "How far away do we need to go when we move away?" "How do we focus our attention on our activity when there is a low risk?" "How do we know when we should do a Safety Plan to avoid a situation and when it is best to try to face a difficult situation?"

→***Orient to ending Encoding Phase.***

"There are many parts of the Safety Plan skill: Levels of Risk, types of Safety Plans, and actions that we take to handle risky situations. How about we move on to practice Safety Planning?"

E-Spiral Phase 3

Elaboration: Linking Previous and New Learning

→***Orient to elaboration activity.*** "Okay, we are going to put all of these new things together into a Safety Plan. Please turn to page 232. The Safety Plan Worked Example 3 looks like this.

Instructions for practice exercise. "We are going to read through this Safety Plan together and talk about it."

- *Review questions.* "What are your thoughts about Safety Plans?"

→**Orient to discussion.**

"Okay, I know you have done Safety Plans in the past; let's talk about that a little bit."

- *Linking questions.* "When have you avoided risky situations in the past?" "How did it work?"
- *Disclosure questions.* "Were there times when you did not use a Safety Plan and wish you had?" "What happened?"
- *Expansion questions.* "What are other skills we use with Safety Plans?" "Are there times in your life that you could use a Safety Plan?" "At work?" "At home?" "With family?" "With friends?"

→**Orient to the end of Elaboration Phase.**

"It sounds like there are times when we need to use Safety Plans. I'm glad we are learning this today!"

E-Spiral Phase 4

Efficacy: Bridge to Future Learning

→**Orient to efficacy activities: *Safety Planning Worksheet 3*.** "Okay, I think we are ready to do a Safety Plan together. Let's turn to page 233. The Safety Plan Worksheet 3 looks like this. Who would like to share a risky situation that happened this week that we could go through and do a Safety Plan for? Very brave, thank you!"

Note: It is important to pick a scenario that is not highly arousing for the volunteer or the group. A medium- or low-risk situation is best to review.

Instructions for efficacy activity. The leader leads the person through the Safety Plan. The therapist focuses on moving through the Safety Plan, rather than stopping to do Expressing Myself or Problem Solving about the situation. The group is encouraged to participate. The leader and group ask questions to foster thinking about different options and check the fit of each. Together the leader, the volunteer, and the group make the Safety Plan.

- *Review questions.* "How do you think the Safety Plan went?" "Do you think the Safety Plan would have helped?" "Do you have any questions about Safety Plans?"

→**Orient to discussion**. "That was very good; everyone was helpful. Before we finish up today, I would like us to talk together about some of the challenges of doing Safety Plans."

- *Barrier questions.* "What is difficult about using a Safety Plan?" "What is it like to have to walk away from situations, especially ones that we enjoy but know are risky?" "What is it like to have to stop doing something we like because of someone else?"
- *Inner-wisdom question.* "Do you think Safety Plans are important for you to use?"
- *Commitment question.* "When can you use Safety Plans in your life?"
- *Coaching question.* "How can you coach yourself to use Safety Plans?"

→**Orienting to home study.** "Great job today! There is a lot to learn about Safety Plans. You know what really helps us learn about Safety Plans? Right—practice! So, this week, please practice noticing risky situations. Think about whether the risk is low, medium, or high. Think about whether you should do a Thinking, Talking, and/or Writing Safety Plan. Also, decide to refocus, move away, or leave the area completely. Are there any questions? Good luck!

Also, "If you want to study skills at home, review all the handouts we have gone over so far. You can also do Safety Plan Worksheets 1, 2, and 3."

→**Orient to group ending.** "As you know, we ring the bell six times at the end of group. We do one ring for each of the Clear Picture Do's. It is a chance to notice what is happening inside and outside of us right now. We take a moment to get a Clear Picture as we go back to our activities. Who would like to ring the bell today?"

Week 6: Handouts to Review in Future Cycles or for Home Study

A. Safety Plan Worksheet 1 (p. 226)

☼ *Teaching Points.* The individual lists specific inside and outside risks that he or she experiences.

B. Safety Plan Worked Example 2 (p. 228)

☼ *Teaching Points.* This worksheet gives worked examples of low-, medium-, and high-risk situations.

C. Safety Plan Worksheet 2 (p. 229)

☼ *Teaching Points.* The individual lists specific low, medium, and high risks on Safety Plan Worksheet 2.

D. Safety Plan Summary Sheet (p. 223)

Week 7: New-Me Activities

Preparing for Group
Handouts Needed
- Skills System Review Sheet (page 179)
- New-Me Activities Handout 1 (page 235)
- New-Me Activities Handout 2 (page 236)
- New-Me Activities Handout 3 (page 238)
- New-Me Activities Handout 4 (page 240)
- New-Me Activity Handout 5 (page 242)

E-Spiral Phase 1

Exploring Existing Knowledge Base: Beginning Group
Welcome group. "Hi, everybody. How are we doing today? Ready for some mindfulness?"

→*Orient to mindfulness activity: breathing and noticing emotions.*

Instructions for mindfulness exercise. "Today we are going to notice our emotions as we listen to the bell. I will ring the bell six times, and we will turn our attention to noticing any emotions we are having. When you mind starts to wander to all the things that are making you feel that way, gently bring your mind back to just noticing emotions. Try not to hold on to any emotions once you notice them. It is important to be able to notice emotions come and let them go without needing to dwell on them or make them stronger by focusing on the issues. Learning to turn our minds from one emotion to another helps us not be consumed by painful emotions. Okay, here goes; let's focus on emotions. Any questions?"

- *Review questions.* "How was that for you?" "What emotions did you notice?" "Did your mind drift?" "Were you able to bring your mind back to your emotions?"

→*Orient to Skills System review.* "Great job with Clear Picture. Okay, how about we do our Skills System review? Please turn to page 179. The Skills System Review questions look like this. Would anyone like to read?"

→*Orient to skills practice.*

"Great, on to homework! How did we do this week practicing Safety Plans?"

- *Review questions.* "Who would like to tell us about a thinking Safety Plan they did this week?" "Who can tell us about doing a talking Safety Plan this week?" "Who can tell us about doing a Writing Safety Plan this week?" "Did anyone wish they had used a Safety Plan this week?"

→*Orient to new skills topic.* "Good start. Safety Plans take time to learn; you all will get it. Now, let's talk about what we know about doing New-Me Activities."

◉ **Discuss existing knowledge about the new topic.**

- *Assessment questions.* "After people walk away from a risky situation, what do they do then?" "What are some activities that help you stay on-track?"
- *Relevant context questions.* "What is the difference between an On-Track Activity and an Off-Track Activity?" "How do we decide if an activity is helpful or not helpful?"

- *Clarifying questions.* "Why do people choose New-Me Activities?" "Why do people choose Off-Track Activities?"

→**Orient to relevant context of new topic.** "New-Me Activities help us in many ways. We are going to learn about how to choose the right activities at the right time to help us reach our goals."

E-Spiral Phase 2

Encoding: Teaching the New Topic

→**Orient to new learning.** "We are going to learn about New-Me Activities today! We are going to read through five New-Me Activity Handouts. Let's turn to page 235. The New-Me Activities Handout 1 looks like this."

Instructions for encoding activity. The group reads through the New-Me Activities handouts and discusses different activities. "Would anyone like to read or should I?"

☼ *Teaching Points for New-Me Activities Handout 1.* "This handout introduces the four different types of New-Me Activities. Different activities help us do different things. Some help us focus, feel better, distract us, and are fun. We have to learn to do many different New-Me Activities and to choose the one that will help us the most in the moment. Handouts 2–5 go into detail about each kind."

→**Orienting to New-Me Activities Handout 2 . (Focus)** "Now let's learn more about Focus New-Me Activities. Please turn to page 236. The New-Me Activities Handout 2 looks like this."

☼ *Teaching Points for New-Me Activities Handout 2.* "Focus New-Me Activities help us focus our attention. We have to concentrate and pay attention carefully when we do these activities. Let's create a brainstorm list on the board of each kind of activity on the handout."

Note: It is particularly important that each individual has accessible activities that fit the individual's means and logistical situation.

- *Content questions.* "What are different things we can organize and sort?" "What king of things can you clean?" "When is it helpful to use Focus New-Me Activities?"

→**Orienting to New-Me Activities Handout 3 (Feel Good).** "Now we are going to look at page 238. It is the New-Me Activities Handout 3 that shows us Feel-Good New-Me Activities. It looks like this."

Review New-Me Activities Handout 3.

☼ *Teaching Points for New-Me Activities Handout 3.* "Feel-Good New-Me Activities make us feel comfortable and happy. When we are feeling stressed or upset, it can help to do an activity that soothes us and makes us feel better. Let's read these and make a brainstorm list on the board of activities that utilize each of our senses that help us feel good."

Content questions.

  ○ "What do you enjoy looking at?"

  ○ "What are things that you enjoy listening to?"

  ○ "What do you enjoy touching?"

  ○ "What do you enjoy smelling?"

○ "What do you enjoy tasting?"

○ "When is it helpful to use Feel-Good New-Me Activities?"

→*Orienting to New-Me Activities Handout 4 (Distraction).* "On to Distraction New-Me Activities Handout 4. It is on page 240, and it looks like this."

☼ *Teaching Points for New-Me Activities Handout 4.* "Sometimes, we are overwhelmed and need to chill out and take a break. If we have done everything we can to fix a situation and just need to relax or focus on something else, Distraction New-Me Activities are great. It is important that we use distraction when we have used all necessary skills in a situation and we need to wait or relax.

"If we distract ourselves when we need to focus, it could lead us off-track. Sometimes we may want to use Distraction New-Me Activities, like watch TV, rather than facing challenging situations. We have to use Clear Picture and On-Track Thinking to figure out whether a Distraction New-Me Activity is helpful at that time. Using a Distraction New-Me Activity (TV) when a Focus New-Me Activity (video game), On-Track Action, or Problem Solving would work better may not be helpful. At other times, it is best to use a Distraction New-Me Activity until the time is right to use other skills. We decide these things in the moment to make sure we pick the best New-Me Activity for the situation. Let's make a brainstorm list on the board of activities that are useful to distract us."

Content questions.

○ "What are things that help you get your mind off of your problems?"

○ "When is it helpful to distract ourselves?"

○ "When is it not helpful to distract ourselves?"

→*Orienting to New-Me Activities Handout 5 (Fun).* "Fun New-Me Activities are next! Please turn to page 242. The New-Me Activities Handout 5 looks like this."

☼ *Teaching Points for New-Me Activities Handout 5.* "It is important to do activities that are fun. Doing activities that we enjoy helps us have a higher quality of life. If you do not do things that give you joy, you tend to get depressed. Let's create a brainstorm list on the board of activities that people find to be fun using the categories in the handout."

Content questions.

○ "What sports do you like to watch?"

○ "What hobbies do you enjoy?"

○ "What kind of crafts do you like to make?"

Note: It is important that the group discusses realistic options, so that the participants can readily integrate the activities into their lives.

→*Orient to ending Encoding Phase.* "We have come up with many great new ideas today. It's time to practice!"

E-Spiral Phase 3

Elaboration: Linking Previous and New Learning

→*Orient to elaboration activity.* "We are going to do a New-Me Activity right now! Here are some markers and paper. We are going to draw for a few minutes."

Note: The trainer hands out paper and drawing tools.

Instructions for practice exercise. "I know that not everyone is going to love this New-Me Activity. So for those of you who think you can't draw or are embarrassed, we are going to do an On-Track Action and give 100 percent effort to drawing. As we are drawing, we may notice our minds starting to insult our drawings or ourselves; we have to allow those Off-Track Thoughts to pass and gently bring our attention back to our picture. Does this sound similar to how we control our attention when we ring the bell? It does to me! We want to stay focused on our picture, not on Off-Track Thoughts or Feelings. We might want to say nice things to other people about their drawings. What skill is that? Right—Relationship Care! If we say nice things to them, they might say our drawing is good. That might make us feel better! You can draw anything you want for five minutes. If you want to share the picture at the end, great. Sharing our pictures might be stressful, so we may have to do another On-Track Action to make ourselves give 100 percent to this activity. Does everyone have something to draw on and to draw with? Any questions?"

Note: The trainer may want to wait until the end of the activity to make compliments, because certain people may get more positive reinforcement for being a good drawer.

- *Review questions.* "Was this activity a Focus, Feel Good, Distraction, and/or Fun New-Me Activity?" "Did you use Clear Picture and On-Track Thinking while you were drawing?" "How was that activity for people?" "What was helpful about it?" "What was difficult about it?" "Did you have to do an On-Track Action?" "Were you able to jump in 100 percent?"

→*Orient to discussion.* "Great, we are going to talk for a few minutes about doing New-Me Activities."

- *Linking questions.* "In the past, have you ever been bored because you did not do enough New-Me Activities?" "What was that like?" "Have you ever had too many New-Me Activities to do?" "What was that like for you?"
- *Disclosure questions.* "Who can describe a time when you used a New-Me Activity that really helped you feel better?" "Who can describe a time when you had to do an On-Track Action because you didn't feel like doing anything?" "Who can describe a time when you chose the wrong New-Me Activity to do?" "What happened?" "How can you tell when your New-Me Activities are in balance?"
- *Expansion questions.* "What other skills do we use with New-Me Activities?" "How can New-Me Activities help you reach your goals?"

→*Orient to the end of Elaboration Phase.*

"That was a great discussion. Guess what? We are going to practice a New-Me Activity again!"

E-Spiral Phase 3

Elaboration: Linking Previous and New Learning

→*Orient to efficacy activities: game.* "That was a great discussion. Guess what? We are going to practice a New-Me Activity again! Game time!"

Note: The skills trainer presents a game that will be fun for the group. This is an opportunity for the group leader to be creative. The trainer can make up an activity or bring in some kind of game that fits the ability level of the group. The game should be simple, short, and fun. The goal is for all members to participate and to experience joy.

Instructions for efficacy activity. The skills trainer gives clear step-by-step directions. Be sure all participants are ready prior to beginning.

- *Review questions.* "Was this activity a Focus, Feel Good, Distraction, and/or Fun New-Me Activity?" "Did you use Clear Picture and On-Track Thinking while you were playing?" "How was that activity for you?" "Did you have fun?" "Was there anything challenging about it?"

→**Orient to discussion.** "Let's talk a little more about some of the challenges we face when we do New-Me Activities."

- *Barrier questions.* "What is difficult about doing New-Me Activities?" "Is it difficult to ask people to join you?" "How can we deal with that?"
- *Inner-wisdom questions.* "Are New-Me Activities important for you to do?" "Do you need to do more New-Me Activities?"
- *Commitment question.* "What new New-Me Activities will you try?"
- *Coaching question.* "How can you coach yourself to do a different New-Me Activities?"

→**Orienting to home study.** "Great group today. Now it is homework time! This week we are going to practice doing all four kinds of New-Me Activities. We will do at least one Focus New-Me Activity, one Feel Good New-Me Activity, one Distraction New-Me Activity, and one Fun New-Me Activity. Skill Masters will try new New-Me Activities! Any questions?

Also, if you want to study skills at home, review all the handouts we have gone over so far. You can also do New-Me Activities Worksheets 1, 2, 3, and 4."

→**Orient to group ending.** "As you know, we ring the bell six times at the end of group. We do one ring for each of the Clear Picture Do's. It is a chance to notice what is happening inside and outside of us right now. We take a moment to get a Clear Picture as we go back to our activities. Who would like to ring the bell today?"

Week 7: Handouts to Review in Future Cycles or for Home Study

A. New-Me Activities Worksheet 1 (p. 321)
  ☼ *Teaching Points.* The client lists New-Me Activities that help him or her focus attention.

B. New-Me Activities Worksheet 2 (p. 322)
  ☼ *Teaching Points.* The participant writes down New-Me Activities that help the individual's body to feel good.

C. New-Me Activities Worksheet 3 (p. 323)
  ☼ *Teaching Points.* The client lists New-Me Activities that help provide distraction.

D. New-Me Activities Worksheet 4 (p. 324)
  ☼ *Teaching Points.* The individual writes down Fun New-Me Activities that he or she likes to do.

E. New-Me Activities Summary Sheet (p. 325)

Week 8: Problem Solving

Preparing for Group

Handouts Needed

- Skills System Review Sheet (page 179)
- Problem Solving Handout 1 (page 245)
- Problem Solving Worked Example 1 (page 246)
- Problem Solving Worksheet 2 (page 249)
- Problem Solving Worked Example 2 (page 248)
- Problem Solving Worksheet 2 (page 249)
- Problem Solving Worked Example 3 (page 250)
- Problem Solving Practice Exercise (page 252)
- Problem Solving Worksheet 4 (page 253)

E-Spiral Phase 1

Exploring Existing Knowledge Base: Beginning Group

Welcome group. "Welcome back! How is everybody today? Ready to go?"

→*Orient to mindfulness activity; breathing and Rating Emotions.*

Instructions for mindfulness exercise. "Last week we noticed emotions when we rang the bell. This week we are going to notice emotions again, and this time we are going to rate the emotions. When the bell rings, we will bring our attention to an emotion. Then we rate the emotion, rate the feeling using the 0–5 scale. Once we have noticed and rated the emotion, we will turn our attention to another emotion. We will rate that emotion and let it pass as well. If you mind drifts to things in the past or future, bring your mind back to Rating Emotions. It is important to be able to focus your attention on a task. It is also important to be able to notice, rate, and allow emotions to pass like clouds in the sky. Any questions?"

- *Review questions.* "How was that exercise?" "What did you notice about rating your emotions?" "Where did your attention go during this exercise?"

→*Orient to Skills System review.* "If you are ready, could we turn to page 179? The Skills System Review Questions look like this. Would anyone like to read these questions today?"

→*Orient to skills practice.* "Great, let's talk about how our practicing of New-Me Activities went this week?"

- *Review questions.* "Who can tell us about the Focus New-Me Activities they did?" "Who can tell us about the Feel Good New-Me Activities they did?" "Who can tell us about the Distraction New-Me Activities they did?" "Who can tell us about the Fun New-Me Activities they did?"

→*Orient to new skills topic.* "Sounds as if we did a lot of interesting things this week. Would it be okay if you talked a little about what we already know about Problem Solving?"

◙ **Discuss existing knowledge about the new topic.**

- *Assessment question.* "How do we know when we have a problem?"
- *Relevant context questions.* "What are some examples of On-Track Problem Solving?" "What are some examples of Off-Track Problem Solving?"

- *Clarifying questions.* "What happens when people try to do Problem Solving when they are upset?" "How does that usually work out?" "What happens if we do Problem Solving when we are clear and calm?" "How does that usually work out?"

→*Orient to relevant context of new topic.* "Knowing how and when to fix problems is important. Life gives us challenges all the time. If we try to fix problems at the wrong time, we can make things worse. If we don't know how to solve problems, we can also make things worse. The goal of our skills is to make our lives better and to reach our goals."

E-Spiral Phase 2

Encoding: Teaching the New Topic

→*Orient to new learning.* "We are going to learn about Problem Solving today. Problem Solving is Skill 6, and it is a Calm-Only skill. That means that we, and anyone we are talking to, have to be below a 3 emotion when we are solving problems. Problem Solving helps us fix problems, so we can reach our goals. Knowing when and how to fix problems is important."

Instructions for encoding activity. "We are going to review several handouts about Problem Solving. We are only going to look at this skill quickly today, because there is a lot to learn about Problem Solving. It is important to remember that Problem Solving is a Calm-Only skill and can be used *only* when we are at a 0–3 emotion."

→*Orienting to Problem Solving Handout 1.* "We will get started by finding page 245. The Problem Solving Handout 1 looks like this. Did everyone find it?"

☼ *Teaching Points after reading Section a.* "There are three basic steps to Problem Solving. First we get a Clear Picture of the Problem. Second, we Check All Options that we have for fixing the problem. Third, we make Plans A, B, and C for solving the problem. Ready to learn more?"

- *Content question.* "Why do you think Problem Solving is a Calm-Only skill?"

→*Orienting to Problem Solving Worked Example 1.* "Let's turn to page , so we can learn more about getting a Clear Picture of the problems by turning Problem Solving Worked Example 1. It looks like this. Everyone all set?"

☼ *Teaching Points for Problem Solving Worked Example 1.* "There are three steps to do when we get a clear picture of the problem. First, we think about what the problem is. In this situation, the person wants to buy sneakers and there isn't enough money. Second, we have to think about what our goal is. It is important to set the goal so that we can figure out how to get there. In this situation, the person's goal is to get new sneakers today."

→*Orienting to Problem Solving Worksheet 2.* "Great, we know what the problem is. We know what we want, and we know we want to fix the problem. Now we move on to Checking all Options. Turn to page to the Problem Solving Worksheet 2. It looks like this."

Note: Leaders or group reads through the worksheet to explain what pros and cons are. The group then switches to the worked example to get a clearer sense of the material.

☼ *Teaching Points for Problem Solving Worksheet 2.* "When we Check All Options, we find many different ways to solve a problem. For each option, we think of the pros and cons. The pros of an option are helpful results." (Make the thumbs-up gesture.) "The cons of an option are the unhelpful results." (Make the thumbs-down gesture.) "Once we look at several options, we check the fit to choose the best option for us."

Note: Some group members may understand pros and cons quickly. Other participants will comprehend the concepts when the worked example is reviewed.

→**Orienting to Problem Solving Worked Example 2.** "It will help us to go through an example of this. Please turn to page 2480to the Problem Solving Worked Example 2 sheet. It looks like this."

Note: Leaders read through the worked example slowly.

Content questions.

    ○ "Can you think of any other options?"

    ○ "What would be the pros of your ideas?"

    ○ "What would be the cons of your ideas?"

    ○ "Which option do you think is the best?"

☼ *Teaching Points for Problem Solving Worked Example 2.* "Problem Solving takes a lot of thinking and focus. This is why it is a Calm-Only skill. When we are calm, we can think of options, pros, and cons. When we are upset, we rush to solutions that make us feel better in the moment. We don't take time to think clearly. In Fuzzy Mind, we have a hard time focusing on what is good in the long term."

- *Content questions.* "How do we know what is best for ourselves?" "What does it mean for something to fit in the short term but not in the long term?" "What is an example of something that is good in the short term, but not good in the long term for us?"

→**Orienting to Problem Solving Worksheet 3.** "We have gotten a clear picture of the problem and checked all the options. Now we are ready to make Plans A, B, and C. How about we turn to page 251 to the Problem Solving Worksheet 3? It looks like this."

Note: The group reads through the worksheet. The skills trainer uses this worksheet to explain introductory information to the group. Once the group understands the basic concepts, the discussion shifts to the worked example.

☼ *Teaching Points for Problem Solving Worksheet 3.* "Once we figure out what our best option is, we have to make plans. We use Clear Picture and On-Track Thinking to help us make the best plan to fix the problem. We call our favorite idea Plan A. Usually we have to take several steps to fix problems well. We plan who we need to talk to. We plan what we are going to say and how we are going to say it. We focus on doing what works to fix our problem.

"Sometimes we start Plan A, and we find out that our favorite plan will not work. It can be upsetting. So, we come up with a Plan B so that we are prepared for when things go wrong with Plan A. Plan B helps us get part of what we want. It may make sense to even make a Plan C, in case Plan A and Plan B do not work. Plan C is better than nothing.

"It is very important to be on-track when solving problems with people. If we have a Clear Picture and use On-Track Thinking, we can find new solutions that we hadn't even thought of before. If we keep an open mind, we may find a new Plan A! It is important to notice good ideas and to use them. Any questions?"

→**Orienting to Problem Solving Worked Example 3.** "Wonderful! Let's keep moving to see how Mary is going to make plans to get her sneakers. Let's turn to page 250. The Problem Solving Worked Example 3 sheet looks like this."

Note: The skills trainer reads through the worked example with the group.

☼ *Teaching Points for Problem Solving Worked Example 3.* "This person creates a Plan A while realizing that many things can go wrong to keep Plan A from happening. Instead of getting upset about that, Mary makes backup plans so that she is ready for anything. Life is very hard to predict.

Things sometimes work out in our favor and sometimes not. We have to be flexible so that we can bend, rather than break, when life does not go exactly our way. If we are flexible, sometimes we can get part of what we want. Any questions?"

→*Orient to ending Encoding Phase.* "Great, are we ready to practice some Problem Solving?"

E-Spiral Phase 3

Elaboration: Linking Previous and New Learning

→*Orient to elaboration activity.* "We have learned about Getting a Clear Picture of a problem, Checking All Options, and making Plans A, B, and C. Now, how about we practice solving a problem together? Please turn to page 252. The Problem Solving Practice Exercise looks like this."

Instructions for practice exercise. The skills trainer reads the instructions that are on the practice exercise sheet and leads a discussion. It may be helpful to write the exercise on the board so that the group is focused on the activity versus looking at their skills books.

- *Review questions.* "What was that exercise like for you?" "Do you feel as if you understand Problem Solving?"

→*Orient to discussion.* "If it is okay with you, I would like to ask a few questions that will help us understand Problem Solving even better."

- *Linking questions.* "Who can describe a time when you have done On-Track Problem Solving in the past?" "What made it on-track?" "Who can describe a time when they did Off-Track Problem Solving in the past?" "What made it off-track?"
- *Disclosure questions.* "How did On-Track Problem Solving make you feel about yourself and your life?" and "How did Off-Track Problem Solving make you feel about yourself and your life?"
- *Expansion questions.* "What other skills do we use with Problem Solving?" "What do we do if we notice we are doing Off-Track Problem Solving?" "What can you do instead?" "What are some parts of your life where Problem Solving can help you?" "At work?" "At home?" "With family?" "With friends?"

→*Orient to the end of Elaboration Phase.* "Very interesting discussion. Problem solving can be pretty complicated. That is why we must be below a 3 emotion. We need to take time to carefully solve problems. We also may need to talk to our friends, coaches, and therapist to help us think things through. Okay, let's step it up another notch. How about we solve one of our own problems?"

E-Spiral Phase 3

Elaboration: Linking Previous and New Learning

→*Orient to efficacy activities: Problem Solving Worksheet 4.* "We are going to practice solving real problems now. Please turn to page 253. The Problem Solving Worksheet 4 looks like this. Who would like to tell us a problem that the group can use to practice our Problem Solving skills on?"

Instructions for efficacy activity. The trainer leads the group through the steps of Problem Solving using an example provided by a group member. The goal of this exercise is to teach the process of Problem Solving. It may make sense to go through more problems in less detail or do one problem in more detail. There are benefits of both tactics; therapists have to make that decision in the moment. It is helpful to choose a relatively simple problem during early cycles through the curriculum; a more complex situation may elicit more emotion and hence increase cognitive load.

- *Review questions.* "What did you learn about Problem Solving in that exercise?"

→*Orient to discussion.* "We are just about done for today, but first how about we chat for a few minutes about the challenges of Problem Solving?"

- *Barrier questions.* Asking one or more barrier questions can help the group improve Problem Solving abilities: "What is difficult about Problem Solving?" "What do we do when we have the urge to do Problem Solving but we are over a 3 emotion?" "Is it hard to think of different ways to solve a problem?" "Is it difficult to do pros and cons?" "Is it challenging to come up with Plans A, B, and C?" "What happens if we tried Plans A, B, and C and none of them worked like we hoped for?"
- *Inner-wisdom questions.* "Is it important for you to know how to solve problems?"
- *Commitment questions.* "Are you going to use Problem Solving?"
- *Coaching questions.* "How can you coach yourself to use Problem Solving?"

→*Orienting to home study.* "Great group; homework time! This week we are going to practice Problem Solving. We will Get a Clear Picture of problems, Check All Options, and make Plans A, B, and C. Any questions?

"Also, if you want to study skills at home, review all the handouts we have gone over so far. You can also do worksheet 1, 2, 3, and 4 if you would like."

→*Orient to group ending.* "As you know, we ring the bell six times at the end of group. We do one ring for each of the Clear Picture Do's. It is a chance to notice what is happening inside and outside of us right now. We take a moment to get a Clear Picture as we go back to our activities. Who would like to ring the bell today?"

Week 8: Handouts to Review in Future Cycles or for Home Study

A. Completing Problem Solving Worksheet 1 (p. 247)

B. Problem Solving Summary Sheet (p. 244)

Week 9: Expressing Myself

Preparing for Group
Handouts Needed
- Skills System Review Sheet (page 179)
- Expressing Myself Handout 1 (page 255)
- Expressing Myself Handout 2 (page 256)
- Expressing Myself Handout 3 (page 257)
- Expressing Myself Handout 4 (page 258)
- Expressing Myself Handout 5 (page 259)

E-Spiral Phase 1

Exploring Existing Knowledge Base: Beginning Group

Welcome group. "Hi, everyone! How are we doing today? Are we ready to get started? Great, it is time to ring the bell."

→*Orient to mindfulness activity: breathing and Noticing Thoughts.*

"Last week we did a mindfulness activity of noticing and rating our feelings. Today we are going to practice the next Clear Picture Do and Notice our Thoughts. Are we ready?"

Instructions for mindfulness exercise. "Okay, I will ring the bell six times. As I ring it, we will notice the thoughts in our minds. We will notice a thought in our mind and let it go. When you notice a thought, watch it pass like a city bus. We are only going to watch thoughts and not get on any of the buses! We will allow thoughts to pass without thinking more about that thought or taking action. We will let the bus pass by and look for another bus. If our attention drifts from Noticing Thoughts, we will gently bring our minds back to our thoughts. Practicing Noticing Thoughts is helpful. There are many times when we need to watch thoughts and not take actions. Any questions?"

- *Review questions.* "What was it like to watch thoughts?" "Did your mind drift at all?" "Were you able to bring your attention back to Noticing Thoughts and allowing them to pass?"

→*Orient to Skills System review.* "Great job. It is time to review our skills. Please turn to the Skills System Review Questions sheet on page . It looks like this. Who would like to read the questions today?"

→*Orient to skills practice.* "We are really getting good at this! How about we talk about how we did using Problem Solving this week?"

- *Review questions.* "Who would like to share how the Problem Solving went this week?" "Did anyone wish they had used Problem Solving this week?"

→*Orient to new skills topic.* "The skill we are going to learn about today often helps us with Problem Solving, Getting It Right, and Relationship Care. Let's spend a few minutes talking about what we know about Expressing Myself."

◉ **Discuss existing knowledge about the new topic.**

- *Assessment questions.* "What does it mean when someone expresses themselves?" "When do we express ourselves?"

- *Relevant context questions.* "Did you have to express yourself to anyone when you were trying to solve problems this week?" "Are there on-track ways to express ourselves?" "Are there off-track ways to express ourselves?"
- *Clarifying questions.* "What happens to our relationships when we do On-Track Expressing?" "Do we reach our goals?" "What happens when we use Off-Track Expressing?" "Do we reach our goals?"

→ ***Orient to relevant context of new topic.***

"Expressing Myself helps us communicate well with other people. Having clear communication helps us feel better about ourselves, our lives, and relationships. It helps us solve problems, get what we want, and keep our relationships in balance."

E-Spiral Phase 2

Encoding: Teaching the New Topic

→ ***Orient to new learning.*** "We are going to learn what Expressing Myself is, why it is helpful, how we can do it well, and when is best to use it. It is important to remember that Expressing Myself is a Calm-Only skill and can be used *only* when we are at a 0–3 emotion. Are we ready to get started?"

Instructions for encoding activity. "Let's begin by turning to page 255. The Expressing Myself Handout 1 looks like this."

Note: Leaders and the group read through the handout. This is an introductory handout. The next four handouts provide more detailed information for these points.

☼ *Teaching Points for Expressing Myself Handout 1.* "This handout will help us begin to understand more about Expressing Myself. We are going to read through this one and move on to a few others that will explain more details."

→ ***Orienting to Expressing Myself Handout 2 (What is Expressing Myself?).*** "Good start. Let's check out the Expressing Myself Handout 2 on page 256. It teaches us what Expressing Myself is. It looks like this. All set?"

Note: Leaders and/or the group read through the handout.

☼ *Teaching points.* "The general goal of this handout is to teach us that communication brings what is inside of us to the outside of us. Section A highlights different things that are inside of us that we communicate. Section B is about different was we communicate. Section C shows us ways that we communicate through using New-Me Activities."

- *Content questions.* "What do you have inside of yourself that you like to communicate?" "What are different ways that we use body language to communicate to people?" "What do you try to communicate through your artwork or dancing?"

→ ***Orient to Expressing Myself Handout 3 (Why We Use Expressing Myself).*** "Okay, so Expressing Myself is communicating with ourselves and with other people. Let's talk about why Expressing Myself is helpful. How about we turn to page 257? The Expressing Myself Handout 3 looks like this."

Note: The group or leaders reads the handout and fosters a discussion about the material.

☼ *Teaching Points for Expressing Myself Handout 3.* "Expressing Myself is a skill that can help us while we are using our other skills."

- *Content questions.*

Section A: "How can Expressing Myself help when doing a Safety Plan?"

Section B: "How can expressing Myself help when we are doing New-Me Activities?"

Section C: "How can Expressing Myself help us in Problem Solving?"

Section D: "How can Expressing Myself help in Getting It Right?"

Section E: "How can Expressing Myself help us in Relationship Care with ourselves and other people?"

→*Orient to Expressing Myself Handout 4* (**How We Use Expressing Myself**). "We have talked about what Expressing Myself is and why we do it. Now we are going to learn about how to best use Expressing Myself. Please turn to page 258. The Expressing Myself Handout 4 looks like this. Everybody set?"

Note: The group or leaders read the handout to cultivate a discussion about the material.

☼ *Teaching Points for Expressing Myself Handout 4.* "We are going to talk together about the answers to questions about Expressing Myself."

• *Content questions.*

Section A: "How do we know when we need to express ourselves?" (Answer: Clear Picture and On-Track Thinking.) "Why is using words the clearest way of communicating?" "Why is it sometimes difficult to communicate with people using words?"

Section B: "Have you ever tried to be a mind reader?" "How well can we really read other people's minds?" "Does reading other people's minds usually help us feel better or worse?"

Section C: "What problems happen when we just use body language and attitude to communicate?" "Why do you think we use body language instead of words sometimes to communicate?"

Section D: "How does our attitude affect a Two-Way-Street relationship?" "How do you feel when the other person has a negative attitude?" "How do other people respond to you when you have an attitude?" "How do we deal with a situation when someone says something we don't like?"

Section E: "What can happen if we misunderstand someone's point?" "Is it difficult to ask people what they mean if we are not sure?" "What other skill do we use when we are afraid to do something that will help us?" (Answer: On-Track Action.)

→*Orient to Expressing Myself Handout 5* (**When We Use Expressing Myself**). "Great discussion. Okay, last handout for today. Now we are going to learn about when we use Expressing Myself. Can we turn to page 259? The Expressing Myself Handout 5 looks like this."

Note: The group or leaders read the handout and cultivate a discussion about the material.

☼ *Teaching Points for Expressing Myself Handout 5.* "Now we are going to talk about this handout. I will ask you questions, and we will talk about the answers."

• *Content questions.*

Section A: "Why does Expressing Myself work best when we are in Clear Mind?"

Section B: "Why do we have strong urges to use Expressing Myself when we are over a 3 emotion?"

Section C: "What feels good about yelling, demanding, blaming others, and dumping our feelings on other people?" and "What feels bad about it?"

Section D: "How can we affect other people when we use Expressing Myself?"

Section E:"How does using Expressing Myself affect how people treat us?"

Section F: "How do you feel about yourself when you treat other people well?" "How do you feel about yourself when you do not treat people well?"

→***Orient to ending Encoding Phase.*** "Wow, that was a great discussion about Expressing Myself. Are we ready to practice Expressing Myself?"

E-Spiral Phase 3

Elaboration: Linking Previous and New Learning

→***Orient to elaboration activity.*** "Today we are going to do some Expressing Myself. I will ask each of us a few questions that will help us express our individual feelings and thoughts."

Instructions for practice exercise. " If you are over a 3 emotion, you can say 'pass.' If you have difficulty answering the questions, it may be helpful to do an On-Track Action and jump in with both feet, answering the questions rather than avoiding them. I will write the answers on the board. Questions:

"1. What is your favorite food?

"2. Say three words that describe your favorite food.

"3. Please tell us one thing in your life that you really care about.

"4. Please tell us how you feel about that thing.

"5. What is one of your goals?"

- *Review question.* "What was it like to use Expressing Myself?"

→***Orient to discussion.*** "Great, I feel like I know you all a little better! Would it be all right if I asked you a few more questions that will help us understand Expressing Myself better?"

- *Linking questions.* "Who can describe a time in the past when you did On-Track Expressing Myself?" "What made it On-Track Expressing Myself?" "Who can describe a time when they did Off-Track Expressing Myself?" "What made it Off-Track Expressing Myself?"

- *Disclosure questions.* "What happened when you used On-Track Expressing Myself?" "How did it make you feel about yourself and your life?" "What happened when you did Off-Track Expressing Myself?" "How did it make you feel about yourself and your life?"

- *Expansion questions.* "What other skills do we use with Expressing Myself?" "What do you do if you notice you are doing Off-track Expressing Myself?" "What can you do instead?" "What are some parts of your life where Expressing Myself can help you?" "At work?" "At home?" "With family?" "With friends?"

→***Orient to the end of Elaboration Phase.*** "Good discussion. It sounds as if Expressing Myself is an important skill."

E-Spiral Phase 3

Elaboration: Linking Previous and New Learning

→***Orient to efficacy activities: role play.*** "Great, I think we are ready for a role play!"

Instructions for efficacy activity. "The situation is, you are at work. A co-worker comes up to you and begins to get too close to you while you are working. You try to move, but he or she keeps coming too close. How would you use Expressing Myself? I am going to play the role of your co-worker. Any questions? Who would like to go first?"

Note: Skills trainers coach the individual to advocate for himself or herself to the co-worker. Leaders may move away and then return to being too close, so the client has to reiterate the expression in a more assertive way. Trainers can also vary responses to the participants. Generally, it is helpful to have a response that is commensurate with the quality of the participant's skill use. For example, if the client is very effective, leaders respond more quickly. If the participant hesitates and lacks effectiveness, skills trainers do not respond, so the individual has to improve Expressing Myself. (It can be helpful to get the group involved. For example, "Why isn't the co-worker responding?" and "Could the person do anything differently?")

- *Content questions (following each role play).* "Did you notice the person communicating with body language?" "Did the person use words that worked well to communicate?"
- *Review questions.* "How was that role play for you?"

→**Orient to discussion**. "Before we finish up for today, we are going to talk about some of the challenges we face when we use Expressing Myself. Okay?"

- *Barrier question.* "What is difficult about Expressing Myself?"
- *Inner-wisdom question.* "Do you want to learn how to use Expressing Myself?"
- *Commitment question.* "When are you going to use Expressing Myself?"
- *Coaching question.* "How can you coach yourself to use Expressing Myself when you need to?"

→**Orienting to home study.** "Good discussion! Time for homework! This week we are going to practice using Expressing Myself. We are going to practice communicating what we think and feel. Remember, Expressing Myself is a Calm-Only skill, so when can we use it? Right—when *both* people are below a 3 emotion! Good luck!

"Also, if you want to study skills at home, review all the handouts we have gone over so far."

→**Orient to group ending.** "As you know, we ring the bell six times at the end of group. We do one ring for each of the Clear Picture Do's. It is a chance to notice what is happening inside and outside of us right now. We take a moment to get a Clear Picture as we go back to our activities. Who would like to ring the bell today?"

Week 9: System Component Handouts to Review in Future Cycles or for Home Study

A. Expressing Myself Summary Sheet (p. 254)

Week 10: Getting It Right

Preparing for Group
Handouts Needed
- Skills System Review Sheet (page 179)
- Getting It Right Handout 1 (page 261)
- Getting It Right Handout 2 (page 262)
- Getting It Right Handout 3 (page 263)
- Getting It Right Handout 4 (page 264)
- Getting It Right Handout 5 (page 265)

E-Spiral Phase 1

Exploring Existing Knowledge Base: Beginning Group

Welcome group. "Hi, everyone. How are we doing today? Ready to build some skills? Excellent! How about we start with mindfulness?"

→*Orient to mindfulness activity: breathing and Noticing Urges.* "Last week we worked on noticing our thoughts. Today we are going to practice the Clear Picture Do of Noticing my Urges. Okay?"

Instructions for mindfulness exercise. "Great. I will ring the bell six times, and we will bring our attention to noticing any urges we have. An urge is a feeling inside of us that makes us want to do something or to take an action. We will notice the urge and allow it to pass without taking action. If your mind drifts to something other than Noticing Urges, gently bring your mind back to the bell and the urges. It is very important to be able to Notice Urges. We have to be able to experience an urge and not take action until we Check It. Any questions?"

- *Review questions.* "What urges did you notice?" "How did you handle the urge?" "Did your mind drift?" "Were you able to bring your attention back to Noticing Urges?"

→*Orient to Skills System review.* "Handling urges is very important; all of us have urges that make us want to go off-track. Noticing the Off-Track Urges and allowing them to pass is difficult *and* important! Can we go over our Skills System Review Questions on page 179? It looks like this. Who would like to read the questions today?"

→*Orient to skills practice.* "Okay, how about we talk about our skills practice for the week? Who would like to share about using Expressing Myself this week?"

- *Review questions.* "What different ways did you use Expressing Myself?" "When did you use it?" "How did it work out for you?"

→*Orient to new skills topic.* "Great job. Today we are going to talk about getting things that we need from people. Let's talk for a little bit about what we already know about getting people to give us what we need and want."

◉ **Discuss existing knowledge about the new topic.**

- *Assessment questions.* "Has anyone ever asked you for something in an on-track way?" "What happened?" "Has anyone ever asked you for something in an off-track way?" "What happened?"

- *Relevant context questions.* "How does it work when people to want to help us?" "Do people want to help us when we are on-track or off-track?" "Why is that?"
- *Clarifying questions.* "How do we feel when people help us?" "How do we feel when people refuse to help us?"

→**Orient to relevant context of new topic.** "It sounds like Problem Solving, Expressing Myself, and Getting It Right are important skills to help us make our lives happier. Knowing what to say and how to say it really helps us reach our goals. Getting It Right can give us more joy; Getting it Wrong can lead us off-track!"

E-Spiral Phase 2

Encoding: Teaching the New Topic

→**Orient to new learning.** "We are going to learn about Getting It Right today; it is Skill 8 in the Skills System. Ready to get started? Let's turn to page 261. The Getting It Right Handout 1 looks like this. Got it?"

Instructions for encoding activity. The skills trainer reads through the handout. This handout functions as an introduction.

→**Orient to Getting It Right Handout 1.** "Getting It Right is how we get what we want from other people. We will go through five handouts to learn how to Get It Right."

☼ *Teaching Points for Getting It Right Handout 1.* "Getting It Right is a Calm-Only skill. This means that we have to be below a 3 emotion if we are going to use it. We have to remember that the person we are talking to has to be below a 3 emotion, too. So, if we notice that the person is starting to get upset or overly excited, we should step back and get a Clear Picture of the situation. We will want to do On-Track Thinking to decide what to do. We have to be careful because when we want things we can get nervous and impatient. These feelings can make us want to rush. Rushing Getting It Right usually makes it turn out wrong."

→**Orienting to Getting It Right Handout 2.** "Let's start with being in the Right Mind. Please turn to page 262. The Getting It Right Handout 2 looks like this. Everyone find the page?"

Note: The group discusses each of the points about how "Clear Mind Helps Me." The individual must understand that being in the Right Mind is critical to reaching goals.

→**Orienting to Getting It Right Handout 3.** "Okay, let's keep going. Please turn to page 263. The Getting It Right Handout 3 looks like this. We are going to learn about talking to the Right Person now. All set?"

Note: The group or therapists read through this handout. A discussion about who people go to for particular issues is helpful. Support teams can be complex systems; an individual with significant cognitive disabilities may not have a clear understanding of who to talk to about certain issues.

→**Orienting to Getting It Right Handout 4.** "Great! Not only do we have to be in the Right Mind and talk to the Right Person, we have to choose the Right Time and Place. Let's turn to page 264. The Getting It Right Handout 4 looks like this. Ready?"

Note: The group and/or skills trainer reads through this handout. The group discusses the reasoning for each of the points.

→*Orienting to Getting It Right Handout 5.* "Awesome! Now let's learn about using the Right Tone. Please turn to page 265. The Getting It Right Handout 5 looks like this. Did you find it?"

Note: The group and/or trainer reads through this handout. The group discusses the reasoning for the each of the points.

→*Orienting to Getting It Right Handout 6.* "Almost there—one more handout to review. Let's turn to page 266. The Getting It Right Handout 6 looks like this. All set?"

Note: The group and/or trainer reads through this handout. The group discusses the reasoning for each of the points.

→*Orient to ending Encoding Phase.* "Okay, let's learn more about how to Get It Right."

E-Spiral Phase 3

Elaboration: Linking Previous and New Learning

→*Orient to elaboration activity.* "Okay, we are going to practice Getting It Right. Let's turn to the Getting It Right Handout 1 on page 261."

Instructions for practice exercise. "First we have to figure out what we want. Who has something that they need from someone that we can use as an example? Then we will go through each step in the Getting It Right Handout 1 to help plan how to make it happen. Any questions?"

- *Review questions.* "How do we decide what to say to people?" (Answer: Clear Picture and On-Track Thinking.) "How can you keep yourself from rushing and skipping steps?" (Answer: Clear Picture, On-Track Thinking, and On-Track Action.) "Why do you think it is important to use Sugar, Explain, Ask, Listen, and Seal a Deal?" "What happens when we don't?"

→*Orient to discussion.* "Let's talk a little more about getting what we want from people."

- *Linking questions.* "Have you ever gotten something from someone in the past?" "What worked?" "Have you ever used Getting It Wrong and not gotten what you wanted?" "What happened?"
- *Disclosure questions.* "What parts of Getting It Right are you good at?" "What parts of Getting It Right do you need to work on?"
- *Expansion questions.* "What other skills do we use with Getting It Right?" "How can Getting It Right help you in your life?" "What is something that you need or want in the future?" "How are you planning to get it?"

→*Orient to the end of Elaboration Phase.* "It is great when we know how to get what we want; let's practice Getting It Right some more!"

E-Spiral Phase 3

Elaboration: Linking Previous and New Learning

Orient to efficacy activities: role play. "Ready for a role play? We are going to do a role play of a person asking his or her boss for more hours. Any volunteers?"

Instructions for efficacy activity. "You are going to talk to your boss—that will be me—about adding another day to your work schedule. You work two days a week now, and you would like to work three days a week in the future. Are you in the Right Mind? Is this the Right Person?

Is this the Right Time and Place? Think about the tone and words that you will want to use. Remember SEALS: Sugar, Explain, Ask, Listen, and Seal a Deal."

Note: Skills trainers will adjust the boss's responses for each participant. Hitting the "pause" button can give the group a chance to chat about what is happening and to offer feedback. Helping the individual shape behaviors to be effective is the goal.

- *Review questions.* "How was that role play for you?" "What did you learn about Getting It Right?"

→*Orient to discussion.* "Before we head home, let's talk about some of the challenges of using Getting It Right."

- *Barrier questions.* "What is difficult about Getting It Right?" "What do you do if you think you have all the steps right and the person still says no?"
- *Inner-wisdom question.* "Do you think that Getting It Right is important for you?"
- *Commitment question.* "When are you going to try to use Getting It Right?"
- *Coaching question.* "How are you going to coach yourself to use Getting It Right?"

→*Orienting to home study.* "Homework time already! This week we are going to practice Getting It Right. What are the parts of Getting It Right?" (Allow the group to answer.) "That is correct: Right Mind, Right Person, Right Place, Right Time, Right Tone, and Right Words. You remembered that after only one day. Very good!

"Also, if you want to study skills at home, review all the handouts we have gone over so far. You can also do Getting It Right Worksheet 1 on page 267. This is a great worksheet to use if you want to make a good plan to Get It Right."

→*Orient to group ending.* "As you know, we ring the bell six times at the end of group. We do one ring for each of the Clear Picture Do's. It is a chance to notice what is happening inside and outside of us right now. We take a moment to get a Clear Picture as we go back to our activities. Who would like to ring the bell today?"

Week 10: System Component Handouts to Review in Future Cycles or for Home Study

A. Getting It Right Worksheet 1 (p. 267)

☼ *Teaching Points.* This worksheet helps the individual plan ahead to do Getting It right successfully. The client can complete this sheet independently or with support.

B. Getting It Right Summary Sheet (p. 260)

Week 11: Relationship Care

Preparing for Group
Handouts Needed
- Skills System Review Sheet (page 179)
- Relationship Care Handout 1 (page 269)
- Relationship Care Handout 2 (page 270)
- Relationship Care Handout 3 (page 272)
- Relationship Care Handout 4 (page 273)
- Relationship Care Handout 5 (page 274)
- Relationship Care Handout 6 (page 276)
- Relationship Care Handout 7 (page 277)
- Relationship Care Handout 8 (page 279)

E-Spiral Phase 1

Exploring Existing Knowledge Base: Beginning Group

Welcome group. "Welcome, everyone! How are we doing today?"

→*Orient to mindfulness activity: six rings, one for each of the Clear Picture Do's.* "We are going to learn about Skill 9, Relationship Care, today! Are we ready to get started with mindfulness?"

Instructions for mindfulness exercise. "Today we are going to go through all six of the Clear Picture Do's as we listen to the bell. I will say 'Breathe' and ring the bell. We will all take a belly breath. Then I will say 'Body Check,' and I will ring the bell. As the bell rings, we will all do a Body Check. Then I will say 'Notice Surroundings' and ring the bell. We will all notice our surroundings. Next I will say 'Label and Rate Emotions.' I will ring the bell, and we will notice and rate our emotions using the 0–5 scale. Then I will say 'Notice Thoughts,' and I will ring the bell. We will all Notice Thoughts that are in our minds. Last, I will say 'Notice Urges.' I will ring the bell, and we will all Notice Urges. If you feel your mind drifting off, gently bring your mind back to following the directions. This exercise helps us pay attention, shift our focus, and practice Clear Picture. Any questions?"

- *Review questions.* "How was that exercise for you?" "Were you able to follow the instructions?"

→*Orient to Skills System review.* "Ready to review our skills? Let's turn to the Skills System Review Questions on page 179. All set? Who would like to read these today?"

→*Orient to skills practice.* "Okay, time to review our skills practice for the week. We were working on Getting It Right."

- *Review questions.* "Who can tell us about using Getting It Right?" "Did anyone Get It Wrong?"

→*Orient to new skills topic.* "We have to use Relationship Care if we are going to Get It Right with people. Let's take a few minutes to talk about what we know about Relationship Care."

◉ **Discuss existing knowledge about the new topic.**

- *Assessment questions.* "What does the word 'relationship' mean?" "What does the word 'care' mean?" "What does it mean to balance a relationship?"
- *Relevant context questions.* "What do people do to keep relationships in balance, or on-track?" "What are things that make relationships go off-track?"
- *Clarifying questions.* "How does it feel when our relationships are on-track?" "What is it like when our relationships are off-track?"

→*Orient to relevant context of new topic.* When we use our skills—Clear Picture, On-Track Thinking, On-Track Actions, Safety Plans, New-Me Activities, Problem Solving, Expressing Myself, and Getting It Right—we are doing Relationship Care. Skill Masters use skills to help his or her relationships with themselves and other people. Knowing about Relationship Care can help us use all of our other skills as well.

E-Spiral Phase 2

Encoding: Teaching the New Topic

→*Orient to new learning: Relationship Care Handout 1.* The skill called Relationship Care helps us know how to care for the relationships we have with ourselves and other people. Ready to get started? How about we turn to page 269? The Relationship Care Handout 1 looks like this."

Instructions for encoding activity. Note: The skills trainer can decide how best to read through the material in all of the Relationship Care handouts. This handout is an introduction for more detailed handouts.

☼ *Teaching points for Relationship Care Handout 1.* "There are three types of Relationship Care that we are going to learn. First, we will learn about building On-Track Relationships with ourselves and other people. Second, we will learn how to Balance On-Track Relationships by having One-Way and Two-Way Street Relationships. Third, we will learn how to Change Off-Track Relationships. There are times when we need to Repair Relationships, and sometimes we have to end off-track ones."

→*Orienting to Relationship Care Handout 2.*

☼ *Teaching Points for Relationship Care Handout 2.* "We build On-Track Relationships with ourselves as we learn skills that help us become more self-aware. We are able to understand what is happening inside and outside of us. When we start being self-aware, we also learn to accept ourselves. The more we find out about ourselves, other people, and life, the clearer it becomes that life is hard for us all sometimes. We realize that we are as perfect as the next person; we are all perfectly human. We learn to accept that we and everyone else are doing the best we can. As we become self-aware and self-accepting, we begin to value things about ourselves. We realize we have strengths. We start believing in our abilities and our skills. We try new things and meet new people. As we keep practicing skills every day, all day, we begin to trust that we can handle most anything that comes our way. We know how to get a Clear Picture, and we stop and think things through. We learn that deep in our hearts that we will be okay—no matter what. So, as we practice skills and Relationship Care with ourselves, we learn to be self-aware, self-accepting, self-valuing, and self-trusting.

"We also learn how to be aware of, accept, value, and trust other people. We use Clear Picture and On-Track Thinking to decide when a relationship is on-track or off-track. We use Safety Plans to be sure we keep relationships safe. We use On-Track Actions to help us handle Off-Track Urges that can harm relationships. New-Me Activities help people in relationships share experiences. Problem Solving helps people work together to fix problems between them and in the world around them. Expressing Myself helps people know how other people think and feel. All these skills are important parts of having On-Track Relationships. Relationship Care makes us aware of all the things we do to keep our relationships on-track. Any questions?"

→**Orienting to Relationship Care Handout 3.** "There are many different types of relationships. Let's turn to page 272, the Relationship Care Handout 3, to see about some of the different kinds. It looks like this."

Note: The group discusses these options and adds more on a brainstorm list on the board. The goal is to teach participants about how different relationships are and the need to be flexible and adapting in each different situation.

→**Orienting to Relationship Care Handout 4.** "Great, how about we move on to Relationship Care Handout 4? This helps us learn different things we can do to make relationships closer and more distant as we need to. It is on page 273 and it looks like this."

Note: The skills trainer can lead a discussion about the points, emphasizing the need to make decisions in the moment that reflect the person's inner wisdom.

- *Content questions.* "When would be a time when you would want to have a closer relationship with someone and you would use Relationship Care behaviors?"

  "When is a time when you would want to get distance in a relationship.?"

→**Orienting to Relationship Care Handout 5.** "Let's turn to Relationship Care Handout 5. This handout introduces Two-Way-Street and One-Way-Street Relationships. It is on page 274. It looks like this."

☼ *Teaching Points for Relationship Care Handout 5.* "Sometimes we have Two-Way-Street Relationships with people. A Two-Way-Street Relationship is when both people talk and listen to each other, taking turns. There is a balanced give-and-take between both people. Both people care about what the other person is thinking, feeling, and saying. A Two-Way-Street Relationship can help people work together well. It takes two people to maintain a Two-Way-Street Relationship. Even when we work very hard to keep a Two-Way-Street Relationship working, there are times when it gets out of balance. We may have to repair the relationship to fix the problem. When we can feel cared-for in a relationship and are able to give caring back, it can add to the quality of our lives.

"There are times when we try to have a Two-Way-Street Relationship with someone, but it doesn't work out. Then it might be a One-Way-Street Relationship. We may feel we are giving, but we do not feel heard or that the other person is giving back. If the other person is bothering us, we may decide that we do not want to have a Two-Way-Street Relationship, and we stop having an equal give-and-take. It is important to notice when relationships are two-way or one-way streets. We use Clear Picture and On-Track Thinking to make relationship decisions in the moment."

→**Orienting to Relationship Care Handout 6.** "Good points. Okay, there are times when we need to change Off-Track Relationships. Since we have relationships with ourselves and other people, let's begin with learning how we get the relationship with ourselves back on-track when it is off-track. If you are ready, turn to Relationship Care Handout 6 to learn more about how to do this. It is on page 276, and it looks like this."

Note: The leader goes through the three points and has a brief discussion about the relevance of each. Additionally, the group talks about challenges related to making the changes from off-track to on-track.

→**Orienting to Relationship Care Handout 7.** "There are times that even in great relationships, things go off-track. It is important to know how to Repair Relationships with other people. Finding Middle Ground and Steps of Responsibility help us get relationships back on-track. In some cases, we decide to end an Off-Track Relationship. Let's go to Relationship Care Handouts 7 and 8 to learn more about this. These are on pages 277 and 279, and they look like this. Okay, we will start with Handout 7."

☼ *Teaching Points for Relationship Care Handout 7.* "There are times when relationships go off-track because we do something to harm the relationship. At other times, the other person does something to make us feel as if they have hurt the relationship. For example, if you forget to call a friend back, you would be harming the bond. If your friend forgets to call you back, he or she is hurting the relationship. There are times in relationships when communication breaks down and feelings get hurt. It is very common for a relationship to get out of balance to the point where the relationship needs to be changed and/or repaired.

"When we figure out that a relationship is off-track, it may helpful to do some things to make it better. If we notice that we are feeling hurt or angry with someone, we may want to use Finding Middle Ground. This skill helps use take a few moments to communicate with the person. When we Talk It Out with the other person, we let them know how we are feeling; we let them know that the relationship needs some attention or repairing. If we are upset, it is hard not to blame the other person sometimes. This is why we need to use Expressing Myself when we are below a 3 emotion. If we blame people for all of the problems, the relationship may not get better. If we start getting more upset, we may want to take a break from the talk and return to the conversation at a later time, when you are calmer.

"As we Talk It Out, we try to have a Two-Way-Street Relationship, making sure to listen to what the other person is saying about the situation. We try to See Both Sides, which means that we try to understand why the person feels how they do and acts how they act. Usually people's behavior makes sense when we take time to listen to them and understand what they are going through.

"Sometimes as we Talk It Out and See Both Sides, we are able to naturally Work It Out. Even though it can be stressful to repair relationships, it makes both people feel better. Sometimes we feel a little better and have to accept some things we don't like. Other times, we can't work it out, and we need to change or end the relationship. Every situation is different, and that is why we have to do Clear Picture and On-Track Thinking to know what we want in each moment. Completing Relationship Care Worksheet 3 can help teach these concepts."

→**Orienting to Relationship Care Handout 8.** "Okay, let's turn now to Relationship Care Handout 8 on the next page."

☼ *Teaching Points for Relationship Care Handout 8.* "When we have made a mistake that hurts another person, it is helpful to do the Steps of Responsibility. Doing these steps can help us keep self-respect and the respect of other people. First, I admit the problem; I tell the person what I did. I try to explain what I did and how I may have harmed the person. This is really difficult, because I may feel ashamed.

"Next, I apologize for what I did that I am sorry for. I have to think about what exactly I wish I had done differently and what I wish I had not done. Then, I Commit to Changing my behavior in the future. I let the person know that I am going to try not to do it again. I finish doing the Steps of Responsibility and then do an On-Track Action that shows the person that I mean what I am saying. Doing the Steps of Responsibility helps me regain self-trust and trust with other people whom I have harmed. Completing Relationship Care Worksheet 4 can help teach the Steps of Responsibility.

"There are times when relationship ends. Sometimes we end relationship, and other times, other people end the relationship. Relationships naturally change and end. People move in different directions and to different locations or people die. We have to use all of our skills to manage the situation when people leave us before we are ready. It is important to get skills coaching in situations when we feel overwhelmed with sadness and hurt.

"Sometimes, we choose to end relationships. If a relationship is off-track and we can't fix it, we may want to end it. We might tell the person we are moving on, or we may just stop paying attention to the relationship so that it just drifts apart. We have to use Clear Picture to know how we feel about our relationships and On-Track Thinking to make sure we do what fits for us. Problem Solving can help us figure out how to fix relationship problems. We are taking good care of ourselves when we keep our relationships in balance and change Off-Track Relationships."

→*Orient to ending Encoding Phase.* "Relationships are complicated! We have to use all of our skills to be able to do Relationship Care. We are going to talk more about different relationships so that we can learn how to handle all the different, changing relationships in our lives."

E-Spiral Phase 3

Elaboration: Linking Previous and New Learning

→*Orient to elaboration activity.* "We are going to learn more about different types of relationships. We are going to make a brainstorm list on the board."

Instructions for practice exercise. "We have all kinds of relationships in our lives. We are going to make a list of all the different relationships that we can think of. For example, I have a relationship with my doctor. I also have a relationship with my stylist. Are those relationships different? Are they Two-Way-Street or One-Way-Street Relationships? When we think we have all of the relationships on the board, we are going to talk about how we care for these relationships. Any questions? Who can think of a relationship that you have?"

- *Review question.* "What did we learn from this exercise?"

→*Orient to discussion.* "Let's talk a little more about how we have used Relationship Care in the past, okay?"

- *Linking questions.* "Can anyone describe a time in the past when you used On-Track Relationship Care with yourself?" "With another person?" "Who can describe one time in the past when you used Off-Track Relationship Care with yourself?" "Another person?"

- *Disclosure questions.* "How do you feel about the time you used On-Track Relationship Care?" "Do you wish you had done things differently?" "How do you feel about the time you used Off-Track Relationship Care?'" "Do you wish you had done things differently?"

- *Expansion questions.* "How do you think Relationship Care could help your relationship with yourself?" "How do you think Relationship Care can help your relationships with other people?"

→*Orient to the end of Elaboration Phase.* "Are we ready to practice Relationship Care? Let's get started!"

E-Spiral Phase 3

Elaboration: Linking Previous and New Learning

→*Orient to efficacy activities: role play.* "Role play time! The situation is that your individual therapist is always ten minutes late for therapy. Let's figure out how you can use your skills to get this relationship back in balance. Any volunteers?"

Instructions for efficacy activity. "You have been seeing your individual therapist, who will be played by me, for two years. I am always on the phone at 10:00 a.m. when you come in to see me. Sometimes we get started fifteen minutes late! It is your job to talk to the group about how to do Relationship Care in this situation. Is this relationship in balance? Some people may not care that the therapist is late; some people may like a shorter therapy time. Every person and situation is different. If you feel the relationship is off-track, what do you need to do to keep this relationship in balance? What skills do you need to use to handle this situation? If you decide to talk to the individual therapist about this problem, I am here. Any questions? Good luck!"

- *Content questions.* "Do you think that the relationship is off-track or in balance?" "Do you think this relationship needs changing?" "Could you try Finding Middle Ground?" "Can you make the therapist do the Steps of Responsibility?" "Do you need to end this relationship?
- *Review questions.* "What was that exercise like for you?" "What did you learn about Relationship Care?"

→*Orient to discussion.* "Before we finish for this week, I would like to ask a few more questions about some of the challenges in using Relationship Care."

- *Barrier questions.* "What is difficult about doing Relationship Care with yourself?" "What is difficult about doing Relationship Care with other people?"
- *Inner-wisdom questions.* "Is it important for you to do Relationship Care with yourself?" "With other people?"
- *Commitment questions.* "What Relationship Care will you do with yourself?" "What Relationship Care will you do with other people?"
- *Coaching questions.* "How can you coach yourself to do Relationship Care with yourself?" and "How can you coach yourself to do Relationship Care with other people?"

→*Orienting to home study.* "This week we are going to practice using Relationship Care with ourselves and other people. Does that sound good? Also, if you want to study skills at home, review all the handouts we have gone over so far. You can also do Worksheets 1–5."

→*Orient to group ending.* "As you know, we ring the bell six times at the end of group. We do one ring for each of the Clear Picture Do's. It is a chance to notice what is happening inside and outside of us right now. We take a moment to get a Clear Picture as we go back to our activities. Who would like to ring the bell today?"

Week 11: Handouts to Review in Future Cycles or for Home Study

A–E. Relationship Care Worksheets 1–4 (p. 271, 275, 278, and 281)

☼ *Teaching Points.* The individual completes the worksheets in group, at home, with therapists, or with staff. The goal is for the individual to expand awareness related to their relationship with themselves and with other people.

F. Relationship Care Summary Sheet (p. 268)

Week 12: Skills Review

Preparing for Group
Handouts Needed
- Skills System Review Sheet (page 179)
- Skills System Skill Master certificate (page 307)

E-Spiral Phase 1

Exploring Existing Knowledge Base: Beginning Group

Welcome group. "Hello, everyone! We have made it to Week 12! How are you all doing today? Ready for the ringing of the bell?"

→*Orient to mindfulness activity: passing the bell and getting a Clear Picture.* "We have to be able to get a Clear Picture in stressful situations, so we can use the rest of our skills. So, during this exercise, I am going to ask you to do more and continue to stay focused. Skill Masters stay focused even in a crisis."

Instructions for mindfulness exercise. "We are going to make things a little harder! We will choose six people to ring the bell and to say one of the Clear Picture Do's. The first person will say 'Breathe' and then ring the bell. When the sound has finished, we will pass it to the next person. That person will say 'Notice Surroundings' and ring the bell. When the sound is gone, the bell is passed. The next person says 'Do a Body Check' and rings the bell. When the bell sound is finished, he or she passes the bell. That person says 'Label and Rate Emotions' and rings the bell. When the sound is gone, the next person gets the bell. That person says 'Notice Thoughts' and rings the bell. When the sound of the bell has disappeared, the bell is passed to the last person. That person says 'Notice Urges' and rings the bell. While all this is happening, we focus on doing the Clear Picture Do that being said at that moment. If you get lost or your mind begins to drift, gently bring your mind back to the bell and the instructions we are being given. Any questions?"

- *Review questions.* "How did that exercise go for you?" "Were you able to stay focused?" "Were you able to bring your mind back?"

→*Orient to Skills System review.* "Ready to review our skills? Let's turn to the Skills System Review Questions on page 179. All set? Who would like to read these today?"

→*Orient to skills practice.*

"Great! Would it be okay if we did our skills review? Let's turn to page 179. The Skills System Review Questions look like this. Who would like to read today?"

→*Orient to skills practice.*

"We are doing really well learning our skills! Okay, it is time to go over our skills practice. Our homework this week was to practice Relationship Care. Who would like to start?"

- *Review questions.* "Who can share about Relationship Care that you did with yourself?" "Who can tell us about Relationship Care that he or she did with other people?"

→*Orient to new skills topic.* "Good job. Today is a review of all of our skills. We are going to talk for a few minutes about how you are doing learning your skills. Okay?"

◎ **Discuss existing knowledge about the new topic.**

- *Assessment questions.* "Which skills do you use the most?" "Which skills do you need more practice with?" Note: Writing the answers on the board may be helpful.
- *Relevant context questions.* "What is easy about learning skills?" "What is hard about learning skills?"
- *Clarifying questions.* "How is life different when people use skills?" "How is life when we don't use skills?"

→*Orient to relevant context of new topic.* "It is hard to remember all of our skills, especially when we are upset. We have to practice our skills a lot to learn them. As we get to know our skills better, we will learn how to put them together to handle tough life situations."

E-Spiral Phase 2

Encoding: Teaching the New Topic

→*Orient to new learning.* "Today we are going to fill out Skills System Skills Quiz 1, on page 285. I know we don't love quizzes. This will help us find out which skills we understand and which ones we need more help with. We will pass in the quizzes and go over the answers when we get done. I brought in sodas and cookies today to celebrate us finishing our twelve weeks. I am very proud of you all. Are we ready to get started?"

Instructions for encoding activity. "If you have a hard time reading and writing, either I or your staff can help you. Let's take a few minutes to make a plan about how we can fill out this sheet. If you do not know the answer, you can guess or leave it blank. The good news is that when you hand in your quiz, you can take a soda and your cookies. Any questions?" (The answers are provided on page 286.)

→*Orient to ending Encoding Phase.* "Great job! I think I saw a lot of people doing On-Track Actions here today."

E-Spiral Phase 3

Elaboration: Linking Previous and New Learning

Orient to elaboration activity. "Okay, let's go over the quiz together."

Instructions for practice exercise. "I will ask the group the questions, and let's come up with the right answers together."

- *Review questions.* "How do you think you did on the quiz?" "How do you think you are doing learning your skills?"

→*Orient to discussion.* "We are going to talk a little more about how we are doing learning skills?"

- *Linking question.* "Has it been hard for you to learn to control yourself in the past?"
- *Disclosure question.* "What are you doing now that works?" "What are you doing that does not work as well?"
- *Expansion question.* "What do you need to do to make skills work better for you?"

→*Orient to the end of Elaboration Phase.* "Great awareness. How about we talk more about how we use our skills together to handle tough situations?"

E-Spiral Phase 3

Elaboration: Linking Previous and New Learning

→*Orient to efficacy activities: skills review activity.* "Let's talk together about the situations in our lives that are really hard to deal with. We can work together to see how our skills can help us in those situations."

Instructions for efficacy activity. "We are going to begin by listing difficult situations that you have faced in the last few months. We are going to make a list of these stressful situations on the board. Then we are going to look at making a skill plan for each of the situations. When we make a skill plan today, we are going to use the number of the skill to show what the plan is. For example, if the situation is one where we think there is risk, we might use 1. Clear Picture, 2. On-Track Thinking, 3. On-Track Action, 4. Safety Plan, and 5. New-Me Activity. So, that skill cluster is a 1-2-3-4-5. If we were bored and wanted to go watch TV, the skill would be a 1-2-5. A 1-2-5 is when we use Clear Picture, On-Track Thinking, and New-Me Activity together. Skill Masters sometimes use all of their skills in certain situations; that would be a 1-2-3-4-5-6-7-8-9. Usually the bigger the number, the more successful we are at reaching our goals. Any questions?"

- *Review questions.* "How was it using the numbers to label skill clusters?" "Did it help you understand it better, or was it more confusing?"

→*Orient to discussion.* "Before we end for the day, let's talk about some of the challenges that we face when we are learning skills. Okay?"

- *Barrier question.* "What is difficult about learning skills?"
- *Inner-wisdom question.* "Do you think it is important for you to learn skills?" "Why?"
- *Commitment question.* "What are you going to do to keep practicing skills?"
- *Coaching question.* "How can you coach yourself to practice your skills?"

→*Orienting to home study.* "This group has done an amazing job. I would like to hand out your certificates now." (The template for the certificate is on page 287). "I will announce your name and the number of cycles you have completed in the Skills System. This is like getting different belts in karate. The more cycles we get, the stronger Skills Masters we become. Fantastic, I am so happy that you are all here and have worked so hard. It is our favorite part: homework! Please practice putting your skills together in skills clusters this week. If you want to study skills at home, review all the handouts we have gone over so far. You can also do any worksheet that you have not completed yet. Thank you all!"

→*Orient to group ending.* "As you know, we ring the bell six times at the end of group. We do one ring for each of the Clear Picture Do's. It is a chance to notice what is happening inside and outside of us right now. We take a moment to get a Clear Picture as we go back to our activities. Who would like to ring the bell today?"

Week 12: System Component Handouts to Review in Future Cycles or for Home Study

A. Skills System Review Questions (p. 179)

B. Skills System Quiz 1 (p. 285)

C. Skills System: Quiz Worked Example (p. 286)

D. Skills Master Certificate of Completion (p. 287)

Subsequent Cycles Through the Skills System Curriculum

Once the group completes a twelve-week cycle through the skills curriculum, the participant has a much better understanding of the skills concepts. For example, the group will have done twelve different mindfulness activities. During each group session, prior learning is reviewed, new learning is introduced, and new learning is linked to all the previous skills that were addressed. Due to the variable strengths of participants, each group member will have integrated different amounts of information.

The skills trainers juggle many things at the same time. Trainers have to teach the group while individualizing interventions for the diverse levels of skills integration and cognitive abilities of each group member. Although certain group members may be able to generalize all nine skills, others may struggle to remember even three names of the skills. Skills trainers must make group an effective learning experience for each participant or find an alternative group for a client who is significantly ahead or behind the rest of the group.

Throughout each cycle of the group, there are opportunities to return to fundamental Skills System concepts and basic commitment to learning and utilizing skills. In general, teaching progresses in the following ways through multiple cycles of the Skills System curriculum:

- Teaching moves from being more general to more specific. For example, as the individual learns about breathing, he or she learns to focus awareness specifically on the nose or belly.

- Teaching integrates more detailed information as the knowledge base increases. For example, as the person understands On-Track Thinking, more of the steps of On-Track Thinking are integrated into the individual's behavior. Initially the person may take a second to think about a decision, while after repetition the client may Stop, Step Back, and Think about what he or she wants, Check It, Turn It, make a skill plan, and use cheerleading.

- Exercises become more realistic to replicate real-life forces in the participant's environment. For example, skills trainers may create distractions during a mindfulness breathing exercise so that the group must master focusing attention while experiencing interfering forces.

- The individual becomes more able to share helpful personal awareness and information related to skills discussions. For example, initially the participant may be hesitant to disclose that he has ever had difficulties related to overwhelming thoughts or emotions. As the individual gains competency managing emotions, he reduces emotional vulnerabilities and increases abilities to participate fully.

- Discussions become increasingly dialectical as group progresses through the curriculum. During preliminary cycles through the curriculum, the group focuses heavily on integrating concrete skill information. As a group develops a skills knowledge base, discussions become more lively and expansive. As capacities increase, alternative views are encouraged and managed in group.

- Discussions related to barriers for skills use become increasingly personal and detailed. As skills trainers become familiar with each participant and group members get to know each other, barriers to integrating skills are clearer. For example, initially the leader may not know that the participant lives with an abusive housemate. Throughout the group experience, individual challenges become evident. It is crucial that group leaders understand the forces that impede generalization of skills in each participant's life. Skills trainers coach participants to manage challenging situations throughout the cycles of the Skills System curriculum.

Skills System group members learn crucial information from both the teaching and social aspects of the curriculum. The participant cycles through the program, building skills that enhance self-awareness, self-acceptance, self-value, and self-trust. As these factors increase, the individual improves her ability to effectively manage relationships. The Skills System helps the individual to skillfully navigate the human experience. A participant gains mastery that allows her to create a fulfilling life that includes freedom and joy.

REFERENCES

American Psychiatric Association. (2000). Diagnostic and statistical manual of mental disorders: DSM-IV-TR. Arlington, VA.

Alloway, T. P. (2010), Working memory and executive function profiles of individuals with borderline intellectual functioning. *Journal of Intellectual Disability Research, 54,* 448–456.

Belmont, J. M., & Butterfield, E. C. (1977). The instructional approach to developmental cognitive research. In R. Kail & Hagen (Eds.), *Perspectives on the development of memory and cognition* (pp. 437–481). Hillsdale, NJ: Erlbaum.

Benson, B. A., Rice, C. J., & Miranti, S. V. (1986). Effects of anger management training with mentally retarded adults in group treatment. *Journal of Counseling and Clinical Psychology, 54,* 728–729.

Carlin, M. T., Soraci, S. A., Dennis, N. A., Chechile, N. A., & Loiselle, R. C. (2001). Enhancing free recall rates of individuals with mental retardation. *America Journal on Mental Retardation, 106,* 314–326.

Crocker, A.G., Mercier, C., Allaire, J. F., & Roy, M. E. (2007). Profiles and correlates of aggressive behaviour among adults with intellectual disabilities. *Journal of Intellectual Disabilities, 51*(10), 786–801.

Cromwell, J. A. (1997). *Academic, Research and Clinical Summary.* University of Surrey.

Dagnon, D., & Sandhu, S. (1999). Social comparison, self-esteem and depression in people with intellectual disability. *Journal of Intellectual Disability Research, 43*(5), 372–379.

Danielsson, H. , Henry, L. , Ronnberg, J., and Nilsson, L. (2010) Executive functions in individuals with intellectual disability. *Research in Developmental Disabilities: A Multidisciplinary Journal,* 31, (6), 1299-1304.

Esbensen, A. J., Seltzer, M. M., & Krauss, M. W. (2008). Stability and change in health, functional ability, and behavior problems among adults with and without Down syndrome. *American Journal on Mental Retardation, 113*(4), 263–277.

Expert Consensus Guidelines [Special Issue]: Treatment of Psychiatric and Behavioral Problems in Mental Retardation. (2000). *American Journal of Mental Retardation, 105*(3).

Gilson, S. F., & Levitas, A. S. (1987). Psychosocial crisis in the lives of retarded people. *Psychiatric Aspects of Mental Retardation Reviews, 6*(6).

Gold, M. W. (1972). Stimulus factors in skills training of retarded adolescents on a complex assembly task: acquisition, transfer, and retention. *American Journal on Mental Retardation, 76*(5), 517–526.

Greenspan, S. I., & Lourie, R. S. (1981). Developmental structuralist approach to the classification of adaptive and pathological personality organizations: Application to infancy and early childhood. *American Journal of Psychiatry, 138*(6).

Greenspan, S. I. (2009). *Overcoming Anxiety, Depression, and Other Mental Health Disorders in Children and Adults: A New Roadmap for Families and Professionals*. Bethesda, Maryland: Interdisciplinary Council on Developmental and Learning Disorders.

Gross, J. J., & Thompson, R. A. (2007). Emotion regulation: Conceptual foundations. In Gross, J. J. (Ed.), *Handbook of emotion regulation* (pp. 3–27). New York: The Guilford Press.

Hemmings, C. P., Tsakanikos, E., Underwood, L., Holt, G., & Bouras, N. (2008). Clinical predictors of severe behavioral problems in people with intellectual disabilities referred to a specialist mental health service. *Social Psychiatry and Psychiatric Epidemiology, 43*(10), 824–830.

Henry, L. A., and MacLean, M. (2002). Working memory performance in children with and without intellectual disabilities. *American Journal on Mental Retardation*, 107, (6), 421-432.

Jahromi, L.B., Gulsrud, A., & Kasari, C. (2008). Emotional competence in children with Down Syndrome: Negativity and regulation. *American Journal on Mental Retardation, 113*(1), 32–43.

Janssen, C. G. C., Schuengel, C., & Stolk, J. (2002). Understanding challenging behavior in people with severe and profound intellectually disability: A stress-attachment model. *Journal of Intellectual Disability Research, 46*(6), 445–453.

Jarrold, C., Baddeley, A.D., and Hewes, A. K. (2000). Verbal short-term memory deficits in Down syndrome: A Consequence of problems in rehearsal? *Journal of Child Psychology and Psychiatry*, 41, 233-244.

Jorm, A. F. (1983). Specific reading retardation and working memory: A review. *British Journal of Psychology, 74*, 311–342.

Koons, C. R., Robins, C. J., Tweed, J. L., Lynch, T. R., Gonzalez, A. M., Morse, J. Q., Bishop, G. K., Butterfield, M. I., & Bastian, L. A. (2001). Efficacy of dialectical behavior therapy in women veterans with borderline personality disorder. *Behavior Therapy, 32*(2), 371–390.

Lew, M., Matta, C., Tripp-Tebo, C., & Watts, D. (2006). DBT for individuals with intellectual disabilities: A program description. *Mental Health Aspects of Developmental Disabilities.*

Lewis, J. J. (2009) Bernice Johnson Reagon Quotes. About Women's History. Retrieved May 1, 2009, from http://womenshistory.about.com/od/quotes/a/reagon_quotes.htm

Lindsey, W. R., (2005). Model underpinning treatment for sex offenders with mild intellectual disability: Current theories of sex offending. *American Association on Mental Retardation, 43*, 428–441.

Linehan, M. M. (1993). *Cognitive behavioral treatment for borderline personality disorder.* New York: The Guilford Press.

Linehan, M. M. (1993b). *Skills training manual for treating borderline personality disorder.* New York: The Guilford Press.

Linehan, M. M., Tutek, D. A., Heard, H. L., & Armstrong, H. E. (1994). Interpersonal outcome of cognitive behavioral treatment for chronically suicidal borderline patients. *American Journal of Psychiatry, 151,* 1771–1776.

Linehan, M. M., Schmidt, H., Dimeff, L. A., Craft, J. C., Kanter, J., & Comtois, K. A. (1999). Dialectical behavior therapy for patients with borderline personality disorder and drug-dependence. *American Journal on Addiction, 8*(4), 279–292.

Linehan, M. M., Dimeff, L. A., Reynolds, S. K., Comtois, K. A., Welch, S. S., Heagerty, P., & Kivlahan, D. R. (2002). Dialectical behavior therapy versus comprehensive validation plus 12-step for the treatment of opioid dependent women meeting criteria for borderline personality disorder. *Drug and Alcohol Dependence, 67*(1), 13–26.

Lynch, T. R., Morse, J. Q., Mendelson, T., & Robins, C. J. (2003). Dialectical behavior therapy for depressed older adults: A randomized pilot study. *American Journal of Geriatric Psychiatry, 11*(1), 33–45.

Mastropieri, M. A., Sweda, J., & Scruggs, T. E. (2000). Putting mnemonic strategies to work in an inclusive classroom. *Learning Disabilities Research & Practice, 15(2),* 69–74.

Matson, J. L. (1984). Social learning approaches to the treatment of emotional problems. In R. Fletcher & F. Menolascino (Eds.), *Mental retardation and mental illness.* Lexington, MA: Lexington.

McClure, K. S., Halpern, J., Wolper, P. A., & Donahue, J. J. (2009). Emotion regulation and intellectual disability. *Journal on Developmental Disabilities, 15,* 38–44.

Merrill, E. C. (1992). Attentional resource demands of stimulus encoding for persons with and without mental retardation. *American Journal on Mental Retardation, 97*(1), 87–98.

Moore, D. G. (2001). Reassessing emotion recognition performance in people with mental retardation: A review. *American Journal on Mental Retardation, 106,* 481–502.

Najjar, L. J. (1996). The effects of multimedia and elaborative encoding on learning. Georgia Institute of Technology.

Nezu, C. M., Nezu, A. M., & Arean, P. (1991). Assertiveness and problem-solving training for mildly mentally retarded persons with dual diagnoses. *Research in Developmental Disabilities, 12,* 371–386.

Nezu, C. M., Nezu, A. M., & Gill-Weiss, M. J. (1992). *Psychopathology of persons with mental retardation: clinical guidelines for assessment and treatment.* Champaign, IL: Research Press.

Nigro, G. N., & Roak, R. M. (1987). Mentally retarded and non-retarded adults memory for spatial location. *American Journal of Mental Deficiency, 91(4),* 392–397.

Petre-Miller, D., Haaven, J., & Little, R. (1989). *Treating intellectually disabled sex offenders.* Burlington, VT: Safer Society Press.

Reiss, S., & Szyszko, J. (1983). Diagnostic overshadowing and professional experience with mentally retarded persons. *America Journal of Mental Deficiency, 87,* 396–402.

Reiss, S., & Rojahn, J. (1993). Joint occurrence of depression and aggression in children and adults with mental retardation. *Journal of Intellectual Disability Research, 37,* 287–294.

Ross, D. M., & Ross, S. A. (1973). Cognitive training for the EMR child: situational problem solving and planning. *American Journal of Mental Deficiency, 78(1),* 20–26.

Rowitz, L. (1981). A sociological perspective on labeling in mental retardation. *Mental Retardation, 19,* 47–51.

Rowitz, L. (1988). The forgotten ones: Adolescents and mental retardation. *Mental Retardation, 6,* 115–117.

Safer, D. L., Telch, C. F., & Agras, W. S. (2001). Dialectical behavior therapy for bulimia nervosa. *American Journal of Psychiatry, 158*(4), 632–634.

Sakdalan, A., & Collier, V. (2009) Conference presentation/PowerPoint presentation. "Staying in the here-and-now," a pilot study on the use of dialectical behavior therapy group skills training with intellectually disabled offenders. *Australasian Society for the Study of Intellectual Disabilities.*

Scott, P. H., Asoko, H. M., & Driver, R. H. (1991) Teaching for conceptual change: A review of strategies. University of Leeds, UK: Children's Learning in Science Research Group.

Spivack, G., & Shure, M. (1980). The cognition of social adjustment. *Advances in Child Clinical Psychology, 5,* 323–373.

Streech-Fischer, A., & Van der Kolk, B. (2000). Down will come baby, cradle and all: Diagnostic and therapeutic implications of chronic trauma on child development. *Australian and New Zealand Journal of Psychiatry, 34,* 903–918.

Sullivan, P. M., & Knutson, J. F. (2000). Maltreatment and disabilities: A population-based epidemiology study. *Child Abuse & Neglect, 24(10),* 1257–1273.

Sweller, J. (1988). Cognitive load during problem solving: Effects on learning. *Cognitive Science, 12,* 257–285.

Sweller, J. (1989). Cognitive technology: Some procedures for facilitating learning and problem solving in mathematics and science. *Journal of Educational Psychology, 81(4),* 457–466.

Telch, C. F., Agras, W. S., & Linehan, M. M. (2001). Dialectical behavior therapy for binge eating disorder. *Journal of Consulting and Clinical Psychology, 69(6),* 1061–1065.

Tomasulo, D. (2005). The interactive-behavioral model of group counseling for people with mental retardation and chronic psychiatric illness. The National Association for the Dually Diagnosed.

Tyrer, F., McGrother, C. W., Thorp, C. F., Donaldson, M., Bhaumik, S., Watson, J. M., & Hollin, C. (2006). Physical aggression towards others in adults with learning disabilities: Prevalence and associated factors, *Journal of Disabilities Research, 50,* 295–304.

Ueker, A., & Nadel, L. (1998). Spatial but not object memory impairments in children with fetal alcohol syndrome. *American Journal on Mental Retardation, 103(1),* 12–18.

van den Bosch, L. M. C., Verheul, R., Schippers, G. M., & van den Brink, W. (2002). Dialectical Behavior Therapy of borderline patients with and without substance use problems: Implementation and long-term effects. *Addictive Behaviors, 27(6),* 911–923.

Van der Molen, M. J., Van Luit, J. E. H., Jongmans, M. J. and Van der Molen, M. W. (2007). Verbal working memory in children with mild intellectual disabilities. *Journal of Intellectual Disability Research, 51,* 162–169.

Verheul, R., van den Bosch, L. M. C., Koeter, M. W. J., de Ridder, M. A. J., Stijnen, T., & van den Brink, W. (2003). Dialectical behaviour therapy for women with borderline personality disorder: 12-month, randomized clinical trial in the Netherlands. *British Journal of Psychiatry, 182,* 135–140.

Vicari, S., Carlesimo, A., & Caltagirone, C. (1995). Short-term memory in persons with intellectual disabilities and Down's syndrome. *Journal of Intellectual Disabilities, 39*(6), 532–537.

Wehmeyer, M. L. & Metzler, C. A. (1995). How self-determined are people with mental retardation? The national consumer survey. *Mental Retardation, 33*(2), 111–119.

Willner, P., Jones, J., Tams, R., & Green, G. (2002). A randomised controlled trial of the efficacy of a cognitive-behavioural anger management group for adults with learning disabilities. *Journal of Applied Research in Intellectual Disabilities, 15*, 224–235.

Wilson, B.J. (1999). Entry behavior and emotion regulation abilities of developmentally delayed boys. *Developmental Psychology, 35*, 214–222.

Whitman, T. L. (1990). Self-regulation and mental retardation. *American Journal on Mental Retardation, 94*(4), 347–362.

APPENDIX A

The Skills List

1. Clear Picture

2. On-Track Thinking

3. On-Track Action

4. Safety Plan

5. New-Me Activities

6. *Problem Solving*

7. *Expressing Myself*

8. *Getting It Right*

9. *Relationship Care*

The Skills System- Handout 2
How Our Skills Help Us

There are NINE Skills in the Skills System.
Here is a list of the nine skills and how they help us.

All-the-Time Skills

 1. **Clear Picture:** Clear Picture helps me notice what is happening inside and outside of me *right now*.

 2. **On-Track Thinking**: On-Track Thinking helps me think things through to do what works to reach my goals.

 3. **On-Track Action**: Once I get a Clear Picture and have On-Track Thinking, I take an On-Track Action to do something positive to move towards my goals.

 4. **Safety Plan**: I use a Safety Plan to handle risky situations that come my way.

 5. **New-Me Activities**: I do New-Me Activities to help me focus my attention, distract me, make me feel better, and to have fun.

Calm Only Skills

 6. *Problem Solving*: Problem Solving helps me fix situations in my life, so that I can be happier and reach my goals.

 7. *Expressing Myself*: Expressing Myself helps me to share what is inside of me with people and the world around me.

 8. *Getting It Right*: Getting It Right helps me work with people to get what I want.

 9. *Relationship Care*: Relationship Care helps me understand how to have on-track relationships with myself and others.

159

The Skills System- Worksheet 1

Name: _____ **Date:**_____

Please fill in the Skills List and Categories of Skills

1. _____

2. _____

3. _____

4. Safety Plan _____

5. _____

_____

_____

0-1-2-3-4-5

6. _____

7. _____

8. _____

9. _____

_____

_____

0-1-2-3

160

The Skills System- Worksheet 2

Name: _____ **Date:** _____

Please fill in the Skills List and Categories of Skills

1. _____

2. _____

3. _____

4. _____

5. _____

⎫ _____

⎬ _____

⎭ **0-1-2-3-4-5**

6. _____

7. _____

8. _____

9. _____

⎫ _____

⎬ _____

⎭ **0-1-2-3**

161

The Skills System- Handout 3

How I Use the Skills System

a.

FEELINGS RATING SCALE

0-1-2-3-4-5

The Feelings Rating Scale is a 0-1-2-3-4-5 scale
I use to rate how strong my feelings are. The Feelings
Rating Scale helps me know what skills and
how many skills I need to use in a situation.

b.

Categories of Skills

**All-the-Time
0-5 Emotion**

**Calm Only
0- 3 Emotion**

There are two Categories of Skills: All-the-Time skills and
Calm Only skills. I can use All-the-Time skills at any level
of emotion: 0-1-2-3-4-5. I can only use Calm Only skills
when I am at a 0-1-2-3 emotion.

c.

Recipe for Skills

The Recipe for Skills helps me know how many skills I
need to use in a situation. The Recipe tells me to add 1
skill for every level of emotion. So, if I am at a 3 sad, I
need to use 4 skills.

Overwhelming Feeling:

Harming myself, others, or property **5**

4 Strong Feeling

FEELINGS RATING SCALE

3 Medium Feeling

2 Small Feeling

1 Tiny Feeling

0 No Feeling

163

Feelings Rating Scale- Handout 2
Helps me know which skill I should use next
AND how many skills I need to use

0 – 1 – 2 – 3 – 4 - 5

| None | Tiny | Small | Medium | Strong | Out-of-Control |

Rating # of the Emotion	Using the Skills System
0	A 0 emotion means that I am not feeling that emotion. For example, a 0- Anger means that I am not feeling angry at that moment.
#1	A 1 is when I feel a **tiny** emotion. I may have a 1 emotion when I am having a tiny reaction to something. A 1 emotion may mean that a stronger feeling is beginning to happen. A 1 may also mean that a stronger feeling is reducing to a lower level. In all of these cases, at a 1 I am able to think clearly and usually able to control my urges, impulses, and actions. Because I am able to think clearly when I am at a 1 emotion, I can use all of my skills; even the Calm Only ones!
#2	A 2 is when I feel a **small** emotion. I may begin to notice my body reacting to the emotion at a 2. I may feel some uncomfortable body sensations, if it is a painful emotion. I may find it a little more difficult to think clearly at a 2 . If I am still thinking clearly and am in control, I can use all of my skills at a 2, even the Calm Only ones.
#3	A 3 emotion is a **medium** emotion. This level of emotion will be causing different body sensations. At a 3, these body sensation may feel uncomfortable. I may notice more off-track thoughts and urges at a 3. It may be getting challenging to focus my attention. I may be able to use my Calm Only skills at a 3, but if my thinking is confused or I am having strong urges, it may be best to use my All-the-Time Skills until I am calmer. If I am over a 3 at all, I DO NOT USE Calm Only Skills!!!
#4	A 4 emotion is a **strong** emotion. At a 4 there may be strong body sensations. My thinking will be affected by the high emotion. I may also have strong action urges because of the 4 emotion. I use my All-the-Time Skills to reduce my emotions and to stay safe. I have to wait to use my Calm Only skills until my emotions have gone down below a 3.
#5	A 5 emotion is an **out-of-control** emotion. A 5 emotion is when I am not in control. The body sensations, thoughts, and urges are over-whelming. At a 5 I have actions that hurt myself, others, or property. I have to use ALL of my All-the-Time skills to stay safe! I do not try to talk about or fix problems until I am below a 3.

Feelings Rating Scale- Worked Examples 1

Name: _____   **Date:** _____

Please list an emotion and events that would make you feel each level of the emotion. Start at 0 and move up to 5

5 *The pizza man screams and grabs my arm.*   *Fear*

Makes me get out of control.   Emotion:

4 *I notice I have no money.*   *Nervous*

Makes me feel a very strong emotion.   Emotion:

3 *I order a pizza.*   *Excited*

Makes me feel a medium emotion.   Emotion:

2 *I see nothing good to eat.*   *Sadness*

Makes me feel a small emotion.   Emotion:

1 *I go to the kitchen.*   *Happiness*

Makes me feel a tiny emotion.   Emotion:

0 *I blink my eyes.*   *No feeling*

Makes me feel no emotion.   Emotion:

Feelings Rating Scale- Worksheet 1

Name: _____   Date: _____

Please list an emotion and events that would make you feel each level of the emotion. Start at 0 and move up to 5

5 _____

Makes me get out of control.   **Emotion:**

4 _____

Makes me feel a very strong emotion.   **Emotion:**

3 _____

Makes me feel a medium emotion.   **Emotion:**

2 _____

Makes me feel a small emotion.   **Emotion:**

1 _____

Makes me feel a tiny emotion.   **Emotion:**

0 _____

Makes me feel no emotion.   **Emotion:**

⚖️ Feelings Rating Scale- Worked Examples 2

Name: _____   Date: _____

Emotion: *FEAR* _____

Choose an emotion. Then list events that would make you feel each level of that emotion. Start at 0 and move to 5.

 **5** *I find out that I killed someone in another car.*

Makes me get out of control.

 4 *On my way to work I skid off the road.*

Makes me feel a very strong emotion.

 3 *I watch the weather and it said there is a blizzard.*

Makes me feel a medium emotion.

 2 *I look outside and see that it is snowing.*

Makes me feel a small emotion.

 1 *I hear the wind blowing outside.*

Makes me feel a tiny emotion.

 0 *I open my eyes first thing in the morning.*

Makes me feel no emotion.

Feelings Rating Scale- Worksheet 2

Name: _____   **Date:** _____

Emotion: _____

Choose an emotion. Then list events that would make you feel each level of that emotion. Start at 0 and move to 5.

5 _____

Makes me get out of control.

4 _____

Makes me feel a very strong emotion.

3 _____

Makes me feel a medium emotion.

2 _____

Makes me feel a small emotion.

1 _____

Makes me feel a tiny emotion.

0 _____

Makes me feel no emotion.

Categories of Skills- Handout 1

Once I know my Level of Emotion (0-1-2-3-4-5),
I know what Category of Skills I can use:

1. Clear Picture

2. On-Track Thinking

3. On-Track Action

4. Safety Plan

5. New-Me Activities

All-The-Time Skills

0-#5 Emotions

6. Problem Solving

7. Expressing Myself

8. Getting It Right

9. Relationship Care

Calm Only Skills

Only 0-#3 Emotions!

Categories of Skills- Worked Examples 1

Name: _____ **Date:** _____

Please circle the skills that can be used when you are having these emotions.

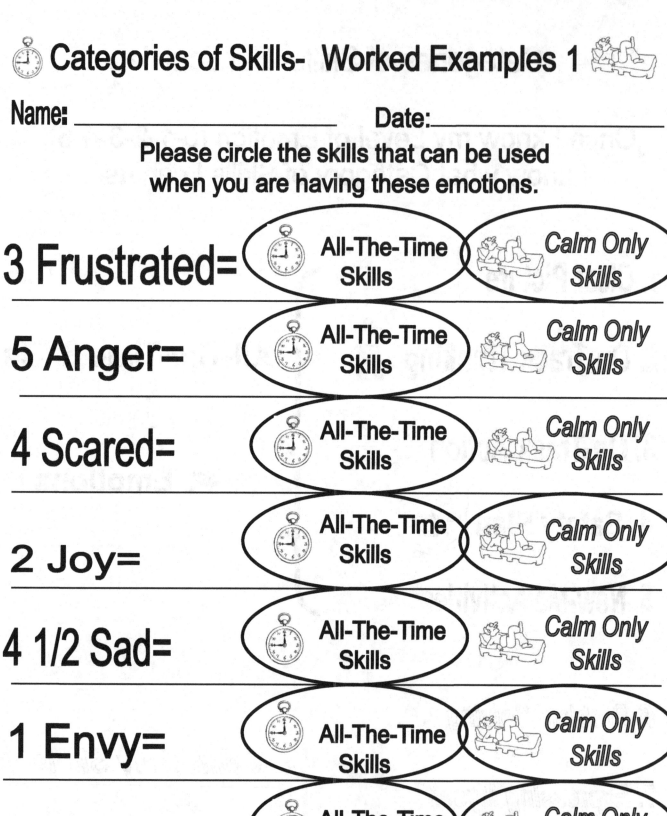

3 Frustrated= All-The-Time Skills | Calm Only Skills

5 Anger= All-The-Time Skills | Calm Only Skills

4 Scared= All-The-Time Skills | Calm Only Skills

2 Joy= All-The-Time Skills | Calm Only Skills

4 1/2 Sad= All-The-Time Skills | Calm Only Skills

1 Envy= All-The-Time Skills | Calm Only Skills

3 Happiness= All-The-Time Skills | Calm Only Skills

3 1/2 Shame= All-The-Time Skills | Calm Only Skills

Categories of Skills- Worksheet 1

Name: _____ **Date:** _____

Please circle the skills that can be used when you are having these emotions.

3 Sad= **All-The-Time Skills**   *Calm Only Skills*

5 Fear= **All-The-Time Skills**   *Calm Only Skills*

4 Disgusted= **All-The-Time Skills**   *Calm Only Skills*

2 Happy= **All-The-Time Skills**   *Calm Only Skills*

4 1/2 Jealous= **All-The-Time Skills**   *Calm Only Skills*

1 Mad= **All-The-Time Skills**   *Calm Only Skills*

3 Love= **All-The-Time Skills**   *Calm Only Skills*

3 1/2 Guilty= **All-The-Time Skills**   *Calm Only Skills*

Categories of Skills- Worksheet 2

Name: _____ **Date:** _____

Please write an emotion and a level of the emotion in the blank (For example: 4 upset). Then circle the skills that can be used when you are having these emotions.

Emotion and Rating

	All-The-Time Skills	Calm Only Skills

_____   All-The-Time Skills   Calm Only Skills

_____   All-The-Time Skills   Calm Only Skills

_____   All-The-Time Skills   Calm Only Skills

_____   All-The-Time Skills   Calm Only Skills

_____   All-The-Time Skills   Calm Only Skills

_____   All-The-Time Skills   Calm Only Skills

_____   **All-The-Time Skills**   Calm Only Skills

 Recipe for Skills

Once I know my level of emotion (0-1-2-3-4-5),
I use the Recipe for Skills to decide how many
Skills to use to DO WHAT WORKS in the situation.
Skill Masters use EVEN MORE!!!

Combine 1 skill
for EVERY level of Emotion:

Level 0 Feeling= 1 Skill

Level 1 Feeling= 2 Skills

Level 2 Feeling= 3 Skills

Level 3 Feeling= 4 Skills

Level 4 Feeling= 5 Skills

Level 5 Feeling= 6 Skills

Recipe for Skills- Worked Examples 1

Name: _____   Date: _____

Please circle the minimum number of skill that
should be used at this level of emotion.

3 Frustrated=   1 - 2 - 3 - ④ - 5 - 6

5 Anger=   1 - 2 - 3 - 4 - 5 - ⑥

4 Scared=   1 - 2 - 3 - 4 - ⑤ - 6

2 Joy=   1 - 2 - ③ - 4 - 5 - 6

4 1/2 Sad=   1 - 2 - 3 - 4 - 5 - ⑥

1 Envy=   1 - ② - 3 - 4 - 5 - 6

3 Happiness=   1 - 2 - 3 - ④ - 5 - 6

3 1/2 Shame=   1 - 2 - 3 - 4 - ⑤ - 6

Name: _____ Date:_____

Please circle the minimum number of skill that
should be used at this level of emotion.

3 Sad=   1 - 2 - 3 - 4 - 5 - 6

5 Fear=   1 - 2 - 3 - 4 - 5 - 6

4 Disgusted=   1 - 2 - 3 - 4 - 5 - 6

2 Happy=   1 - 2 - 3 - 4 - 5 - 6

4 1/2 Jealous=   1 - 2 - 3 - 4 - 5 - 6

1 Mad=   1 - 2 - 3 - 4 - 5 - 6

3 Love=   1 - 2 - 3 - 4 - 5 - 6

3 1/2 Guilty=   1 - 2 - 3 - 4 - 5 - 6

175

Recipe for Skills- Worksheet 2

Name: _____ Date: _____

Please write an emotion and the rating of
the emotion in the blank. (For example 3 sad)
Then circle the minimum number of skills that
should be used at this level of emotion.

Emotion and Rating:

1 - 2 - 3 - 4 - 5 - 6

_____

1 - 2 - 3 - 4 - 5 - 6

_____

1 - 2 - 3 - 4 - 5 - 6

_____

1 - 2 - 3 - 4 - 5 - 6

_____

1 - 2 - 3 - 4 - 5 - 6

_____

1 - 2 - 3 - 4 - 5 - 6

_____

1 - 2 - 3 - 4 - 5 - 6

Week 2- Group Practice Activity

Instructions: Please work together to fill in the blanks in this story.

Story:

Mary was running late for work.

She was feeling _____ at a level _____ .

She was thinking: _____ .

That made her feel _____ at a level _____ .

Mary had the urge to _____ .

She knew she had to use her skills.

At that second she was feeling _____ at a level _____ .

Mary knew that she could use her_____ skills at
   any level of emotion.

She remembered that her All-the-Time skills were: _____,

_____, _____, _____,

and _____ .

Because Mary was at a level _____ of emotion, she _____ use her
   Calm Only skills.

Her Calm Only sills are: _____, _____,
_____, and _____ .

Because she was at a _____ level of emotion, Mary knew she needed to use
   _____ skills.

Week 2- My Practice Activity

Instructions: We will fill this sheet in during group with each person .

What was a stressful situation that you noticed this week:

_____

_____

Feelings Rating Scale Practice:

I felt _____ at a level _____ .

Categories of Skills Practice:

Could I use my All-the-Time skills?   YES or NO

I can use my All-the-Time skills when I am at a _____ to a _____ emotion.

Could I use my Calm Only skills YES or NO

I can use my Calm Only skills when I am at a _____ to a _____ emotion.

Recipe for Skills Practice:

I am at a _____ emotion, so I need to use _____ skills.

Skills System Review Questions

1. What is skill 1?
2. What is skill 2?
3. What is skill 3?
4. What is skill 4?
5. What is skill 5?
6. What is skill 6?
7. What is skill 7?
8. What is skill 8?
9. What is skill 9?

10. Who can tell us about the Feelings Rating Scale?

11. What are the Categories of Skills?

12. Which skills are All-the-Time skills?

13. At what level of emotion can we use the All-the-Time skills?

14. Which skills are the Calm Only skills?

15. At what level of emotion can we use the Calm Only skills?

14. What is the Recipe for Skills?

15. What are the six Clear Picture Do's?

1. Clear Picture - Summary Sheet

Getting a Clear Picture

Clear Picture is an All-the-Time skill. I use my Clear Picture Do's at all levels of emotion, 0-1-2-3-4-5. Every time I notice that my feelings or situation changes, I take a moment to get a Clear Picture of what is happening inside and outside of myself. I do the six Clear Picture Do's.

1. First, I **Breathe**. I notice the air going in and out. I notice and accept the breath. Paying attention to my belly breathing helps me focus my attention 100%. I allow the air to come and go out without holding on to the breath.

2. Second, I **Check my Surroundings**. I notice what is going on around me. I look around to see what is happening in the situation *right now*. I see what is real; I focus on the facts.

3. Third, I do a **Body Check**. I notice my body sensations; doing a body scan helps me know how my body is feeling and how I am reacting to the situation. Different body sensations help me know how I am feeling. I notice the sensations come and go.

4. Fourth, I **Label and Rate** my emotions. I notice what I am feeling. I label feelings such as: sadness, happiness, hurt, fear, jealousy, guilt and anger. Once I label the emotion, I rate how strong it is, using my 0-1-2-3-4-5 scale. I notice that feelings come and go; I allow the emotions to pass like clouds without holding on to them.

5. Fifth, I notice my **Thoughts**. I watch my thoughts come and go, like watching city buses pass by. I pay attention to thoughts that will help me reach my goals. I notice other thoughts, but I let them pass without taking action, just like I let buses pass that are not going where I want to go. I focus more on thoughts that will take me to my goal. If I pay attention to off-track thoughts, I will end up somewhere where I don't want to be. Don't get on the wrong bus!

6. Sixth, I notice my **urges**. Urges make me want to take actions. I only take on-track actions. I notice that urges come and go; I do not have to take actions until I do On-Track Thinking .

Having a Clear Mind:

- I am the boss of my mind. I control my attention.
- When I do Clear Picture, I focus my mind 100%.
- I notice this one moment. I see and accept this moment AS IT IS.
- I focus on what is happening inside and outside of me *right now*, not the past or future.
- I shift my attention to things that are helpful.
- When I focus on how things should be different, it makes me more emotional.
- When my mind drifts off-track, I gently bring it back to what is helpful.
- It helps me focus when I bring my attention back to my breathing. My breath is always there to help!
- My breath is like an anchor that keeps me steady when feelings and thoughts pull me in different directions.
- When feelings and thought are difficult or painful, I remember that they will pass. I remind myself that I have skills to help be more comfortable and to fix problems (when I am below a 3 emotion).
- My mind gets fuzzy when I rush or do too many things at once.
- When I SEE and ACCEPT the present moment AS IT IS, I can deal with the moment using the right skills to reach my goals.

1. Clear Picture - Handout 1

Focus 100% on the Clear Picture Do's

1. Breathe

2. Check my Surroundings

3. Body Check

4. Label & Rate my Emotions

0-1-2-3-4-5

5. Notice my Thoughts

6. Notice my Urges

181

1. Clear Picture - Worked Examples 1

Name: _____ Date:_____

Situation: _I hear my housemate arguing with staff_

I take a deep belly breath

I am in my room and my housemate is in the kitchen.

I feel tired and have a headache.

I am frustrated at a level 3.

I wish he would just learn to use his skills.

I would like to go out there and tell him to shut up.

1. Clear Picture - Worksheet 1

Name: _____   Date: _____

Please write the name of the Clear Picture Do next to the picture.

_____

_____

_____

_____

_____

_____

1. Clear Picture - Worksheet 2

Name: _____ Date:_____

Write down what is happening *Right Now*

Situation: _____

_____

_____

_____

_____

_____

_____

184

1. Clear Picture: Breathing- Handout 1

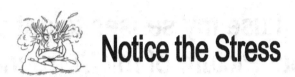 Notice the Stress

 Turn Attention to My Breathing

Feel the air going in and out of my nose

Feel my Chest Rise and Fall

 Pull Air into My Belly & Feel My Belt get Tighter

Take Deep Belly Breathes

1. Clear Picture: Notice Surroundings- Handout 1

**I use my senses to get a
Clear Picture of my Surroundings**

SEE

TOUCH

HEAR

SMELL

TASTE

Name: _____   Date: _____

Please Check Around and write down what you notice.

Situation: _____ *I am sitting in my livingroom.* _____

👁 I SEE _____ *the TV, the furniture, and my housemate* _____

👂 I HEAR _____ *the TV and my housemate on the phone* _____

I TASTE _____ *the tea I am drinking* _____

I SMELL _____ *the lemon in my tea* _____

✋ I TOUCH _____ *the warm cup, and I am sitting on the soft couch*

1. Clear Picture: Notice Surroundings - Worksheet 1

Name: _____   Date: _____

Please Check Around and write down what you notice.

Situation: _____

I SEE _____

I HEAR _____

I TASTE _____

I SMELL _____

I TOUCH _____

Name: _____ Date: _____

Please sit or lie down. Starting at your feet, tighten and then relax the muscles in each part of your body.

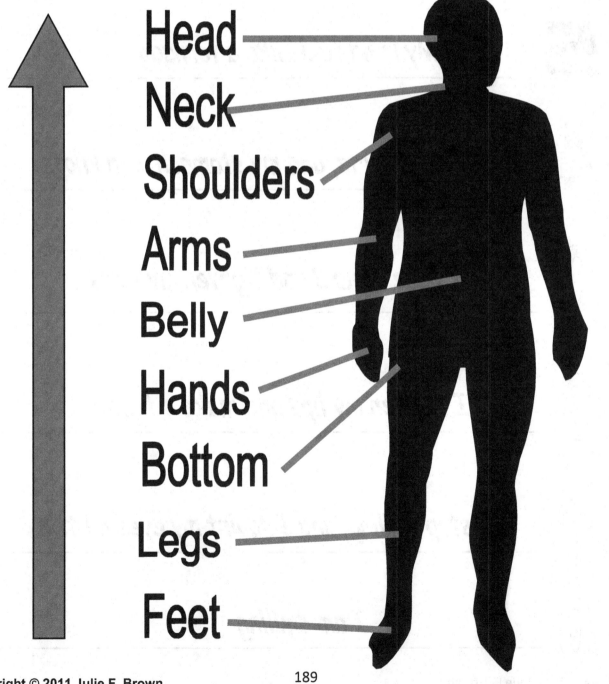

Head

Neck

Shoulders

Arms

Belly

Hands

Bottom

Legs

Feet

Name: _____   Date:_____

Please choose an emotion. List body sensations
for each level of the emotion.

Emotion: _Anger_ _____

5 _My mind feels like a tornado_ _____

4 _My head hurts, and my stomach is in knots_ ____

3 _I pace around and tighten my fists_ _____

2 _I tighten my lips and make a frown_ _____

1 _I stop smiling, and I squint my eyes a little_ __

0 _I am smiling_ _____

1. Clear Picture: Body Check- Worksheet 1

Name: _____ Date: _____

Please choose an emotion. List body sensations for each level of the emotion.

Emotion: _____

5 _____

_____

4 _____

_____

3 _____

_____

2 _____

_____

1 _____

_____

0 _____

Add to This List of Different Body Sensations

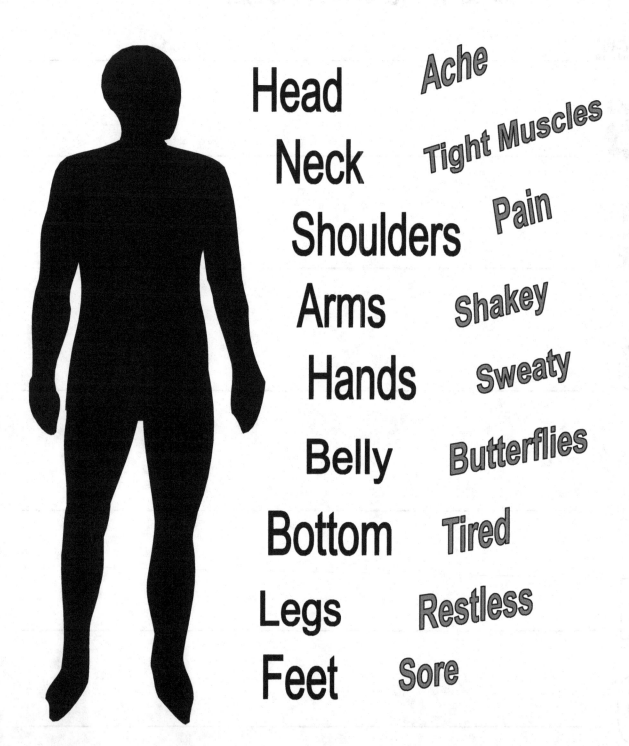

Head   Ache

Neck   Tight Muscles

Shoulders   Pain

Arms   Shakey

Hands   Sweaty

Belly   Butterflies

Bottom   Tired

Legs   Restless

Feet   Sore

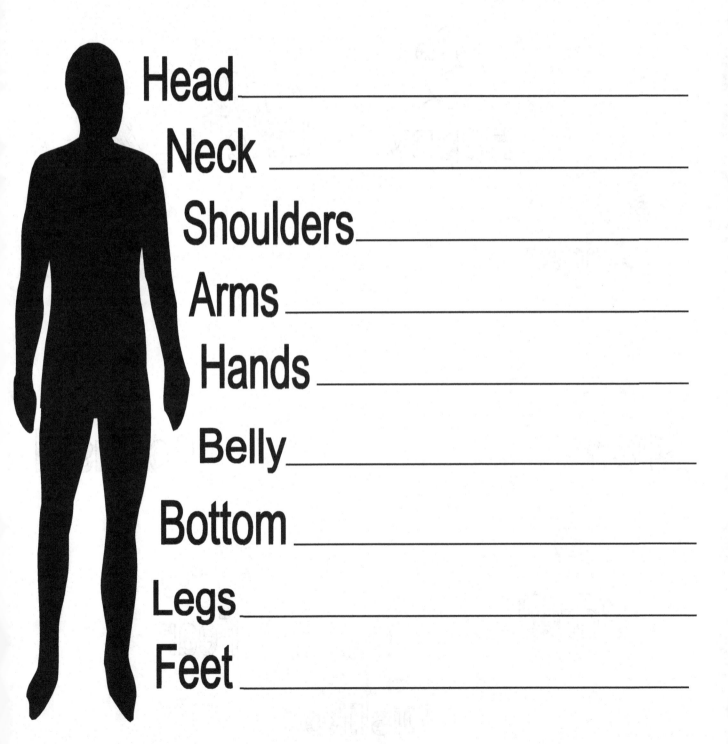

1. Clear Picture: Body Check - Worksheet 2

Name: _____ Date: _____

What sensations do we feel in each part of our body?

Head _____

Neck _____

Shoulders _____

Arms _____

Hands _____

Belly _____

Bottom _____

Legs _____

Feet _____

1. Clear Picture: Label and Rate Emotions- Handout 1

Name: _____   Date: _____

Please make a brainstorm list of all possible emotions.

Happy

Love

Sad

Anger

Shame

Confused

Bored

Dislike

Fear

194

 Situations cause emotions

Emotions make feelings in my body

 Emotions change my face

 Emotions make me feel like doing things

1. Clear Picture: Label and Rate Emotions- Worked Example 1

Name: _____   Date: _____

Please list situations that may make you feel each emotion.

Happiness: _Going out to dinner with my friends_

Love: _When I think about my best friend_

Sad: _Thinking about family members who have died_

Confused: _When my doctor told me about my medications_

Fear: _On the first day of a new job_

Dislike: _When my staff treated me like a child_

Bored: _When I have nothing to do_

Shame: _When I think about hurting people in the past_

Anger: _When someone steals my stuff_

1. Clear Picture: Label and Rate Emotions- Worksheet 1

Name: _____   Date: _____

Please list situations that may make you feel each emotion.

Happiness: _____

Love: _____

Sad: _____

Confused: _____

Fear: _____

Dislike: _____

Bored: _____

Shame: _____

Anger: _____

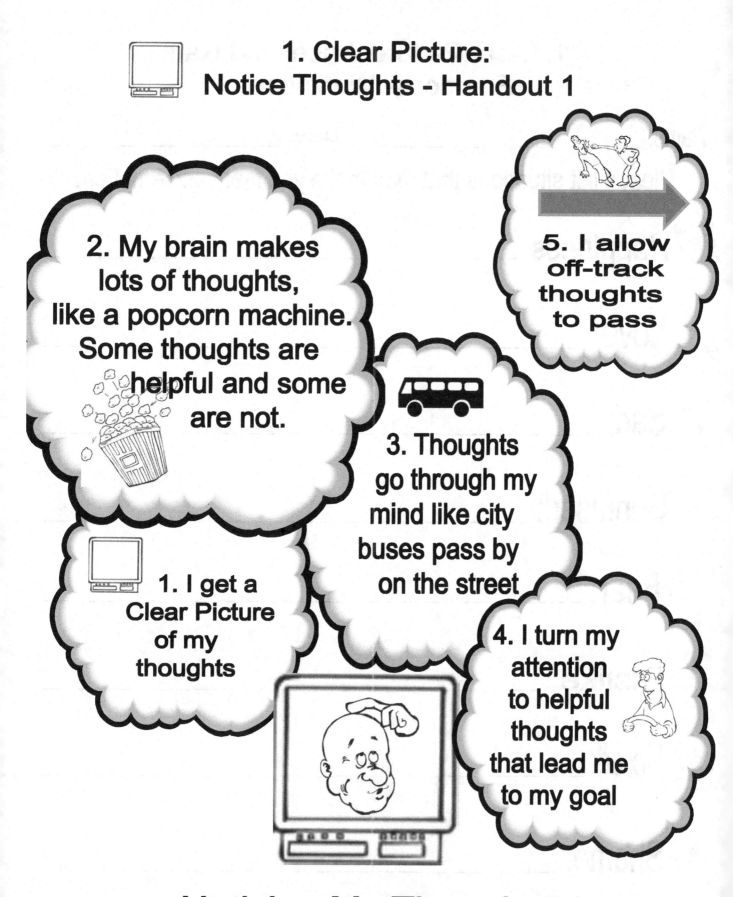

5. I allow off-track thoughts to pass

2. My brain makes lots of thoughts, like a popcorn machine. Some thoughts are helpful and some are not.

3. Thoughts go through my mind like city buses pass by on the street

1. I get a Clear Picture of my thoughts

4. I turn my attention to helpful thoughts that lead me to my goal

Noticing My Thoughts

1. Clear Picture:
Notice Thoughts- Worked Example 1

Name: _____ Date: _____

Please list thoughts you have had that led you to feel each emotion.

Happiness: _"I am doing a good job!"_

Love: _"My brother is my best friend."_

Sad: _"I miss my mother."_

Confused: _"I don't know what I am doing."_

Fear: _"That man is going to yell at me."_

Dislike: _"That woman was mean to me."_

Bored: _"I just want to watch TV."_

Shame: _"I am ugly."_

Anger: _"I hate how she looks at me."_

1. Clear Picture:
Notice Thoughts- Worksheet 1

Name: _____ Date: _____

Please list thoughts you have had that led you to feel each emotion.

Happiness: _____

Love: _____

Sad: _____

Confused: _____

Fear: _____

Dislike: _____

Bored: _____

Shame: _____

Anger: _____

How Emotions Help Us

Emotions get us to do things!

Our emotions show other people how we feel about things

Emotions help us know what is important to us

Name: _____ Date: _____

Please list action urges that each emotion gives you.

Happiness: *Clap my hands*

Love: *Hug*

Sad: *Look down*

Confused: *Avoid*

Fear: *Scream*

Dislike: *Move away*

Bored: *Complain*

Shame: *Hide*

Anger: *Yell*

1. Clear Picture: Notice Urges - Worksheet 1

Name: _____   Date: _____

Please list action urges that each emotion gives you.

Happiness: _____

Love: _____

Sad: _____

Confused: _____

Fear: _____

Dislike: _____

Bored: _____

Shame: _____

Anger: _____

1. Clear Picture:
Notice Urges- Worked Examples 2

Name: _____ Date: _____

Please choose an emotion. List action urges for each level of the emotion.

Emotion: _____ *Nervous* _____

5 _____ *Storming around and yelling* _____

4 _____ *Cry* _____

3 _____ *Pace around the room* _____

2 _____ *Talk a lot* _____

1 _____ *Get figity* _____

0 _____ *Relaxed* _____

Name: _____   Date: _____

Please choose an emotion. List
action urges for each level of the emotion.

Emotion: _____

5 _____

4 _____

3 _____

2 _____

1 _____

0 _____

2. On-Track Thinking- Summary Sheet

On-Track Thinking is an All-the-Time skill. I use On-Track Thinking at every level of emotion, 0-5.

First, I get a Clear Picture. When I notice an urge, I **Stop and Step Back** to do On-Track Thinking; I do not take action until I have done On-Track Thinking.

I **Check the Urge**. I give it a *thumbs-up* if it is a helpful urge. Helpful urges help me to be on-track to my goals. I give the urge a *thumbs-down*, if the urge is off-track. Off-track urges do not help me reach my goals.

I **Turn It** to Thumbs-Up Thinking. If my thoughts are not helpful, I turn them to being thumbs-up thinking. I need lots of thumbs-up thinking to help me in tough situations and to cheer myself on to keep using skills. I can do it!

Then I make a **Skills Plan**.

- I start by thinking about my level of emotion again using the 0-1-2-3-4-5 scale.

- Next, I use the *Categories of Skills* to help me decide which skills I can use. If I am below a 3 emotion, I can use all nine skills- even the Calm Only ones. I have to be focused and thinking clearly when using Problem Solving, Expressing Myself, Getting It Right, and Relationship Care. When I am below a 3, I am better able to interact with people in positive ways.

  If I am over a 3, even a little bit, I use my All-the-Time skills. My All-the-Time skills are : Clear Picture, On-Track Thinking, On-Track Action, Safety Plan, and New-Me Activity.

- Then I use the *Recipe for Skills*. The recipe tells me how many skills I need to use. I add 1 skill to my level of emotion. So, at a 3 emotion, I need to use at least 4 skills. The more skills the better!

- Now, I can *choose my skills*. I decide which skills will work the best to help me reach my goals. I use one skill after the other to handle situations that arise in my life. I join skills together to make powerful skills clusters that help me reach my goals. Clear Picture and On-Track Thinking lead me to know which other skills need to be used so that I stay on-track.

  Making a Skill Plan happen can be challenging. I may have to make sacrifices and not get exactly what I want. I have to be brave and strong to be a Skill Master. I cheer myself on to give myself the strength and courage to take On-Track Actions! It may be hard, but I can do it!

STOP & Step Back  *Think about what I want*

CHECK the Urge

Not Helpful?

Helpful?

TURN IT to Thumbs –Up Thinking

 I allow Off-Track Thoughts and urges to pass

Make a Skill Plan:

0-1-2-3-4-5?

How many skills?

Can I use Calm Only skills?

What skills will help me reach my goal?

Take an *On-Track Action*

2. On-Track Thinking- Worked Example 1

Name: _____ Date: _____

Situation: _*I am at work and I feel sick.*_____

STOP **STOP & Step Back**- Think about what I want

♡ **Check the Urge:** ___*I want to quit my job*_____

Helpful? 👍 ♡ ⟨👎 **Not Helpful?**⟩ ·····················➤ *"Let it Pass"*

👍 **TURN IT to Thumbs-Up:** ___*I need this job!*_____

Make a Skill Plan: I am at a: 0 - 1 - 2 -③- 4 - 5

Can I use Calm Only skills now? ⟨YES⟩ or NO

How many skills should I use: ___**4**___

Circle skills will help me reach my goal?

(🖥) (🚂) (🚂) (🛡) (🍴☕) (🚗) (🧍) (📦) (🚢)

My plan: ___*I will use Clear Picture to know what is going on inside and out.*___

___*I will use On-track Thinking to think things through.*___

___*I will use Expressing Myself to see if I can go home early.*___

___*I am afraid to talk to my boss, so I will use On-track Action. I will*___

___*keep my head up and look her in the eyes.*___

🚂 **On-Track Action:** ___*I will go talk to my boss.*___

2. On-Track Thinking- Worksheet 1

Name: _____   Date: _____

Situation: _____

STOP STOP & Step Back- Think about what I want

♡ **Check the Urge:** _____

"Let it Pass"

Helpful? 👍 ♡ 👎 Not Helpful? ....➤

👍 **TURN IT to Thumbs-Up:** _____

Make a Skill Plan: I am at a: 0 - 1 - 2 - 3 - 4 - 5

Can I use Calm Only skills now? YES or NO

How many skills should I use: _____

Circle skills will help me reach my goal?

My plan: _____

_____

_____

_____

_____

On-Track Action: _____

2. On-Track Thinking- Handout 2

 STOP & Step Back: *Think about what I want*

 Check It: Helpful?  Not Helpful?

 Turn It:

Thumbs-up thoughts
keep us on-track to our goals!

 # Off-Track Thoughts and Urges

are NOT Helpful and keep us from our goals

 # Let Them Pass!

2. On-Track Thinking- Worksheet 2

Name: _____   Date: _____

STOP **STOP & Step Back----- Check Urges**

👍 = Helpful urges

👎 = Off-track urges

Please think about your personal goals.
Circle whether the urge is helpful 👍 or not helpful 👎 .

1. I feel like hitting that girl.   👍   👎

2. I want to focus in group.   👍   👎

3. I want to drive too fast.   👍   👎

4. I want to steal a CD.   👍   👎

5. I want to be healthy.   👍   👎

6. I want to put myself down.   👍   👎

7. I want to make some new friends.   👍   👎

8. I want to scream at that guy.   👍   👎

3. On-Track Action- Summary Sheet

On-Track Action is an All-the-Time skill. This means that I can use On-Track Action at any level of emotion, 0-1-2-3-4-5. First, I get a Clear Picture; then I do On-Track Thinking. I Stop & Step Back, Check The Urge, Turn It, and make a Skills Plan. Once I have made an On-Track Skills Plan, I decide what my On-Track Action will be.

I use On-Track Action when I take a **Step Toward My Goal.** I do something positive to be On-Track. I may already be on-track, and I choose to do an On-Track Action to stay on-track.

I **Switch Tracks** when I have urges to go off-track. I also use Switching Tracks to Get back on-track after I have gone off-track. When I do go off-track, it is VERY important to get back on-track AS SOON AS POSSIBLE-ASAP! The longer I wait, the more difficult it may be! Skill Masters realize when they are off-track and do several On-Track Actions to be sure that they are on the right road to their goals!

I give 100% effort to an On-Track Action. Sometimes I do the opposite of off-track urges to make sure I am really on-track. For example, if I feel like avoiding work, instead I do opposite and give work 100% effort. Even though it might be hard, I give 100% effort to the On-Track Action.

I make **On-Track Action Plans** to help myself stay on-track. I do things to keep myself and my life in balance. When I am in balance, I am able to manage life and relationships better. I balance my eating, exercise, health, work, and have fun. For example: I take walks, get enough sleep, eat healthy food, take proper medications, go to work, and talk to friends as part of my On-Track Action Plan each day.

There are times when I do the On-Track Action of **Accepting the Situation.** When I have done all I can in a situation, I may have to Accept the Situation. There are many times when I can't fix problems right away or I have to wait for something that I want. I also may have to do things that I don't want to do. Other times, people do things that affect me that I don't like. Things happen in life that I can't control. In all these situations, I may need to do the On-Track Action of Accepting the Situation. It is important for me to use my other skills to handle the stress that these situations cause me.

There are times when I have to **Let It Pass and Move On**. I may have the urge to hang on to certain thoughts, feelings, memories, and urges to the point where it begins to cause me a problem. I have to pay attention to when "enough is enough." I have to be careful to focus on things that help me and to notice when something is no longer helpful. At that point I may need to do the On-Track Action of Letting It Pass and Move On toward my goals.

212

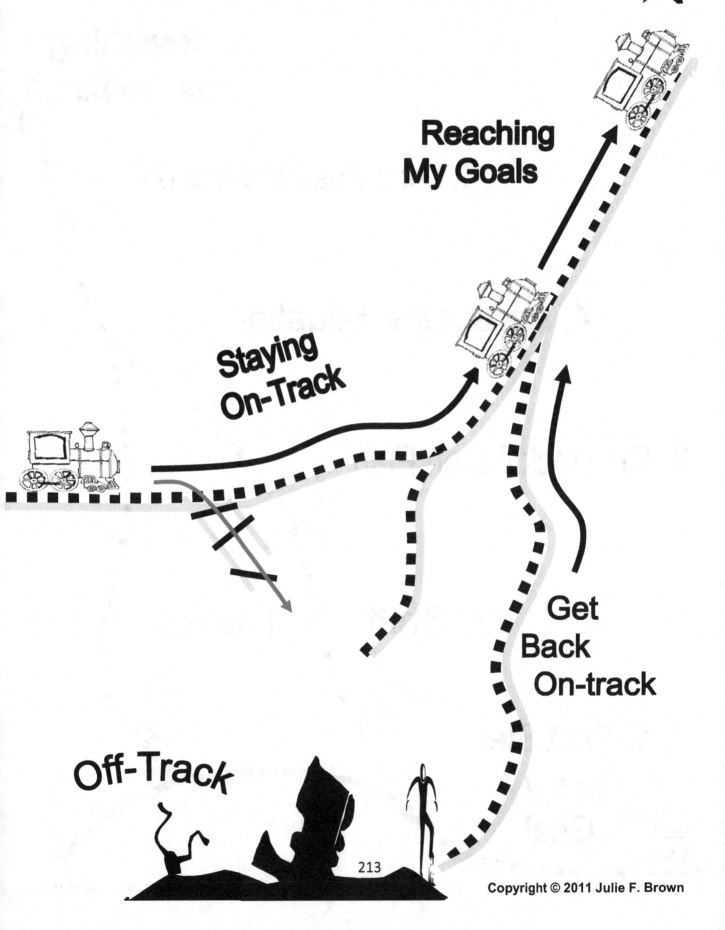

Reaching
My Goals

Staying
On-Track

Get
Back
On-track

Off-Track

213

3. On-Track Action- Handout 2

Reaching my Goals ☆

5. Let It Pass & Move on

4. Accept the Situation

3. On-Track Action Plan

2. Shift Tracks

1. First Step to my Goal

3. On-Track Action- Practice Exercise

Instructions: We are going to read this scenario. Then we will think of On-Track Actions that will be helpful for the person.

Scenario:

I am in the kitchen. I see the last piece of chocolate cake on the counter. There is a sticker with my housemates name on the plastic wrap. I am hungry at a level 4. I feel my stomach growling. I really love cake and I have had a really bad day. I have the urge to grab a fork and take the cake into my room to eat.

I stopped and stepped back to check whether eating Mary's cake was a good idea for me. I thought about how mad she would be. I thought about my own diet. Eating the cake was looking less and less helpful. I am Mary's friend; what if she has had a bad day too? I think eating the cake would be off-track. I think I give that urge a thumbs-down. Now I have to make a skills plan. What skills should I use?

What will my On-Track Action be?

Take a Step Towards My Goal

Switch Tracks

Do the Opposite of Off-Track Urges

Jump in with Both Feet!

216

On-Track Action Plans

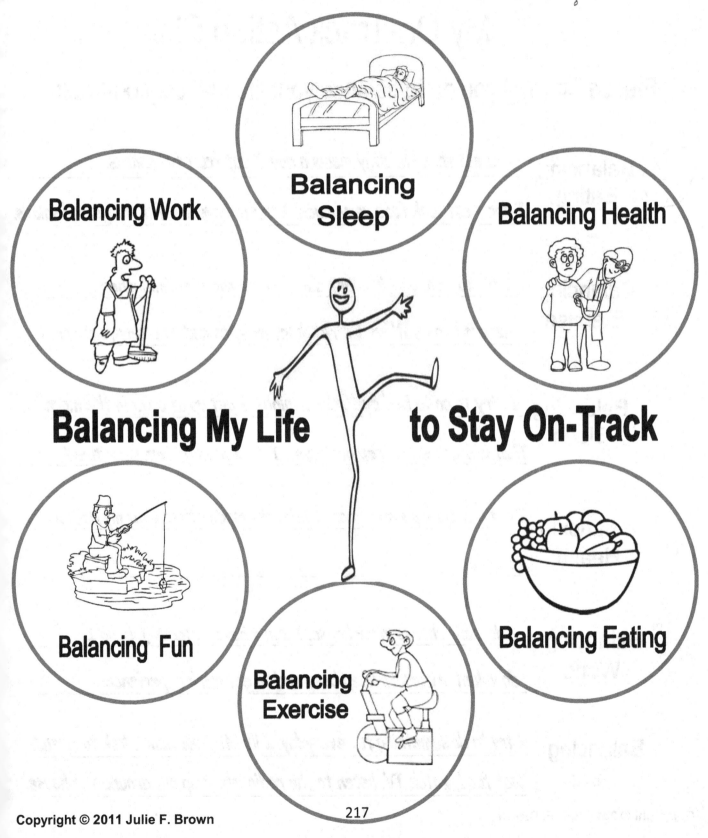

Balancing Sleep

Balancing Work

Balancing Health

Balancing My Life

to Stay On-Track

Balancing Fun

Balancing Exercise

Balancing Eating

217

3. On-Track Action- Worked Examples 1

Name:_____   Date:_____

 # My On-Track Action Plan

Please list what you do to balance your life and stay on-track.

Balancing Eating: _I eat three healthy meals a day. I eat fruit for snacks. I don't eat junk food very much. I try to have low-fat things and salads._

Balancing Exercise: _I try to take a walk every day. I go on the treadmill when there is bad weather. I stretch my muscles and do a few yoga poses._

Balancing Sleep: _It try to go to bed by 10:00 at night. I get up at 6:00 in the morning. That is 8 hours of sleep per night. I take naps if I am very tired._

Balancing Health: _I get a check-up every year. I take the medications that my doctor gives me._

Balancing Work: _I do many chores in my house. I don't have a steady job, so I do volunteer work to keep busy and to get work experience._

Balancing Fun: _I try to do something fun everyday. I like to take walks, talk to friends, cook food, watch TV, listen to the radio, and help out around the house._

218

3. On-Track Action- Worksheet 1

Name:_____ **Date:** _____

My On-Track Action Plan

Please list what you do balance your life and stay On-Track.

**Balancing
Eating:** _____

_____

**Balancing
Exercise:** _____

_____

**Balancing
Sleep:** _____

_____

**Balancing
Health:** _____

_____

**Balancing
Work:** _____

_____

**Balancing
Fun:** _____

_____

Accepting the Situation

Letting It Pass AND Move On

Get Stuck in

Worries

Memories

Painful Emotions

Off-Track Urges

or...

Worries

Off-Track Urges

Painful Emotions & Memories

Let It Pass

AND

Move On

Once we have used:
1. Clear Picture
2. On-Track Thinking
3. On-Track Action

We Shift Tracks to the other skills:

4. Safety Plan- Summary Sheet

Safety Plan is an All-the-Time Skill. That means that I can use Safety Plan when I am at any level of emotion, 0-1-2-3-4-5.

First, I use Clear Picture and On-Track Thinking. If I notice any risks, I may choose to do a Safety Plan. For example, if I am near a certain person that will cause me or the other person to feel stress, problems, or danger I use a Safety Plan to handle the situation. It is best to do a Safety Plan before there is a big problem. If I do take an Off-Track Action, go near risk, or do something dangerous, Safety Plans can help me get back on-track.

The first step in Safety Plan is to get a **Clear Picture of the Risk**. There are Inside-of-Me Risks, such as Off-Track Thoughts, Urges, Feelings and Fantasies (TUFFs). There are also Outside-of-Me Risks, like people who are a risk or situations which are dangerous. I handle Inside and Outside-of-Me Risks before I do things that are off-track.

Next, I rate Level of Risks as either **Low, Medium**, or **High**.
* In *low risk* situations the problem is far away or contact may cause stress.
* In *medium risk* situations the danger is in the area or contact may cause problems.
* In *high risk* situations the danger is close or contact may cause serious damage.

It is important not to over-rate or under-rate risk. Over-rating risk can cause me to avoid activities that are helpful to engage in. Under-rating risk can lead me into danger and harm because I have not taken the necessary steps to manage the problem.

Once I have a Clear Picture of the Risk and know what Level of Risk the situation is, I think about what kind of Safety Plan is best.

There are 3 Types of Safety Plans: **Thinking, Talking and Writing.**
* A *Thinking Safety Plan* is when I think about how I am going to handle the risk. I usually use Thinking Safety Plans in *low risk* situations.
* A *Talking Safety Plan* is when I decide to tell someone about the risk and problems that may happen. This helps me handle the risk in an on-track way; the other person knows that it is important to help me stay on-track. I usually use Talking Safety Plans in *medium* and *high risk* situations.
* A *Writing Safety Plans* is when I write down the possible risk and dangers; I write down plans to handle the risk in safe ways. I usually use Written Safety Plans in *high risk* situations or when I know I will be heading into a difficult situation. It helps to review how I will keep myself safe!

There are 3 Ways to Handle Risk: **Refocus on a New-Me Activity, Move Away** and **Leave the Area.**
* *Refocus on a New-Me Activity*: This means that I put my attention on what I am doing, rather than focusing on the risk. I only pay enough attention to the risk to be sure I am safe and that the situation is not getting worse. I refocus in a low-risk situation and if the risk goes up I may need to Move or Leave.
* *Move Away:* This means that I go to a safer area. I go to a safer area or get distance between myself and the risk. After I move and Refocus on a New-Me Activity. I move away in *medium risk* situations.
* *Leave the Area*: In *high risk* situations, I need to leave the area to where I cannot hear, see, talk to, or touch the risk. I should go to a safer area and do a Refocus New-Me Activity. If I am in the community, it may be helpful to return home.

4. Safety Plan- Handout 1

Safety Plans help us handle risks that come from inside and outside of us.

Inside-of-Me Risks

Outside-of-Me

Risks

Thoughts

Urges

Feelings

Fantasies

 People

 Places

 Things

4. Safety Plan- Worked Examples 1

Name: _____ Date: _____

Please list a few of your inside risks.

Thoughts: _____ I hate his guts. _____

Urges: _____ I want to smack him. _____

Feelings: _____ He cheated on me, and I am jealous. _____

Fantasies: _____ I would like to throw him off the bridge. _____

OUTSIDE

List things in your surroundings that are an outside risks.

RISKS

People: _____ That woman who stole my boyfriend. _____

Places: _____ They both work at Walmart. _____

Things: _____ When I hear 'our song' I get mad. _____

225

4. Safety Plan- Worksheet 1

Name: _____ **Date:** _____

Please list a few of your inside risks.

Thoughts: _____

Urges: _____

Feelings: _____

Fantasies: _____

OUTSIDE

List things in your surroundings that are an outside risks. **RISKS**

People: _____

Places: _____

Things: _____

3 Levels of Risk

HIGH Risk ➡️

Contact with the risk will cause serious damage

Danger is CLOSE

MEDIUM Risk ➡️

Contact will cause problems

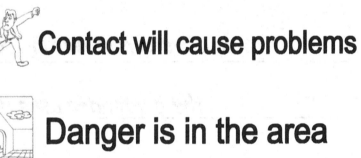 Danger is in the area

LOW Risk ➡️ Contact will cause stress

 Danger is far away

4. Safety Plan- Worked Example 2

Name: _____   Date: _____

Please list your High, Medium, and Low risk situations.

HIGH Risk Situations: (Close by &/or will cause serious damage)

I am drunk and want to drive.

_____

_____

MEDIUM Risk Situations: (In area &/or will cause problems)

I am in a restaurant waiting for a table before dinner, and

the bartender asks if I want a drink.

_____

LOW Risk Situations: (Far away &/or will cause stress)

I am an alcoholic, and my friends ask me to go out to a bar.

_____

_____

228

4. Safety Plan- Worksheet 2

Name: _____ **Date:** _____

Please list your High, Medium, and Low risk situations.

HIGH Risk Situations: (Close by &/or will cause serious damage)

_____

_____

_____

MEDIUM Risk Situations: (In area &/or will cause problems)

_____

_____

_____

LOW Risk Situations: (Far away &/or will cause stress)

_____

_____

_____

3 Types of Safety Plans

 ## Thinking Safety Plans:

A Thinking Safety Plan is when I think about how to handle risky situations. I think about whether I should Refocus on a New-Me Activity, Move Away, or Leave the Area. Thinking Safety Plans are helpful in low-risk situations.

 ## Talking Safety Plans:

In Talking Safety Plans I talk to someone and let them know about my safety concerns. When I tell someone about my risks, they can help me make safe decisions. I talk about whether it is best to Refocus, Move Away, or Leave the Area. It is important to be honest and get support In medium- and high-risk situations.

 ## Writing Safety Plans:

In Writing Safety Plans I write down any possible risks that I am concerned about and make a plan to handle each of the risks. In low-risk situations, I plan to Refocus on a New-Me Activity. For medium risks, I Move Away and in high-risk situations, I Leave the Area. If I know that a situation is going to be high-risk, I may want to do Thinking, Talking, and Writing Safety Plans to be sure I will be safe.

230

3 Ways to Handle Risk

 Leave the Area

 in HIGH Risk Situations

This means that if the situation is high risk I leave the area or community activity and go to a safer place. It is important to go where I can't hear, see, talk to, or touch the risk. Leaving, talking to someone, and focusing on a New-Me Activity will help me be on-track.

Move Away
in MEDIUM Risk Situations

This means I move away from the risk. For example, if I am having a problem with my housemate, I should go to my room, close the door, and refocus on a New-Me Activity.

Refocus on a New-Me Activity
in LOW Risk Situations

Refocusing means that I turn my attention from the risk to something on-track. When I stare at the risk I get more unsafe and emotional. When I focus on a New-Me Activity I am able to think more clearly .

231

4. Safety Plan- Worked Example 3

Writing Safety Plan

Name: _____ Date: _____

Getting a Clear Picture of the risk:

What is the risk: *I feel like running away from my program.*

Who is involved: *My staff and my housemate*

Where is the risk: *Downstairs in the kitchen and the den*

When is the risk happening: *8:00 at night--- Right now*

Is the risk: LOW (MEDIUM) HIGH

Making a Safety Plan:

LOW Risk= Refocus on New-Me Activities

What activity will I focus on: _____

MEDIUM Risk= I move away and focus on an activity

Where will I go: *I will stay in my room*

Who can I talk to: *I will call my therapist for skills coaching.*

What activity will I do: *Play video games and listen to music*

HIGH Risk= I leave the area, talk to someone, and do an activity.

Where will I go: _____

Who will I talk to: _____

What activity will I do: _____

232

Writing Safety Plan

Name: _____ Date: _____

Getting a Clear Picture of the risk:

What is the risk: _____

Who is involved: _____

Where is the risk: _____

When is the risk happening:_____

Is the risk: LOW   MEDIUM   HIGH

Making a Safety Plan:

LOW Risk= Refocus on New-Me Activities

What activity will I focus on: _____

MEDIUM Risk= I move away and focus on an activity

Where will I go:_____

Who can I talk to:_____

What activity will I do: _____

HIGH Risk= I leave the area, talk to someone, and do an activity.

Where will I go: _____

Who will I talk to: _____

What activity will I do: _____

5. New-Me Activities- Summary Sheet

New-Me Activities are an All-the-Time skill. This means that I can use New-Me Activities at any level of emotion, 0-1-2-3-4-5.

New-Me Activities are the on-track activities that I do during each day. Different New-Me Activities help me in different ways. It is important to choose the right activities at the right time. There are 4 Types of New-Me Activities:

- **Focus Activities**: Focus activities improve my attention and focus in the moment. When I do sorting, organizing, following step-by-step instructions, and/or counting, my mind becomes more focused. Examples: Solitaire, cooking with a recipe, counting money, folding clothes, cleaning, reading, and playing video games.

- **Feel Good Activities**: I do Feel Good New-Me Activities when I need to soothe myself. I use my senses to enjoy pleasant things. I see, listen to, smell, taste and feel things that make me feel good. I also may do self-care to feel better. Examples: Walking on the beach, using hand lotions which smell good, listening to nice music, drinking a cup of tea, washing my face, taking a bath, and eating chocolate..

- **Distraction Activities**: I do Distraction Activities when I have done everything I can in a situation and just need to hang-out or wait. Examples: Watching TV, movies, video games, and reading.

- **Fun Activities**: Fun Activities make me feel happiness and joy. I like doing different things and that is the spice of life! Examples: Drawing, playing sports, video games, working, cooking, cleaning, reading, watching TV, listening to music, talking to friends, going out, and studying skills, etc.

I want to pick New-Me Activities that help me most in the moment. For example:

- If I am getting upset or confused, I should choose a Focus New-Me Activity to increase focus and to think more clearly.
- If I am feeling uncomfortable or stressed, I may want to do Feel Good New-Me Activities to help myself relax and feel better.
- If I have to wait for a few hours and I want to keep my mind off of it, I should use Distraction New-Me Activities.
- If I want to feel good about myself and my life, I do Fun New-Me Activities.

Some New-Me Activities do more than one thing for me. For example: Video games may help me focus, distract me from my worries, and they are fun! A phone call to a friend may make me feel good and be fun at the same time.

I need to have a few different New-Me Activities that I can do when I am unfocused, worried, feeling bad, or bored. Sitting around being miserable often takes me off-track.

I have to remember to try new things! Keep an open mind and be WILLING! I need to use Clear Picture, On-Track Thinking, and Take On-Track Actions to do many of these activities each day!

I like to do New-Me Activities with people. I have to remember that when I interact with people, I should be below a 3 emotion. The other person should also be below a 3 emotion. If I am over a 3, I should do New-Me Activities by myself.

New-Me Activities help me to:

FOCUS

FEEL GOOD

DISTRACT Myself

Have FUN

FOCUS New-Me Activities

FOCUS New-Me Activities
help me get control of my mind!

 CONFUSED → FOCUSED

Organizing   **Cleaning**   **Counting**   **Sorting**   **Folding**

Following a recipe   **Reading**   **Video games**   **Computer**   **Playing cards**

5. New-Me Activities- Worksheet 1

Name: _____ **Date:** _____

Please list New-Me Activities that help you focus your mind.

My FOCUS New-Me Activities

_____

_____

_____

_____

_____

_____

_____

_____

_____

I do FEEL GOOD New-Me Activities to relax and soothe myself.

STRESSED ➡ FEEL BETTER

I Look	I Listen	I Smell	I Taste	I Touch

Pleasant Things

I enjoy nature

I listen to music

I smell nice things

I enjoy healthy food

I do self-care

5. New-Me Activities- Worksheet 2

Name: _____   **Date:** _____

Please list New-Me Activities that help your body feel good.

_____

_____

_____

_____

_____

_____

_____

_____

_____

_____

 I use DISTRACTION New-Me Activities when I need to turn my mind away from things or actions that are not on-track to my goal.

Distracting myself is helpful when I have done everything I can in a situation & I need to chill out and wait.

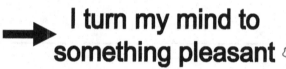 FRUSTRATION → I turn my mind to something pleasant

---

I watch shows or sports on TV

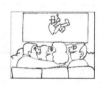

I watch movies

I play video games

I read magazines or books

5. New-Me Activities- Worksheet 3

Name: _____ **Date:**_____

Please list New-Me Activities that help you get your mind off of things.

DISTRACTION New-Me Activities

_____

_____

_____

_____

_____

_____

_____

_____

_____

I do FUN New-Me Activities to add joy and happiness to my life!

I do Fun New-Me Activities when
I need to turn my mood around.

Grumpy Mood ➡ **Find the Joy**

I do sports

I make crafts

I play games

I watch TV & movies

I read

I sing

I dance

I chat

I hang out

I go out

5. New-Me Activities- Worksheet 4

Name: _____ Date: _____

Please list New-Me Activities that help you have fun!

My FUN New-Me Activities

_____

_____

_____

_____

_____

_____

_____

_____

_____

_____

243

6. Problem Solving- Summary Sheet

Problem Solving is a Calm Only skill. This means that I can use Problem Solving when I am below a 3 emotion. When I try to do Problem Solving over a 3 emotion I usually make things worse for myself. I rush, forget to look at all my options, and choose options that may feel good in the short-term, yet are not helpful to me in the long-term. Problem Solving over a 3 takes me off-track from my goals. The person I am speaking with also should be below a 3 emotion.

1. When I notice that there is something bothering me in my life, I try to get a **Clear Picture of the Problem**. I think about what I want to have happen. I notice what is in the way of me reaching that goal. I continue doing Clear Picture and On-Track Thinking to help me handle the problem.

2. Once I have a Clear Picture of the Problem, I **Check All Options**. First, I think about different options. Options are all the things I could do to fix the problem. Then, I check my options by thinking about the pros and cons of each one. Pros are the possible on-track or helpful results of an action; cons are the not helpful possible results. Usually each option has both pros and cons, positive and negative outcomes. Pros get a thumbs-up and cons get a thumbs down. When an option has many pros or thumbs-up, it may be an On-Track Action. I take some time to think about all of the options and their pros and cons before deciding which action will help me reach my goal best.

3. Next, I make **Plan A**. Plan A is the plan that I think will work best to fix the problem. I put 100% effort and focus into my plan. I think about all the steps that I need to take. I think about all the people I need to talk to, what I need to say, and how I will say it. I think about all the other skills I need to use to solve the problem.

After I make Plan A, I think about the fact that sometimes Plan A doesn't work. Sometimes I have to be ready to compromise with the person. I make **Plan B** to have a back-up plan that will help me get part of the problem solved. Plan B may help me make the situation better, at least for now, until I can figure out another Plan A that will work better.

I realize that even Plan B doesn't work out sometimes, so I accept the fact that I may need to make a Plan C. **Plan C** may be to do an On-Track Action of Accepting the Situation. Perhaps doing a Focus New-Me Activity will help me stay on-track as plans fall apart. A Safety Plan might be necessary if I am having urges to take my frustration out on other people.

Problem Solving:

 Clear Picture of the Problem

 Check all Options

 Make Plans A, B, & C

> Problem Solving is a Calm Only skill. I have to be at a 0-3 emotion to do Problem Solving. I have to be focused so that I can think things through to reach my goals.

Name: __MARY__   Date:_____

🖥 Clear Picture of the Problem

⭐ **What is my goal in the situation?**

To get my new sneakers today

_____

🐎 **What is keeping me from my goal?**

I only have $12.00, and the ones I want are $25.00

_____

🖥 **What is the problem?**

I need to go to the mall to buy new sneakers, and

I do not have enough money to buy the ones I want.

6. Problem Solving- Worksheet 1

Name: _____ Date:_____

Clear Picture of the Problem

What is my goal in the situation?

_____

_____

What is keeping me from my goal?

_____

_____

What is the problem?

_____

_____

6. Problem Solving- Worked Example 2

Name: _MARY_   **Date:** _____

👍 **Check all Options** 👎

I think of lots of ways to fix my problem

Check the Pros 👍 and Cons 👎 for each option.

1. _I can get extra money from my house manager from my personal needs._

👍 Results: _I will see her today and maybe get my sneakers._

👎 Results: _If I don't see her, I will have to wait until tomorrow._

2. _I can call my sister to see if she will loan me the money._

👍 Results: _I might not have to pay my sister back._

👎 Results: _She will have to send it, and I won't get the money until next week._

3. _I can save my work money and go next week._

👍 Results: _I won't have to beg my sister and feel bad._

👎 Results: _I will have to wait until next week to get my sneakers._

4. _I can go to the mall and buy cheaper sneakers._

👍 Results: _I will get new sneakers today._

👎 Results: _I will not be buying my favorite sneakers._

Which is the best fit? _Talk to my manager_

6. Problem Solving- Worksheet 2

Name: _____ **Date:** _____

👍 **Check all Options** 👎

I think of lots of ways to fix my problem

Check the Pros 👍 and Cons 👎 for each option.

1. _____

👍 Results: _____

👎 Results: _____

2. _____

👍 Results: _____

👎 Results: _____

3. _____

👍 Results: _____

👎 Results: _____

4. _____

👍 Results: _____

👎 Results: _____

Which is the best fit? _____

6. Problem Solving- Worked Example 3

Name: **MARY**   Date: _____

Make Plans A, B, &C ☆

The plan I think will work best is Plan A.
I list the steps I will take to make Plan A work.

A Plan A: *I can get extra money for my house manager from my personal needs.*

Steps to Plan A: *Call my house manager on her cell phone*

Use Getting It Right to ask for extra money

Talk to staff about getting a ride to the mall

I make Plan B in case Plan A does not work out.
Plan B is my second best option.

B Plan B: *I want these sneakers, so I would rather wait.*

I would rather not bother my sister, so I will use my work money.

Just in case Plan A and Plan B do not work, I will make Plan C.
Plan C may be to Make Lemonade out of Lemons!

C Plan C: *If I can't go today, I will watch a movie instead.*

 Accept What I Can't Change

250

6. Problem Solving- Worksheet 3

Name: _____ Date: _____

Make Plans A, B, &C ☆

The plan I think will work best is Plan A.
I list the steps I will take to make Plan A work.

A Plan A: _____

Steps to Plan A: _____

_____

_____

I make Plan B in case Plan A does not work out.
Plan B is my second best option.

B Plan B: _____

_____

Just in case Plan A and Plan B do not work, I wil make Plan C.
Plan C may be to Make Lemonade out of Lemons!

C Plan C: _____

 Accept What I Can't Change

251

Copyright © 2011 Julie F. Brown

6. Problem Solving- Practice Exercise

Instructions: Listed below is a problem (or create another one). We are going to write down 5 possible options for fixing the problem. Then we are going to talk about the pros and cons for the options and choose the best fit. Next we are going to make a Plan A, B, and C.

PROBLEM: I do not like my housemate.

Different Problem: _____

CHECK MY OPTIONS: (Think about the pros and cons of each)

1. _____

2. _____

3. _____

4. _____

5. _____

What is the best option? _____

Plan A: _____

_____

_____

Plan B: _____

_____

Plan C: _____

6. Problem Solving- Worksheet 4

CLEAR PICTURE OF MY PROBLEM:

_____

_____

_____

CHECK MY OPTIONS: (Think about the pros and cons of each)

1. _____

2. _____

3. _____

4. _____

5. _____

What is the best option? _____

Plan A: _____

_____

_____

Plan B: _____

_____

Plan C: _____

7. Expressing Myself- Summary Sheet

Expressing Myself is a Calm Only skill. That means that I can use Expressing Myself only when I am below a 3 emotion. This also means that I can not communicate with another person unless he or she is also below a 3.

What is Expressing Myself:

- Expressing Myself is how I communicate what I think or feel. I bring what is happening on the inside of myself to the outside. For example, inside of myself I have: feelings, thoughts, ideas, concerns, hopes, and dreams.

- I Express Myself in many different ways. I talk, laugh, cry, and use my body language. I express what is inside of me when I do certain New-Me Activities. I Express Myself when I write, play music, & dance.

Why do I Express Myself?

- It often feels good to Express Myself. When I describe my thoughts and emotions, it helps me understand myself better. When I share what is inside I have a chance to feel connected with myself and the world around me. The connection can help me experience a sense of self-respect.

- Expressing Myself also helps me to do what works. When I need to get something done, usually it helps to communicate with people who are involved. Expressing Myself is an important tool when we need to do Problem Solving.

- Expressing Myself helps me adjust my relationships. People I want to be close to me, I communicate more with. People that I do not feel comfortable with, I share less with. I use Expressing Myself to balance my relationships.

- Expressing Myself helps me keep control in my life. I can let everyone know what I will do and will not do. When I am not sure, I say maybe.

- Talking to people and getting advice from people helps me. It does not mean that they are in control of my life. Listening to others does not mean I have to do what people say to do. I think things through and make my own decisions. Getting advice from people who care makes me happy and wise!

When do I Express Myself

- I use Expressing Myself when I am a 3 or below. Expressing emotions might make a feeling get a little stronger, so I need to keep using Clear Picture and On-Track Thinking to make sure I am still on-track. When I use Expressing Myself, I am careful how I treat people. When I treat people well, they tend to treat me better. When I treat people well, I feel self-respect.

- When I am over a 3 there is a good chance I will have urges to Express Myself. Unfortunately, that is when I have difficulty focusing my mind and saying helpful things. When my mind is fuzzy, I am not as careful. When I am not careful, I can harm my relationships. I have to let the urges to Express Myself pass when I am over a 3. I can Express Myself later when I am calmer, focused, and have used On-Track Thinking.

- There are times when it would help if I used Expressing Myself, but I am afraid to share my feelings and thoughts with people. For example, if I am lonely or I have a problem, Expressing Myself might be useful. If Expressing Myself makes sense, but I am afraid to share my feelings and thoughts, it is a chance to do an On-Track Action to do what works.

How I use Expressing Myself

- Using words is often the clearest way to communicate with people. It is hard for people to understand me if I just use my actions, my looks, or attitudes to communicate. I use Clear Picture and On-Track Thinking to change how I use Expressing Myself to do what works and reach my goals.

- It is sometimes hard for me to know what other people are really thinking and feeling. When I act like a mind-reader, I am often wrong. It works best to ask if I am wondering what someone is thinking.

- Sometimes I do not like what other people communicate to me. I do the Clear Picture Do's and On-Track Thinking before I take any actions.

Getting good at Expressing Myself helps me deal with my emotions, stay more safe, solve problems, get what I want, and have good relationships!

What is Expressing Myself?

Expressing Myself is Communication

Why do I use Expressing Myself?

 Expressing Myself feels good and helps me balance myself, my relationships, and my life.

How do I use Expressing Myself?

 I get a Clear Picture and use On-Track Thinking to help me know how to Express Myself best.

When do I use Expressing Myself?

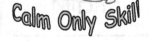 I Express Myself when I am at a 0-3 emotion.

Calm Only Skill

255

7. Expressing Myself- Handout 2

What is Expressing  Myself?

A. **I Communicating things that I think and feel.**

 Share my feelings   **Thoughts**   **Ideas**   **Concerns**  **Hope & Dreams**

B. **I Communicate in many different ways.**

 Talk   **Body Language**   **Laugh**  **Cry**

C. **I Express Myself when I do New-Me Activities...**

 Writing   **Music**   **Dance**   **Drawing**   **Acting**

Why do I use Expressing Myself?

On-Track sharing can help make my life better
Expressing Myself helps me when I use other skills

 It helps me explain what my risks are

 It helps me have fun & work with people

 It helps me negotiate and fix problems

 It helps me use the Right Words

 It helps me have 2-Way Street Relationships

7. Expressing Myself- Handout 4

How do I use Expressing Myself?

A. HEL !

Using words is often the clearest way to Express Myself.

B.

Mindreading often makes things worse.

C.

Communicating just with body language is give a Fuzzy Picture

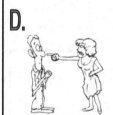
D.

Having an attitude shuts down a 2-Way Street Relationship

E.

If I don't know what someone means, I ask them to make it clearer

When do I use Expressing Myself?

Calm Only Skill

A. Expressing Myself works well when I am in Clear Mind.

B. When I am over a 3 emotion, my mind is fuzzy I may have strong urges to Express Myself.

C. In fuzzy mind I may yell, be demanding, and blame people. I may dump my emotions on others.

D. When I Express Myself, I am careful about how I effect other people.

E. How I treat people affects how they treat me.

F. How I treat people affects how I feel about myself.

8. Getting It Right- Summary Sheet

Getting It Right is a Calm Only skill. That means that I can use Getting It Right only when I am below a 3 emotion. It also means that the person I do Getting It Right with must also be below a 3 emotion.

I use Getting It Right to get things that I want from people.

- First, I make sure I am in the **Right Mind**. I have to be prepared and focused. I have to have a Getting It Right Plan. If my mind is fuzzy instead of clear, I may forget important steps in Getting It Right. In Fuzzy Mind, I might Get It Wrong.

- Then I have to choose the **Right Person** to talk to. In some situations, I may have to call him or her to set up a time to talk. I have to use my other skills while I am waiting to talk to the Right Person. Learning how to wait without losing focus or getting more upset are important skills!

- Choosing the **Right Time and Place** is important. I want people to be able to focus on me, my needs, and how they can help me. I want to DO WHAT WORKS, so waiting for the best time may increase my chances of being successful.

- Using the **Right Tone** is also a must! I use Clear Picture and On-Track Thinking to decide what tone will work. Usually being wimpy makes people not take me seriously. Often being demanding makes people pull away, stop listening, and think that I am not skillful. When I have an aggressive tone, it may stress the relationship so much that the person will never want to help me again or they will make things more difficult for me.

- Finally, I have to use the **Right Words: SEALS**
  - <u>S</u>ugar: Using Sugar means I am nice and polite to the person; I make them want to help me.
  - <u>E</u>xplain the Situation: I explain why it is important that the person help me. When helping me makes sense and is good for the other person, he or she is more likely to help me.
  - <u>A</u>sk for What I Want: I ask for what I want in a clear and direct way; AFTER using Sugar and Explaining the situation!
  - <u>L</u>isten: I listen carefully to what the other person says so that I can figure out how to Seal a Deal.
  - <u>S</u>eal a Deal: If the person agrees to help me, then I Seal a Deal and hash-out the details. If he or she does not agree, I try to either go to Plan B or step back from the situation and re-think the Getting It Right plan.

Getting What I Want!

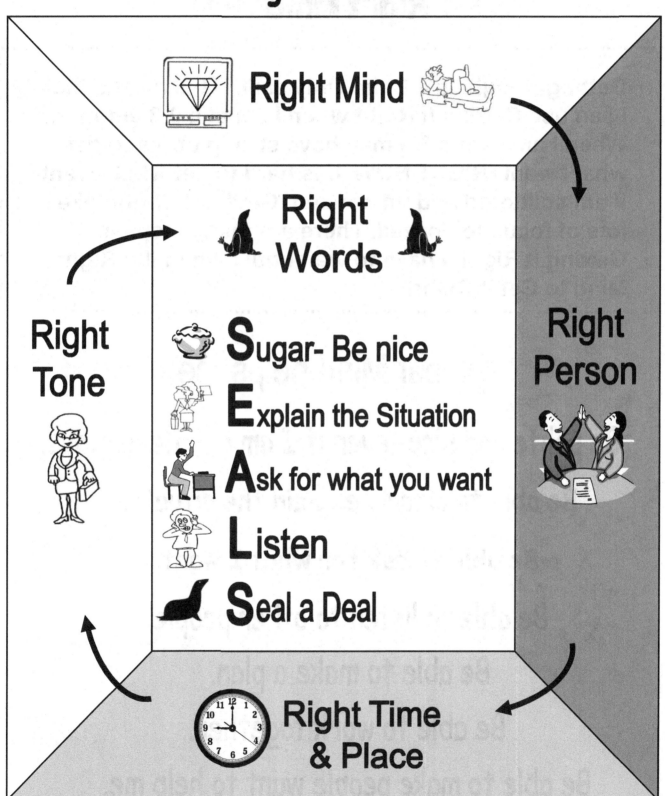

Right Mind

Right Words

Sugar- Be nice

Explain the Situation

Ask for what you want

Listen

Seal a Deal

Right Tone

Right Person

Right Time & Place

Right Mind

Getting It Right is a Calm Only skill. This means that I can use Getting It Right when I am at a 0-3 emotion. When I am over a 3, I may have strong urges to get what I want- RIGHT NOW. It is hard to get what I want if am scattered and unfocused. Getting It Right takes lots of focus to do well. There are many steps in Getting It Right. I have to wait until I am in the Right Mind to Get It Right!

 ## Clear Mind helps me:

Be polite and nice- even if I am a little nervous.

Be able to clearly explain the situation.

Be able to ask for what I want.

Be able to listen to other people.

Be able to make a plan.

Be able to work together.

Be able to make people want to help me.

Right Person

I have to choose the Right Person to talk to when I use Getting It Right. I pick the person who can get me what I want the best. It is usually worth waiting to talk to the Right Person. Talking to the wrong person can keep me from getting what we want. Each situation is different; I use Clear Picture and On-Track Thinking to help me choose the Right Person.

The Right Person is usually the person who is in control of what I want:

 If I want a raise, I usually talk to by boss.

 If I want to change my medications, usually I speak to my doctor.

If I want my housemate to turn down his music, usually I speak to my housemate.

Right Time & Place

Choosing the Right Time and Place is important. I want the person to be able to focus on me, my needs, and how they can help me. If the person is busy or distracted, he or she will not be 100% focused. I want to DO WHAT WORKS so waiting for the BEST time may increase my chances of being successful. While I am waiting, I need to use my other skills to stay on-track.

 # Choosing the Right Time and Place:

Speaking to the person in a quiet and private area can help me focus my attention.

I have to be able to focus on using the Right Tone and Right Words.

It may work best if the person is able to focus on what I am saying.

If the person is distracted by something else, it may affect their decisions.

Right Tone

Using the Right Tone is very important! Each situation is different; I use Clear Picture and On-Track Thinking to decide what tone will work best. Sometimes I want to be gentle, while other times it is best to be firm. I have to think about what tone will make the person hear what I am saying. I want to use a tone that makes the person want to help me.

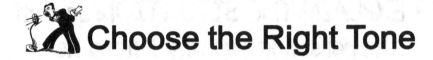

Choose the Right Tone

Being wimpy can make people not take me seriously.

When I have respect and need in my voice the person can feel how important the issue is to me.

Respect ⚖ Need

Being demanding can make the person pull away.

Having an aggressive tone can make the person want to work against me!

 **Right Words**

Using the Right Words is important too! I might be nervous when I am Getting It Right, so I plan ahead and practice so that the words come out smoothly.

 I use SUGAR to help the person want to help me.

 I EXPLAIN THE SITUATION so that the person knows why I need help.

 Then I ASK FOR WHAT I WANT in a direct and clear way.

 Then I LISTEN carefully so that I clearly understand what the person is saying.

 I SEAL A DEAL to get what I want!

 If the person says "no", I do Clear Picture and On-Track Thinking to figure out how to deal with my emotions and to get my needs met.

8. Getting It Right- Worksheet 1

Name: _____ **Date:** _____

Getting It Right Plan

What do I want? _____

Who will I talk to? _____

When and where will I talk to him or her? _____

_____

What kind of tone will I use? _____

What will I say to use **S**UGAR? _____

How will I **EX**PLAIN my situation? _____

_____

How will I **A**SK for what I want? _____

_____

Will I **L**ISTEN to what he or she says? _____YES   _____NO

What is the Deal I want? _____

_____

How will I **S**EAL a DEAL? _____

267

9. Relationship Care- Summary Sheet

Relationship Care is a Calm Only skill. That means that I can use Relationship Care only when I am below a 3 emotion. It also means that the person I am talking with must also be below a 3 emotion. Building On-Track Relationships, Balancing On-Track Relationships, and Changing Off-Track Relationships are aspects of Relationship Care

I use Relationship Care to Build On-Track Relationships with myself and other people.
- An On-Track relationship with myself means that I am getting a stronger Core Self. There are four parts of the Core Self:
  1. Self-awareness: I use Clear Picture to be aware of this moment. I see myself and my life *as it is right now*. I also pay attention to my goals. When I know what I want it is much easier to make a Skills Plan to reach my goals. It is hard to see what is really happening, but in the long run it makes me stay on-track and feel better about myself. As I learn to see myself clearly, I can see others more clearly as well.
  2. Self-Acceptance: When I see and handle myself, it is easier to accept myself and other people. As I interact with others, I see that we are all different and that is OK! That's what makes life interesting! When I notice my thoughts and urges to put myself down, I Turn It to On-Track Thinking about myself instead.
  3. Self-Value: As I use my skills to reach goals, I get more of what I want. I feel good about my abilities to handle my emotions, relationships, and my life. I manipulate things in a good way! Doing what works makes me feel better about myself. When I value me, it is easier to value other people.
  4. Self-Trust: Using my skills, I am able to stay on-track in more challenging situations. I try new things, which makes me happier. I know I can handle anything that comes my way! As I trust myself, I am more able to trust other people. A stronger core self helps me have better relationships.

I use Relationship Care to Balance my On-Track Relationships with myself and other people.
- There are many different types of relationships in my life. I use Clear Picture, On-Track Thinking, and my other skills to make on-track choices to keep them in balance.
- I use Relationship Care behaviors to keep my relationships closer, and I use Relationship NOT Care behaviors when I want to distance myself from someone.
  - Examples of Relationship Care behaviors are when I focus on the person, make thoughtful comments, call on the phone, have appropriate touch, pay compliments, and invite the person to do activities.
  - Examples of Relationship NOT Care behaviors are when I act distracted, change the subject, act disrespectfully, fail to return calls, or act over-controlling.
- A 2-Way Street Relationship is when I have an equal give and take between me and another person. Both of us listen and talk. We work together. Respect flows back and forth between us.
- A One-Way Street Relationship is when I feel that I am giving and the other person is not. I also have One-Way Street Relationships when I do not give or take in a relationship.

I use Relationship Care to Change Off-Track Relationships with myself and other people.
- When I get off-track with myself, I sometimes lose track of my goals, put myself down, and do Off-Track Actions. I get back on-track with myself when I have a Clear Picture of my goals, do thumbs-up thinking about myself, and stop off-track habits.
- When I get off-track with others I can Repair Relationships. Sometimes I cause the problem and have to fix it, and sometimes other people do things that I have to talk to them about.
  - When I have a relationship problem with another person, first I try to Find the Middle Ground. I Talk It Out, try to See Both Sides of the situation, and Work It Out together in a way that fits for us both.
  - When I know I have done something to hurt another person, I do the Steps of Responsibility. I clearly Admit the Problem, Apologize, Commit to Change, and Take an On-Track Action that fits for me and makes the relationship better.
  - When I have tried to find Middle Ground and there are still serious relationship problems, I may have to use Problem Solving to figure out if I need to end Off-Track Relationships and how best to do it.

268

9. Relationship Care- Handout 1

Relationship Care is a Calm Only skill. This means that I can only use Relationship Care when I and the other person are at 0-3 level of emotion. When either person is over a 3, he or she may not be thinking clearly enough to manage relationships well. I use Clear Picture and On-Track Thinking to build, balance, and change my relationships.

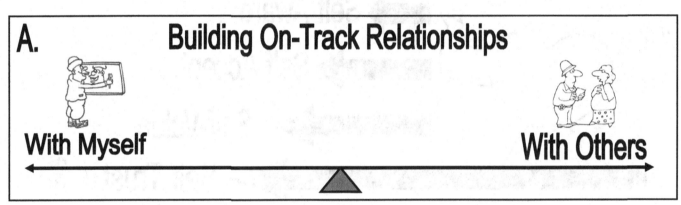

A. Building On-Track Relationships

With Myself   With Others

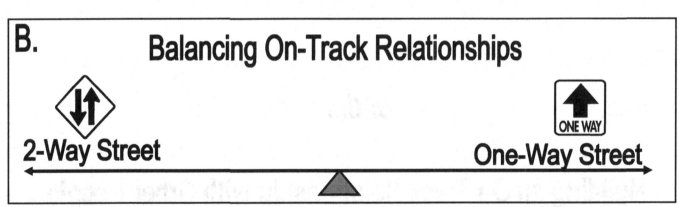

B. Balancing On-Track Relationships

2-Way Street   One-Way Street

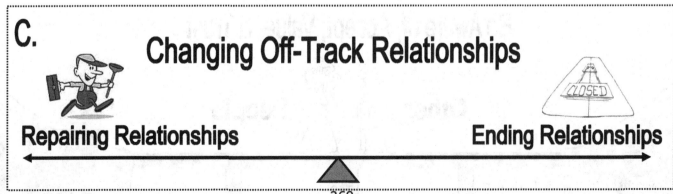

C. Changing Off-Track Relationships

Repairing Relationships   Ending Relationships

A. ## Building On-Track Relationships

Building an On-Track Relationship with Myself

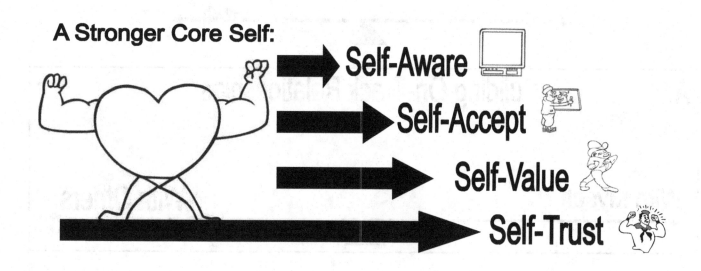

A Stronger Core Self:

→ Self-Aware

→ Self-Accept

→ Self-Value

→ Self-Trust

and...

Building an On-Track Relationship with Other People

Be Aware of, Accept, Value, & Trust

Other **People**

270

9. Relationship Care- Worksheet 1

Name: _____   Date: _____

A. **Building On-Track Relationships**

Things I do to build an
on-track relationship with myself:

_____
_____
_____
_____
_____
_____

and...

Things I do to build on-track
relationships with other people:

_____
_____
_____
_____
_____
_____

271

B. Balancing On-Track Relationships

Different Types of Relationships

 Dating

Supprt Staff

Friends

Housemates

Co-workers

Family

Me

B. Balancing On-Track Relationships

Balancing Relationship Behaviors

Relationship Care Behaviors

Relationship NOT Care Behaviors

We are Both Important ⟷ **It's All About Me**

Focused on the Person ⟷ **NOT Paying Attention**

Make Thoughtful Comments ⟷ **Change the Subject**

Paying Compliments ⟷ **Being Disrespectful**

Doing Things Together ⟷ **Being Over-Controlling**

273

B. **Balancing On-Track Relationships**

 2-Way Street Relationships

 I listen and I talk

 I give and I take

and...

 One-Way Street Relationships

I feel the other person is not participating

 I do not give or take

274

9. Relationship Care- Worksheet 2

Name: _____ Date: _____

B. Balancing On-Track Relationships `ONE WAY`

List things that you do to make
2-Way Street Relationships?

_____

_____

_____

_____

_____

and...

List things you do to make
One-Way Street Relationships `ONE WAY`

_____

_____

_____

_____

_____

C. Changing Off-Track Relationships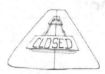

Changing Self-Relationships

 Getting Back On-Track with Me

 Instead of a Fuzzy Picture About My Goals, I Get a Clear Picture of My Goals

 Instead of Putting Myself Down, I do On-Track Thinking

 Instead of Off-Track Habits, I Take On-Track Actions to Care for My Body

C. Changing Off-Track Relationships

Changing Relationships with Others

Repairing Relationships

 When I create a relationship problem

When the other person creates a relationship problem

 Finding Middle Ground

Relationship Problems	Talk It Out	See Both Sides	Work It Out	Relationship Care

Name: _____ Date: _____

Finding Middle Ground

Talk It Out:
What is the relationship problem?

_____

_____

See Both Sides:
What do I need to tell the person about my side?

_____

_____

See Both Sides:
How can I get to know the other side?

_____

_____

Work It Out:
What can I do to try to work it out?

_____

C. Changing Off-Track Relationships

Changing Relationships with Other People

Steps of Responsibility

| Relationship Problems | Admit the Problem | Apologize | Commit to Change | Take an On-Track Action |

Ending Off-Track Relationships

| Relationship Problems | Clear Picture | On-Track Thinking | Problem Solving | Relationship Care |

Name: _____ Date: _____

Steps of Responsibility

Admit the problem

_____

_____

Apologize for the harm that was done

_____

_____

Commit to change the behavior

_____

_____

Take an On-Track Action

_____

_____

9. Relationship Care- Worksheet 4

Name: _____ Date: _____

C. Changing Off-Track Relationships

Things I do to get back on-track with me:

_____

_____

_____

_____

_____

and...

Things I do to get back on-track with others:

_____

_____

_____

_____

_____

_____

Using My Skills- Worksheet 1

(when under a 3 emotion)

Name: _____ Date: _____

Breathe ☐ Yes ☐ No

Surroundings: _____

Body check: _____

1. Clear Picture

RIGHT NOW

Feeling: _____ Rating: 0 - 1 - 2 - 3 - 4 - 5

Thought: _____

Urge: _____

2. On-Track Thinking:

STOP, Step Back & Think about what I want ☐ Yes ☐ No

Goal: _____

Check It: ☐ 👍 Helpful Urge   ☐ 👎 Not Helpful Urge

Turn It to 👍 Thinking: _____

Skill Plan: My Level of Emotion RIGHT NOW: _____ How many skills do I need? _____

What Category of Skills can I use:

All-the-Time Skills 0-5 emotion: ☐ Yes ☐ No

Calm Only Skills 0-3 emotion: ☐ Yes ☐ No

Have I used Clear Picture? ☐ Yes ☐ No

Am I using On-Track Thinking right now? ☐ Yes   No

Should I take an On-Track Action? ☐ Yes ☐ No

Should I use a Safety Plan? Is there any Risk? ☐ Yes ☐ No

☐ Thinking   ☐ Talking   ☐ Written

☐ Low Risk   ☐ Medium Risk   ☐ High risk

☐ Refocus   ☐ Move Away   ☐ Leave Area Entirely

I will go: _____

Should I do New-Me Activities? ☐ Yes ☐ No

Focus: _____

Feel Good: _____

Distraction: _____

Fun: _____

(page 2)

Should I do Problem Solving? ☐ Yes ☐ No ☐ YES, when I am Calmer

Clear Picture of my problem: _____

Check All Options: Helpful 👍 Not Helpful 👎

    Option: _____ 👍 👍

    Option: _____ 👍 👍

    Option: _____ 👍 👍

Plan A: _____

Plan B: _____

Plan C: _____

Should I Express Myself? ☐ Yes ☐ No ☐ YES, when I am Calmer

What do I need to share: _____

Who do I need to share with: _____

How will I share it: _____

Should I use Getting It Right? ☐ Yes ☐ No ☐ YES, when I am Calmer

Right Mind: _____

Right Person: _____

Right Time & Place: _____

Right Tone: _____

Right Words- Sugar: _____

    Explain: _____

    Ask: _____

    Listen _____

    Seal a Deal: _____

Should I use Relationship Care? ☐ Yes ☐ No ☐ YES, when I am Calmer

Relationship Care with myself: _____

Relationship Care with others: _____

Should I have a 2-Way street relationship by listening and talking? ☐ Yes ☐ No

Should I repair a relationship? ☐ Yes ☐ No

Should I change an off-track relationship? ☐ Yes ☐ No

Thumbs-Up Thinking: _____

⭐ What is my goal: _____

Do I have a 👍 Skills Plan? ☐ Yes ☐ No

What will my On-Track Action be: _____

Cheer myself on: _____

283

Using My Skills- Worksheet 2
(when over a 3 emotion)

Name: _____ Date: _____

Breathe ☐ Yes ☐ No

1. Clear Picture

RIGHT NOW

Surroundings: _____

Body check: _____

Feeling: _____ Rating: 0 - 1 - 2 - 3 - 4 - 5

Thought: _____

Urge: _____

2. On-Track Thinking:

STOP STOP, Step Back & Think about what I want ☐ Yes ☐ No

Goal: _____

Check It: ☐ 👍 Helpful Urge ☐ 👎 Not Helpful Urge

Turn It to 👍 Thinking: _____

Skill Plan: My Level of Emotion RIGHT NOW: _____ How many skills do I need? _____

What Category of Skills can I use: All-the-Time Skills 0-5 emotion: ☐ Yes ☐ No

Calm Only Skills 0-3 emotion: ☐ Yes ☐ No

Should I use a Safety Plan? Is there any Risk? ☐ Yes ☐ No

☐ Thinking   ☐ Talking   ☐ Written

☐ Low Risk   ☐ Medium Risk   ☐ High risk

☐ Refocus   ☐ Move Away   ☐ Leave Area Entirely

I will go: _____

Should I do New-Me Activities? ☐ Yes ☐ No

Focus: _____

Feel Good: _____

Distraction: _____

Fun: _____

Skill Plan I will use: 🖥 ☕ 🚂 🛡 🍰☕ 🍰☕   Is that enough? Yes ☐ No ☐

3. On-Track Action: _____

Skills System- Skills Quiz 1

Name: _____ **Date:** _____

1. What skill do I use all the time? _____

2. What skill do I always use after Clear Picture?

   _____

3. What are the numbers of the two skills I use first in all

   situations? _____ and _____

4. What is the skill that I use when I do something positive to

   step towards my goals? _____

5. What skill helps me handle risky situations?

   _____

6. What skill helps me focus, feel better, distract myself, and to

   have fun? _____

7. What skill helps me fix situations?

   _____

8. What skill helps me communicate with people?

   _____

9. What skill helps me get what I want from people?

   _____

10. What skill helps me have a positive relationship with myself?

   _____

11. What skill helps me have positive relationships with other

   people? _____

Skills System- Skills Quiz 1 Answer Sheet

Name: _____ **Date:** _____

1. What skill do I use all the time? *Clear Picture*

2. What skill do I always use after Clear Picture?

    On-Track Thinking

3. What are the numbers of the two skills I use first in all

    situations? *1 and 2*

4. What is the skill that I use when I do something positive to

    step towards my goals? *On-Track Action*

5. What skill helps me handle risky situations? *Safety Plan*

6. What skill helps me focus, feel better, distract myself, and to

    have fun? *New-Me Activity*

7. What skill helps me fix situations? *Problem Solving*

8. What skill helps me communicate with people?

    Expressing Myself

9. What skill helps me get what I want from people?

    Getting It Right

10. What skill helps me have a positive relationship with myself?

    Relationship Care

11. What skill helps me have positive relationships with other

    people?

    Relationship Care

The Skills System

SKILL MASTER:

_____

Cycle #:_____   Date:_____

Group Leader: _____

APPENDIX B

Instructions

The Skills System Planning Sheet is designed to help group leaders (1) make initial plans for group and (2) monitor topics addressed. The group leader may alter preliminary plans and not cover anticipated material. This form allows the trainer to keep track of topics so that planning in future cycles through the material can be adjusted accordingly.

Skills System Group Planning Sheet Group Leader: _____ **Date:**_____

Participants: _____

Check If Done	Intervention	Description
	Exploring Existing Knowledge *Welcome group*	
	Instructions for introductions	
	Orient to mindfulness activity	
	Mindfulness exercise	
	Instructions for mindfulness	
	Review questions re. mindfulness	
	Orient to Skills System review	
	Skills System review	
	Orient to reviewing skills practice	
	Review skills practice	
	Review questions	
	Orient to new skill topic	
	Discussing existing knowledge about the new topic	
	Assessment questions about topic	
	Relevant context questions	
	Orient to relevant context of topic	
	Orient to new learning activity	
	Encoding: Teaching new topic *Encoding activity*	
	Instructions for encoding activity	
	Which handouts were reviewed	
	Handout content questions	
	Orient to the end of Encoding Phase	

	Elaboration: Linking previous and new learning *Practice exercise*	
	Orient to Elaboration exercise	
	Instructions for exercise	
	Review questions	
	Orient to discussion	
	Linking question	
	Disclosure question	
	Expansion questions	
	Orient to the end of Elaboration	
	Efficacy: Integrating learning *Efficacy activity*	
	Orient to Efficacy activities	
	Instructions for activity	
	Review questions	
	Orient to discussion	
	Barrier question	
	Inner-wisdom question	
	Commitment questions	
	Coaching question	
	Orient to home study	
	Orient to group ending	
	Ring bell to end group	

APPENDIX C

These scenarios can be used in various ways. A skills trainer can read them during training sessions to explain how skills are used within a given context. Support providers can utilize the scenarios to better understand how to provide skills coaching. Participants can read or listen to these stories as home study to deepen awareness of skills.

Scenario 1

The following scenario is an example of an individual using skills in a work situation.

Clear Picture.

I was at work, and I was focusing on my job. I sort different things into three different bins. As I was sorting, my co-worker Mike came over to me. He said, "This is my job now; you are supposed to do something else." I noticed I was confused by what he said. I felt confused at a 3. I also noticed my stomach started doing flip-flops. I thought, *What is he talking about?* I had the urge to tell him to mind his own business. I took a second to Take a Breath. I could feel that I was upset at a 3 now also. I coached myself to take a few more breaths. When I focus on my breathing, it helps me to get a Clear Picture of what is happening right now.

On-Track Thinking.

As I was breathing, I knew I had to do some On-Track Thinking. I stopped and stepped back to think things through. I thought about what I wanted to happen in this situation. I had the urge to tell him off, but I Checked It and decided it was not helpful. Telling him to mind his own business got a thumbs-down from me. So, instead, I Turned It; I thought about what would help me more. I want more hours and to make more money, so having a problem with my co-worker would not get me there. I needed to make a Skills Plan. I am at a 3, so I can use all nine of my skills. But, if I am not careful, I might say something off-track.

I kept focusing on doing my job, which was a New-Me Activity for me. Actually, refocusing on a New-Me Activity is a Safety Plan, too. *Wow*, I thought, *I have already done Clear Picture, On-Track Thinking, Safety Plan, and New-Me Activities! I really am a Skills Master!*

I kept thinking about what other skills I needed to do. I was trying to decide whether it was best to do a Safety Plan and Move Away … or should I Express Myself and ask Mike what he was talking about so I had a better understanding of the situation? If I had been over a 3, I would have done a Talking Safety Plan and Moved Away and talked to my supervisor about the situation. But, since I was not over 3, I decided to ask my co-worker what he meant by the comment. *If I do this right*, I thought, *it might be good Relationship Care, too. Also, if there is a problem, I can do Problem Solving with my supervisor about it, rather than getting mad at Mike.*

On-Track Action and Expressing Myself.

My On-Track Action was going to be to use Expressing Myself and ask Mike to explain. I had to be careful that my tone was on-track. I wanted to try to keep a Two-Way-Street Relationship with him. So I said, "What do you mean, Mike? I don't understand."

He said, "I don't know, the boss wants you to go over there to do something else, and I was supposed to come do this."

Skills Review.

This person was at a 3 confused. He did Clear Picture, On-Track Thinking, On-Track Action, Safety Plan, New-Me Activity, and Expressing Myself. He only had to use four skills, and he used six skills effectively.

Scenario 2

Clear Picture.

Right away I saw that Mike was just as confused as I was about the situation. I took a deep belly breath and got a Clear Picture. I noticed that I felt relieved that he was not being a jerk. I also thought about how when I did Relationship Care and saw the situation from both sides, I understood that he was actually trying to help me. I felt relieved at a 2. Even though I felt better, I was still a little confused at a 2 about what I was supposed to do next. My body was more relaxed, and my urge was to figure out what was going on.

On-Track Thinking.

I kept doing my work as I used On-Track Thinking. I stopped, stepped back, and thought about what I wanted. I took a second to Check My Urge. I wanted to figure out what I needed to do next. That was a thumbs-up urge. Now, I needed to make a Skills Plan. I am not over a 3, so I can use my Calm-Only skills. I took a few moments to think about which skills would help me right now. First, I usually check to see whether I need to use a Safety Plan. I did not feel that there was any risk, so I did not think it was necessary. I wanted to know what was going on, so I think that I need to use Getting It Right to get that information. I will go talk to my supervisor now to get the information I need. Before I go, I want to do Relationship Care with Mike.

On-Track Action and Relationship Care.

My On-Track Action was to be sure that Mike was all set at my work station and to tell him what was going on.

I said to him, "Mike, thanks for coming over. I don't really know what I am supposed to do, so I am going to go talk to our supervisor. Are you all set here?"

Mike said, "No problem, Jeff. I am all set."

Skills Review.

Jeff was at a 2 emotion. He needed to use three skills. Instead, he used five skills. In addition to Clear Picture, On-Track Thinking, and On-Track Action, he used Relationship Care in two different ways. First, Jeff used finding Middle Ground and saw the situation from both sides. Later in the situation, he used on-track relationship behaviors to let Mike know that he cared. Jeff was doing his part to have a Two-Way-Street Relationship. In a way, he was also doing Relationship Care with his boss by making sure that the job was getting done.

Scenario 3

Clear Picture.

On my way to see my supervisor, Mrs. Ford, I got a Clear Picture. I took a few breaths as I walked. I noticed that I was nervous at a 3 by now. I thought about how I hoped the conversation would go well, but that I might be in trouble for something. There were a few butterflies in my stomach, and my hands were a little sweaty. I had the urge to put my head down and avoid eye contact.

On-Track Thinking.

I knew On-Track Thinking would help me right then. While walking I thought about how to use Getting It Right. I wanted to find out what was going on. Being at a 3, I know I was in the Right Mind. Mrs. Ford was the Right Person, and she was not busy in her office. It seemed like the Right Time and Place. As I walked, my head was down, and I was feeling afraid to talk to her. I hoped my tone wasn't going to be very wimpy and like a mouse. That would not be the Right Tone. Was acting like that going to help me show my boss that I was ready to take on more hours and be paid more money? No! So, I Checked It and gave it a thumbs-down. I wanted her to take me seriously, so I thought about doing an On-Track Action of looking up, rather than down. I wanted to use a tone that was strong, but not aggressive and demanding. I decided to do opposite of my urge to avoid and jump into the conversation with both feet!

On-Track Action and Getting It Right.

I did an On-Track Action; I knocked on Mrs. Ford's office door and smiled at her. She motioned for me to come in. I began Getting It Right with Mrs. Ford by using the Right Words. I wanted her to want to help me, so I began with using some sugar.

"Hi, Mrs. Ford, how are you today?"

She smiled and said, "Great, Jeff. Thanks for asking. How can I help you?"

I knew that I had to explain the situation so that my supervisor had a Clear Picture. "Mrs. Ford, Mike came to my area and said that he was doing my job now. I was unsure what to do. I thought it was a good idea to come talk to you about it." Then I asked directly for what I wanted: "Mrs. Ford, could you please let me know what I need to be doing right now?" I knew that I had to listen carefully to her responses, even if I did not like what she said.

Mrs. Ford said, "I'm sorry, Jeff. I should have spoken to you about this myself sooner. I would like you to move over to packing boxes and preparing them for shipping. You have done such a great job sorting that I think you can take on more responsibility in the future. I was wondering if you would like to be trained to do the new job. It will mean that you have to work on Saturdays now. Can you do that?"

Skills review.

Jeff was at a 3 emotion, and he had to use four skills. He utilized fours skill in this scenario. He got a Clear Picture, did On-Track Thinking, did an On-Track Action, and used Getting It Right. When Jeff heard about his new position, he began having other emotions. He needed to get another Clear Picture and use On-Track Thinking to make sure his next steps were On-Track Actions.

Scenario 4

Clear Picture.

Mrs. Ford's words were shocking to me. I noticed I was excited at a 4. My heart was racing. My thoughts were spinning about the good news. I thought about how great it was that I had reached a personal goal. Unfortunately, I also remembered that the house car was not available on Saturdays, so I might not have transportation. This made me feel anxious at a 4. I had the urge say yes to the offer right away. I realized that I had to focus, so I tried to take a few breaths to settle down.

On-Track Thinking.

As I took a few breaths, I Stopped, Stepped Back, and Thought about what I wanted. I checked my urge to say yes right away to the job, because I did not want to promise something that I could not follow through on. It was hard to resist the urge to say yes, but I gave it a thumbs-down. Instead I Turned It to thumbs-up thinking and coached myself not to rush. I made a Skills Plan. If I did rush, there was a risk that I would mess up this opportunity. I would have to do Problem Solving later. This job was important to me, and I had things to work out. I decided that a Thinking Safety Plan was a good idea. I thought that if I could refocus on a New-Me Activity, it would help me become more focused. I thought about how starting the new job training might make me upset again. Instead I thought that sorting at my bins was a good focus New-Me Activity that would help me stay on-track.

On-Track Action and Safety Plan.

"Mrs. Ford, thank you very much. I am really happy about this. There are some problems with transportation on Saturdays that I will have to figure out. If it would be all right with you, could I give you my answer tomorrow about this?" Mrs. Ford agreed.

I said, "Would it be okay if I returned to my bins to finish there for the day?" Mrs. Ford thought that was a good plan.

Skills Review.

Jeff is doing a great job handling things. He was at a 4 and did not use Calm-Only skills. He needed to use five skills, and he did: Clear Picture, On-Track Thinking, On-Track Action, Safety Plan, and New-Me Activities. It was really difficult not to agree right away to taking the new job, but he allowed that urge to pass. In addition, he figured out a way to become more focused by bringing his attention to the New-Me Activity.

APPENDIX D

Skills System Test

Name: _____   Date: _____

Skills Instructor: _____

1. How many skills are in the Skills System? _____

2. What are the System Tools? _____

3. What is Skill 1? _____

4. What is Skill 2? _____

5. What is Skill 3? _____

6. What is Skill 4? _____

7. What is Skill 5? _____

8. What is Skill 6? _____

9. What is Skill 7? _____

10. What is Skill 8? _____

11. What is Skill 9? _____

12. What two things does the Feelings Rating Scale help us do?
    1) _____
    2) _____

13. What are the two Categories of Skills and the level of emotions they are used at?

    Category name:_____ Levels of emotion: _____
    Category name:_____ Levels of emotion: _____

14. What does the Recipe for Skills help us know? _____
_____

15. At a 3 emotion, how many skills do we use?_____

16. At a 3 emotion, which skills can we use? _____
_____

17. What are the six steps of Skill 1?
    1) _____
    2) _____
    3) _____
    4) _____
    5) _____
    6) _____

18. What does Skill 1 help us do? _____

19. What Category of Skill is Skill 1? _____

20. What are the four parts of Skill 2?
    1) _____
    2) _____
    3) _____
    4) _____

21. What does Skill 2 help us do? _____

20. What are the five parts of Skill 3?
    1) _____
    2) _____
    3) _____
    4) _____
    5) _____

21. What does Skill 3 help us do? _____

22. What Category of Skills is Skill 3? _____

23. What does Skill 4 help us do? _____

24. What are the three Levels of Risk? _____

25. What are the three kinds of Safety Plans? _____

26. What are the three ways to manage risk?
    1) _____
    2) _____
    3) _____

27. What Category of Skills is Skill 4? _____

28. What are the four types of Skill 5?

    1) _____

    2) _____

    3) _____

    4) _____

29. What Category of Skills is Skill 5? _____

30. How does Skill 6 help us? _____

31. What are the three steps in Skill 6?

    1) _____

    2) _____

    3) _____

32. What is the Category of Skills of Skill 6? _____

33. How does Skill 7 help us? _____

34. What are examples of ways to do Skill 7? _____

35. What Category of Skills is Skill 7? _____

36. How does Skill 8 help us? _____

37. What are the Right Things in Skill 8?

    • _____

    • _____

    • _____

    • _____

    • _____

    • _____

38. What are the Right Words?

    • _____

    • _____

    • _____

    • _____

    • _____

39. What Category of Skills is Skill 8? _____

40. How does Skill 9 help us? _____

41. Who do we do Skill 9 with? _____

42. What are the three functions of Skill 9?

    1) _____

    2) _____

    3) _____

43. What are the four parts of the Core Self?

    1) _____

    2) _____

    3) _____

    4) _____

44. How do we act in Two-Way-Street Relationships? _____

45. What are examples of relationship behaviors that make relationships closer?

_____

46. What are examples of relationship behaviors that make relationships more distant?

_____

47. What are the three steps of Finding Middle Ground?

    1) _____

    2) _____

    3) _____

48. What are the four Steps of Responsibility?

    1) _____

    2) _____

    3) _____

    4) _____

49. What two skills do we always use to figure out what skills we need to use?

    • _____

    • _____

50. How many times per day do Skill Masters use skills? _____

Answer Key for Skills System Test

1. Nine

2. Feelings Rating Scale, Categories of Skills, Recipe for Skills

3. Clear Picture

4. On-Track Thinking

5. On-Track Action

6. Safety Plan

7. New-Me Activities

8. Problem Solving

9. Expressing Myself

10. Getting It Right

11. Relationship Care

12. (1) Rate our emotions (2) Tell us what Category of Skills to use

13. (1) All-the-Time skills; 0–5 emotions (2) Calm-Only skills; 0–3 emotions

14. How many skills to use

15. Four skills

16. All nine skills

17. (1)Take a Breath (2) Notice Surroundings (3) Body Check (4) Label and Rate Emotions (5) Notice Thoughts (6) Notice Urges

18. Have a Clear Picture of what is happening inside and outside of us in the current moment

19. All-the-Time

20. (1) Stop, Step back, and Think about what I want (2) Check the Urge or Check It (3) Turn It to Thumbs-Up Thinking (4) Make a Skills Plan

21. Take a Positive Step toward our goal

22. All-the-Time

23. Handle risky situations

24. (1) Low (2) Medium (3) High

25. (1)Thinking, (2) Talking, (3) Writing

26. (1) Refocus on New-Me Activity (2) Move Away (3) Leave the Area

27. All-the-Time

28. (1) Focus (2) Feel better (3) Distraction (4) Fun

29. All-the-Time skill

30. Solve problems

31. (1) Clear Picture of the problem (2) Check All Options (3) Make Plans A, B, and C

32. Calm Only

33. Communicate with people

34. Examples: Words, body language, laugh, cry, sports, singing, dancing, art, et cetera

35. Calm Only

36. Gets us what we want

37. Right Mind, Right Person, Right Time, Right Place, Right Tone, and Right Words

38. SEALS: Sugar, Explain what you want, Ask for what you want, Listen, Seal a deal

39. Calm Only

40. Helps us have good relationships with ourselves and other people

41. Ourselves and other people

42. (1) Building On-Track Relationships (2) Balancing On-Track Relationships (3) Changing Off-Track Relationships

43. (1) Self-awareness (2) Self-acceptance (3)Self-value (4) Self-trust

44. Talk and listen; give and take

45. Examples: value the other person, focus on person, make thoughtful comments, pay compliments, do things together

46. Examples: Focus on self only, do not pay attention to the other person, change the subject, be disrespectful, be overly controlling

47. (1) Talk It Out (2) See Both Sides (3) Work It Out

48. (1) Clearly admit the problem (2) Apologize (3) Commit to change (4) Take an On-Track Action

49. Clear Picture and On-Track Thinking

50. Any amount that represents a lot or all day

GLOSSARY

Accept the Situation: Accept the situation is the fourth element within On-Track Action. It may be helpful to accept the situation once the individual has done everything possible to improve the circumstances. Acceptance helps the individual remain focused and aware of situations so that he can continue to use skills to manage the events effectively.

All-the-Time skills: All-the-Time skills is a Category of Skills. The first five skills are labeled as All-the-Time skills: Clear Picture, On-Track Thinking, On-Track Action, Safety Plan, and New-Me Activities. These skills can be used at any time and at any level of emotional escalation, 0–5.

Barrier questions: Barrier questions are asked by the skills trainer to prompt the participant to evaluate possible pitfalls to skills use. For example, "What is difficult about doing a Safety Plan?" These types of queries are designed to stimulate troubleshooting and promote adjustments, thus improving efficacy and generalization.

Body Check: Body Check is the third part of Clear Picture. When the participant is doing the Clear Picture Do's, she does a brief body scan to increase awareness of physical sensations that are happening in the present moment. For example, the individual may notice an increased heart rate. Doing a Body Check helps the person Label and Rate Emotions.

Balancing On-Track Relationships: Balancing On-Track Relationships is the second component within the Relationship Care skill. The individual learns about various types of relationships, different relationship behaviors used to balance relationships, One-Way-Street Relationships, and Two-Way-Street Relationships.

Building On-Track Relationships: Building On-Track Relationships is the first element of the Relationship Care skill. The individual works to develop a stronger self-relationship. This Core Self includes enhancing self-awareness, self-acceptance, self-value, and self-trust. As the individual improves these capacities, relationships with others strengthen as well.

Breathe: Taking a few breaths is the first task when doing the Clear Picture skill. When a person notices an internal or external change, he commences the six-step process of getting a Clear

Picture by taking a breath. This action leads the individual to become aware of the moment and ultimately execute an effective Skills Plan.

Calm-Only skills: Calm Only is a Category of Skills. The last four skills are labeled Calm Only: Problem Solving, Expressing Myself, Getting It Right, and Relationship Care. These skills can only be used when the individual is at or below a 3 emotion.

Categories of Skills: The Categories of Skills is one of the System Tools that helps the individual know which skills are appropriate to use at his given level of emotional escalation in the present moment. There are two Categories of Skills: All-the-Time skills and Calm-Only skills. All-the-Time skills can be used when the individual is experiencing any level of emotional arousal, 0–5. Calm-Only skills are used when the person is at or below a 3 emotion.

Changing Off-Track Relationships: Changing Off-Track Relationships is the third component of Relationship Care. The individual may become aware that she or the other person in the relationship has done something to make the relationship go off-track. In this case it is possible to repair the relationship. The person can use Finding Middle Ground, use the Steps of Responsibility, or end the relationship.

Checking All Options: Checking All Options is the second step in Problem Solving. When the individual gets a Clear Picture of the problem, he can compile a brainstorm list of all possible options to fix the problem. It is helpful to review the positive and negative outcomes of each option to decide which option fits best.

Checking the Urge: Check the Urge is the second step in On-Track Thinking. The individual takes a moment to appraise whether the current urge will help her reach her goal or not. A thumbs-up represents a helpful urge that is worthy of action, while a thumbs-down signal symbolizes an urge that should pass without prompting action.

Clear Picture: Clear Picture is the first skill in the Skills System. Getting a Clear Picture leads the individual through six steps to become aware of his internal and external experiences within the current moment. The person Takes a Breath, Notices Surroundings, does a Body Check, Labels and Rates Emotions, Notices Thoughts, and Notices Urges.

Clear Picture of Risk: Getting a Clear Picture of Risk is the first step in doing a Safety Plan. The individual evaluates the kind of risk and the Level of Risk (low, medium, and high) within dangerous situations to make an effective plan to manage the event.

Coaching questions: Skills trainers ask coaching questions to prompt reflection about possible skills use in a given situation—for example, "What skills do you think you could use in that situation?" This type of cognitive rehearsal improves efficacy and generalization of skills.

Cognitive Load Theory: Cognitive Load Theory (Sweller, 1988) is a model that describes how the design of teaching interventions/interactions impact an individual's ability to process information. Sweller (1988) explains that instructors need to be aware of the design of interventions because certain types of questions and interactions can increase cognitive load demands, thus reducing intellectual processing performance.

Cognitive overload: Sweller (1988) explains that cognitive overload is when an individual's capacities to perform cognitive processing decrease due to managing extraneous information.

Commitment questions: The skills trainer asks commitment questions to prompt a participant to make a public commitment to doing a certain skill or behavior—for example, "Are you willing to practice getting a Clear Picture this week?" This type of question is intended to enhance efficacy and integration of skills into the person's life context.

Dialectical behavior therapy (DBT): Dialectical behavior therapy (DBT) (Linehan, 1993, 1993b) is a comprehensive cognitive-behavioral, empirically validated model that was designed to treat individuals with borderline personality disorder (BPD). The utilization of DBT has expended to include other individuals who experience complex Axis I and Axis II diagnoses and experience emotional, cognitive, and behavioral dysregulation.

Disclosure questions: Skills trainers ask disclosure questions to elicit personal information from participants—for example, "Have you ever had off-track behaviors?" This kind of inquiry helps expand and link information, thus promoting elaboration of learning.

Distraction New-Me Activity: Distraction New-Me Activities are activities that take the participant's focus intentionally away from a given emotion, thought, urge, person, or situation. Distraction is most helpful to assist an individual to wait or deploy attention away from off-track things that may serve to escalate emotions. For example, the individual may watch TV while waiting to go out to dinner.

Efficacy Phase: The Efficacy Phase is the fourth part of the E-Spiral framework. During this portion of the teaching process, interventions focus on reducing barriers to skills use and helping the individual mobilize skills execution within the context of the participant's life.

E-Spiral framework: The E-Spiral framework is a four-phase teaching model that outlines essential teaching interventions that promote learning for individuals with learning challenges. The E-Spiral phases are: (1) Exploring Existing Knowledge, (2) Encoding, (3) Elaboration, and (4) Efficacy. As the skills trainer progresses through this teaching process, it broadens and deepens learning to enhance generalization of adaptive coping skills.

Elaboration Phase: The Elaboration Phase is the third phase in the E-Spiral framework. During this stage of teaching, the skills trainer assigns activities and leads discussions that link past and present learning. This period of expansion helps improve connections between topics and increases recognition and recall. Practice exercises and individual instruction are examples of activities that promote elaboration.

Encoding Phase: The Encoding Phase is the second segment of the E-Spiral framework. These interventions are designed to input information into the participant's memory. Direct instruction and handouts are frequently utilized during the Encoding Phase. The trainer also poses progressions of simple questions to enhance the encoding of information in a way that creates a reciprocal learning experience.

Expansion questions: Skills trainers use expansion questions to help broaden the individual's understand of a situation—for example, "You have said that Safety Plans are helpful at home; what about at work?" This kind of expansion of awareness facilitates elaboration and generalization of skills.

Exploring Existing Knowledge: Exploring Existing Knowledge is the first phase of the E-Spiral framework. During this initial stage, the skills trainer introduces a topic and then prompts discussions that investigate the participant's current awareness of the topic and related subjects.

Expressing Myself: Expressing Myself is the sixth skill in the Skills System and it is a Calm-Only skill. Expressing Myself teaches the individual the benefits of communication, the utility of using Expressing Myself with the other skills, and how and when to communicate with people.

Feel Good New-Me Activity: Feel Good New-Me Activities are activities that make the individual feel more comfortable. For example: drinking a cup of tea, putting fragrant lotion on, and taking a warm bath are Feel Good New-Me Activities. These activities are used when the person needs to do self-soothing.

Feelings Rating Scale: The Feelings Rating Scale is one of the System Tools. It is a 0–5 scale that the individual uses to rate the intensity of feelings. For example, "I am a 3 anger." A 0 emotion means that he is not feeling the sensations of an emotion. A 1 is a tiny sensation, while a 2 is a small reaction. At these low levels of emotion, the person can begin to feel body sensations that are caused by the emotion. For example, the individual may notice his heart rate increasing slightly. A 3 emotion is a medium feeling. This level of emotion is the cutoff point for using Calm-Only skills, because at emotions ranking over a 3, the individual may had difficulty thinking clearly and executing interactive skills effectively due to the increasing effects of the emotion on the body and mind. A 4 feeling is a strong feeling. At this intensity, the individual may be experiencing strong body sensations, such as a rapid or pounding heartbeat. Cognitive processing is likely impacted at a 4 emotion, which is why it is not recommended to use Calm-Only skills that are predominantly interactive. Lastly, a 5 is an overwhelming feeling; at this high level, the individual takes an action that harms self, others, and/or property.

First Step toward the goal: The general description of an On-Track Action is when an individual takes a First Step toward her goal. For example, if I want to go exercise, turning off the TV and getting off the couch might be my On-Track Action. These behaviors would lead me toward my goal of working out. An Off-Track Action might be to go to the kitchen and get the box of doughnuts to eat.

Focus New-Me Activities: Focus New-Me Activities are activities that help the individual focus attention. Tasks such as sorting, organizing, counting, and following step-by-step directions encourage attentional control. For example, folding clothes carefully, sorting cards by suit or number groups, playing video games, and counting money are Focus New-Me Activities.

Fun New-Me Activity: Fun New-Me Activities are activities that provide fun and enjoyment. Going out to eat, playing sports, attending social events, and doing hobbies are examples of Fun New-Me Activities. It is important that the individual have a broad repertoire of these to sustain and improve the person's quality of life.

Getting a Clear Picture of the Problem: Getting a Clear Picture of the Problem is the first step in Problem Solving. The individual reflects on what he wants and highlights the barriers to fulfilling his needs.

Getting It Right: Getting It Right is the eighth skill in the Skills System, it is a Calm-Only skill. This skill helps the individual get what she needs from people. By being in the Right Mind, speaking to the Right Person, acting at the Right Time, acting in the Right Place, using the Right Tone, and saying the Right Words, she is more likely to get needs met.

Inner-wisdom questions: The skills trainer uses inner-wisdom questions to prompt the participant to self-reflect about personal beliefs, values, and perspectives related to her life. For example, the trainer may ask, "Do you feel that using Clear Picture would benefit you?" This strategy is intended to stimulate personal reflection, create opportunities for effective self-determination, and improve efficacy.

Labeling Emotions: The individual labels emotions during the fourth part of Clear Picture. For example, he or she may notice that "I feel sad right now." It is helpful for the individual to expand his vocabulary associated with labeling emotions; the ability to associate words with feelings can help the individual cope and communicate about his experiences more effectively.

Letting It Pass and Moving On: Let it Pass and Move On is the fifth and final aspect in the On-Track Action Skill. There are times when the individual needs to realize that enough time and energy has been expended in relation to a given emotion, thought, or situation, and he needs to Let It Pass and Move On to focus attention on another, more on-track topic.

Levels of Risk: The Levels of Risk are a component of Safety Plan. The individual evaluates whether a situation is low, medium, or high risk. A low-risk situation is one where the risk factor is far away and/or contact will cause stress. A medium risk is when the factor is closer and/or contact will cause problems for the individual or the other person. A high-risk situation is when the risk factor is nearby and/or contact will lead to harm to self, others, or property.

Linking questions: The skills trainer asks linking questions to help the individual link current learning to past behavior—for example, "You mentioned that last week you yelled at your housemate; do you think what we have learned today would have helped you in that situation?" This type of question is intended to facilitate elaboration.

Making Plans A, B, and C: Making Plans A, B, and C is the final step in Problem Solving. The individual first crafts Plan A to get the problem solved in a way that is most beneficial. It is helpful to also make a Plan B, in case aspects of Plan A are not possible. Plan B is useful during the negotiation process. Plan C is a backup plan so that the individual can be prepared for when the interactions do not go as expected or desired.

Mindfulness activity: Mindfulness activities are done during the initial phases of skills-training sessions. In the 12-week curriculum, a Tibetan bell (singing bowl) is used to guide various activities that prompt the participant to focus and control attention. For example, the trainer may ring the bell six times (one for each of the Clear Picture Do's), and the participant may notice the breath. Following this exercise, the group discusses the experience.

Mnemonics: Mnemonic strategies assist memory by facilitating associating a new topic with something he has learned in the past.

New-Me Activities: New-Me Activities is the fifth skill in the Skills System; it is an All-the-Time skill. There are four types of New-Me Activities: Focus, Feel Good, Distraction, and Fun. Each of these serve a different function for the individual, and it is important for the person to choose the best activity for the situation. For example, if the individual is upset and unfocused, a Focus New-Me Activity (like sorting cards) may help him get back on-track.

Noticing Surroundings: Noticing surroundings is the second task in Clear Picture. The individual scans the environment to become aware of the environment and the people in the area.

Noticing Thoughts: Noticing thoughts is the fifth task in Clear Picture. The person watches her mind to observe thought passing through it.

Noticing Urges: Noticing urges is the sixth step in Clear Picture. The individual notices any urges that he is experiencing. The person then transitions to On-Track Thinking to take a moment to Check the Urge.

One-Way-Street Relationships: "One-Way-Street Relationship" is a term used in the Balancing On-Track Relationships portion of Relationship Care. When a relationship is not reciprocal (when it is not a two-way street), it is classified as a one-way street. There are times when the person may decide to create one-way streets or it may inadvertently happen. The participant may notice that others are not fully participating in a relationship with him, which can also generate One-Way-Street Relationships.

On-Track Thinking: On-Track Thinking is the second skill in the Skills System; it is an All-the-Time skill. There are four parts: Stop, Step Back, and Think about what I want; Check the Urge; Turn It to Thumbs-Up; and make a Skills Plan. The individual uses Clear Picture and then immediately moves to do the steps of On-Track Thinking.

On-Track Action: On-Track Action is the third skill in the Skills System; it is an All-the-Time skill. There are five components of this skill: the Positive Step toward the goal; Switching Tracks; On-Track Action Plan; Accepting the Situation; and Letting It Pass and Moving On. The individual uses Clear Picture and On-Track Thinking before taking an On-Track Action.

On-Track Action Plans: On-Track Action Plans are the third part of On-Track Action. The individual creates an On-Track Action Plan to do various New-Me Activities throughout each day that serve to proactively help the person remain focused, healthy, and fulfilled.

Orienting to new topics and transitions: Orienting is a foundational teaching strategy that is utilized throughout skills-training sessions. The trainer orients the person to upcoming transitions and seeks permission for the movement ahead. This strategy helps create a reciprocal learning relationship that assists the individual to feel clear about future events, which reduces cognitive load demands. Additionally, orienting provides the individual with an opportunity to give informed consent to the intervention.

Problem Solving: Problem Solving is the sixth skill in the Skills System; it is a Calm-Only skill. There are three parts of this skill: Getting a Clear Picture of the problem; Checking All Options; and making Plan A, B, and C.

Quick-Step Assessment: The Quick-Step Assessment is a foundational teaching strategy and is used throughout skills-training sessions. The purpose of this framework is to help the trainer to continually be planning and executing teaching interventions that maximize learning. There are three parts of the Quick-Step Assessment: (1) Assessing the cognitive load of the intervention; (2) Assessing the cognitive functioning of the individual; and (3) Choosing and shaping interventions.

Rating Emotions: Rating Emotions is the fourth step in the Clear Picture Do's. The individual labels the current emotion and then uses the Feelings Rating Scale to rate the emotion as a 0–5—for example, "I am a 2 frustrated right now." The feeling rating is a key task, because depending on the number, the individual knows which Category of Skills to use and how many skills to utilize by following the Recipe for Skills.

Relationship Care: Relationship Care is the ninth skill in the Skills System; it is a Calm-Only skill. The individual uses this skill to learn to build, balance, and change relationships with himself and others. The concept of the Core Self helps an individual understand the self-relationship. The participant learns about various types or relationships, relationship behaviors, and One-Way-Street and Two-Way-Street Relationships to Balance On-Track Relationships. Repairing Relationships, Finding Middle Ground, taking the Steps of Responsibility, and ending Off-Track Relationships are strategies used to Change Off-Track Relationships.

Recipe for Skills: The Recipe for Skills is a System Tool that helps the individual know how many skills are needed in any given situation. As the person creates a Skills Plan during On-Track Thinking, he adds one skill for every level of emotion, including 0. For example, if the individual is at a 2 emotion, he uses three skills; at a 3 emotion, four skills are used.

Relevant context questions: The skills trainer asks relevant context questions as he or she is Exploring Existing Knowledge in a training session to help orient the group to the importance of the topic—for example, "Are there situations in your life when your emotions get very strong and you have urges to go off-track?" This type of question helps the individual review her personal life to explore whether skills would be helpful for her; this process increases motivation and creates contextual learning opportunities.

Review questions: The trainer asks review questions to have the participants share observations and insights with the group—for example, "What did you notice during that exercise?" Sharing after activities helps the individual work on building the Core Self as well as teaching him about how people are very different and that that is all right.

Right Mind: Right Mind is the first component of Getting It Right. Getting It Right is a Calm-Only skill, so being in the Right Mind means that the participant is below a 3 emotion. Additionally, the individual should be prepared for conversations where she is trying to get needs met.

Right Person: The Right Person is the second element in Getting It Right. The individual must choose the Right Person to talk to when trying to get what she needs. The Right Person is the one who has the ability and power to fulfill the need.

Right Time and Place: The Right Time and Place is the third aspect of Getting It Right. Once the participant has chosen the Right Person, it is vital that the conversation happen at the Right Time and in the Right Place. It is often most effective to talk to someone when he can focus attention; speaking in private generally helps as well.

Right Tone: Using the Right Tone is the fourth component of Getting It Right. The Right Tone is often assertive, without being passive or demanding.

Right Words—SEALS: The Right Words is the fifth element of Getting It Right. SEALS describes what the Right Words are to get what the individual wants: **S**ugar, **E**xplain, **A**sk, **L**isten, **S**eal a deal. "To use sugar" means to be nice and polite. Next, the participant clearly explains what he wants. The individual then asks for that he needs. It is important that the individual listen to the reply to be able to discuss the options. Lastly, the person Seals a Deal to pin down the details of the agreement.

Safety Plan: Safety Plan is the fourth skill in the Skills System, and it is an All-the-Time skill. The individual uses Thinking, Talking, and Writing Safety Plans to manage low, medium, and high Levels of Risk. The person decides to refocus on a New-Me Activity, Move Away, or Leave the Area in response to risk.

Skills Plan: A Skills Plan is the fourth element of On-Track Thinking. Once the person has checked the Urge and Turned It, she makes a Skills Plan to determine which Category of Skills and how many skills (according to the Recipe for Skills) will help in the given situation.

Skills Practice Review: The Skills Practice Review is a portion of a skills-training session when the participants go over the basic concepts in the Skills System. This process helps the individual remember the basic concepts so that when he is emotionally escalated, the person is able to recall the skills.

Skills System: The Skills System is a set of nine skills and three System Tools that help individuals manage emotions, thoughts, and actions to reach personal goals.

Skills System coach: A skills coach is an individual who knows the Skills System and helps guide another person through the process of using skills.

Skills System trainer: A skills trainer is a professional who teaches the Skills System to other people. Generally, skills trainers are master's-level clinicians who have expertise with the populations that they are training.

Shifting Tracks: Shifting Tracks is the second element within On-Track Action. The person does an action that Switches Tracks when he is heading off his preferred track. For example, if the individual speaks with an aggressive tone to a staff member, he may Shift Tracks and use a gentler tone of voice.

Simplification: Simplification is one of the foundational teaching strategies in the Skills System. As the trainer uses the Quick-Step Assessment, he or she may determine that the language used in describing a topic needs to be simplified to enhance learning.

Stop, Step Back, and Think about what I want: Stop, Step Back, and Think about what I want is the first step in On-Track Thinking. This gives the individual a brief moment to engage in On-Track Thinking prior to reacting to an urge. As the person pauses for a few seconds, she is able to reflect on personal goals rather than reacting impulsively.

System Tools: The System Tools in the Skills System are the Feelings Rating Scale, Categories of Skills, and the Recipe for Skills. These tools help the individual combine skills effectively to manage each situation that arises in her life.

Task analysis: Task analysis is a foundational teaching strategy in the Skills System. This strategy is when the trainer breaks down concepts into discrete parts to teach individual components of complex skills.

Turning It to Thumbs-Up Thinking: Turning It to Thumbs-Up Thinking is the third part of On-Track Thinking. This is when the individual replaces Off-Track Thinking with positive thoughts that are moving in the direction of his goals. For example, "If I hit that person, I will get arrested; I want to have a good life, so I need to do a Safety Plan." Turning Off-Track Thinking to Thumbs-Up Thinking leads the person to the next step of creating an On-Track Skills Plan to manage the situation.

Two-Way-Street Relationship: A Two-Way-Street Relationship is an element within the Balancing On-Track Relationships portion of Relationship Care. A Two-Way-Street Relationship is one that includes reciprocal communication and respect. Both people are able to actively participate in an equal relationship that benefits both parties.

Types of Safety Plans: There are three types of Safety Plans: Thinking, Talking, and Writing. A Thinking Safety Plan is when the person thinks about the Level of Risk and then executes maneuvers to manage the issue. A Talking Safety Plan is when the individual talks to another person to discuss options for managing the danger. A Writing Safety Plan is when a person writes down potential and/or current risks and options for handling the danger effectively.

Ways of managing risk: There are three ways to manage risk within a Safety Plan. In low-risk situations, the person can refocus on a New-Me Activity to handle the issue. In medium-risk situations, it may be best to move away from the problem. In high-risk situations, the individual should leave the area where he cannot see, hear, talk to, or touch the risk.

Worked examples: A worked example (Sweller, 1989) is a foundational teaching strategy in the Skills System model. This intervention presents a completed example of a topic so that the participant learns an accurate version of the material. This tactic reduces cognitive load and helps the individual integrate a contextual understanding of the information in a way that minimizes intellectual demands.